I0894992

THE CARS OF THE 50S

A HISTORY OF CARS MANUFACTURED AND ASSEMBLED IN AUSTRALIA DURING THE 1950S

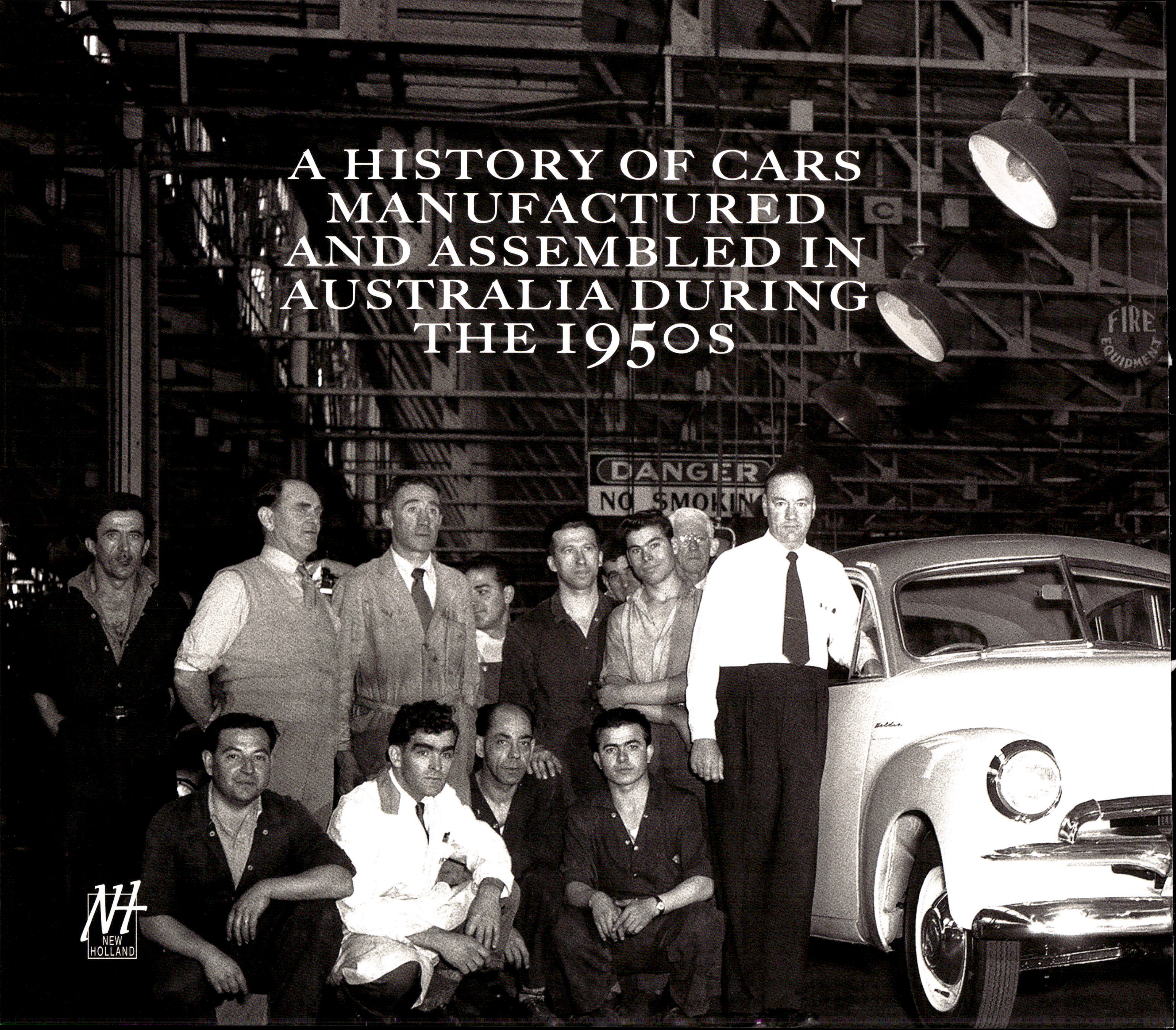

NEW HOLLAND

THE CARS OF THE 50s

GAVIN FARMER

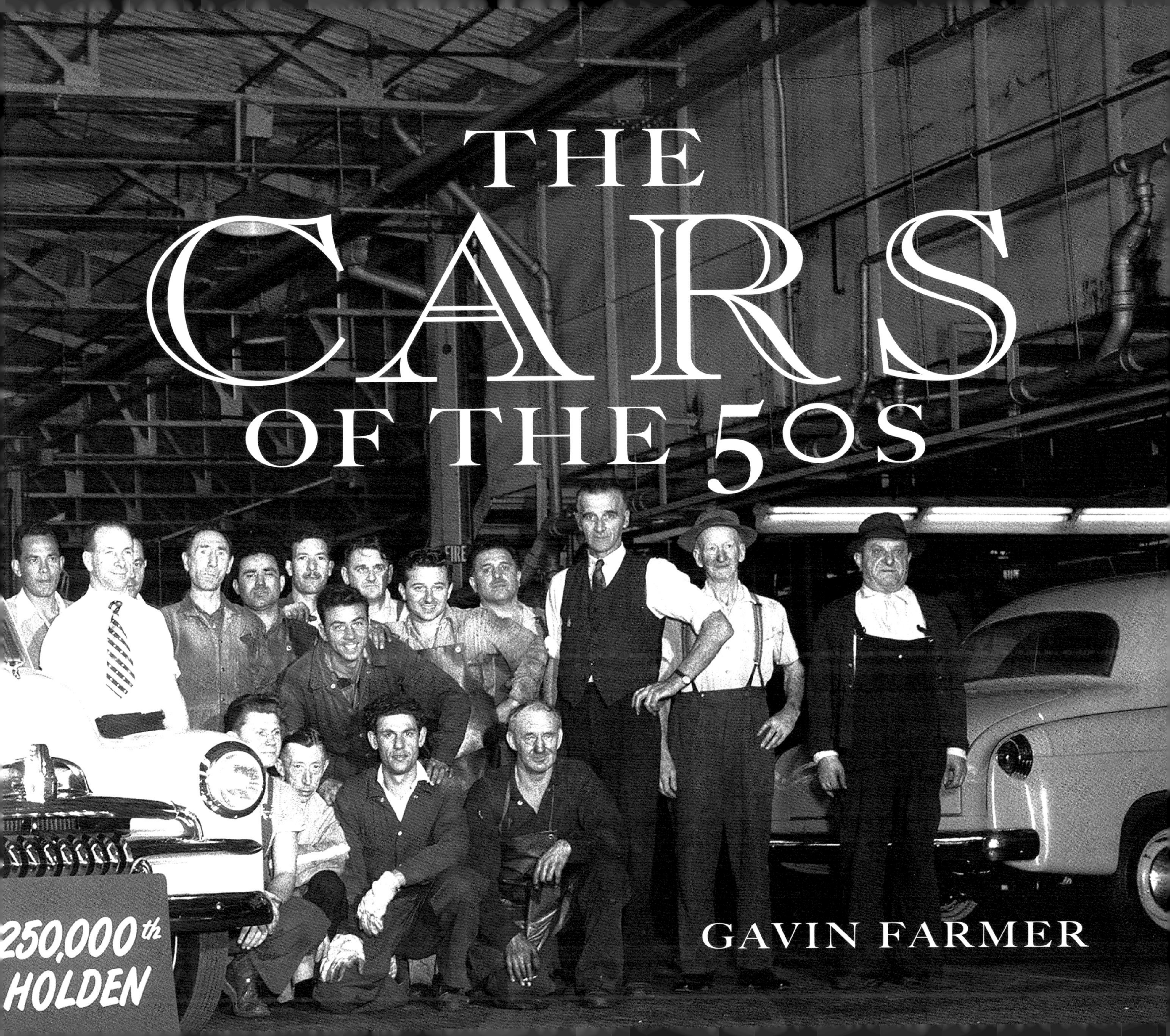

First published in 2022 by New Holland Publishers
Sydney

Level 1, 178 Fox Valley Road, Wahroonga, NSW 2076, Australia

newhollandpublishers.com

Copyright © 2022 New Holland Publishers
Copyright © 2022 in text: Gavin Farmer
For image credits see page 191

All rights reserved. No part of this publication may be reproduced, stored in a retrieval system or transmitted, in any form or by any means, electronic, mechanical, photocopying, recording or otherwise, without the prior written permission of the publishers and copyright holders.

A record of this book is held at the National Library of Australia.

ISBN 9781760795252

Group Managing Director: Fiona Schultz
Copy editor: Matthew Farmer, FUSE Editing
Designer: Andrew Davies
Production Director: Arlene Gippert
Printed in China

10 9 8 7 6 5 4 3 2 1

Keep up with New Holland Publishers:

NewHollandPublishers
@newhollandpublishers

CONTENTS

ACKNOWLEDGEMENTS

A history book as comprehensive as this would not have been possible without the assistance of many people from the motor industry and car clubs around the country.

In no particular order these enthusiasts include Eric Parker from the Barossa Junction Motel who was a Chevrolet expert; the late Peter Tavener along with Matthew Lambert and Leighton Passant who are Rootes Group enthusiasts; Ross Kerslake from Vanguard Triumph Wholesale in Lilydale (a suburb of Melbourne) who advised on Standard and Triumph cars; Vin Youngman and Bill Watson from the Morris Register in Adelaide; Ralph Drage and Ron Burchett for help with the Austin history; John Roberts, David Robinson, Annie Wittup and Monica Kruger from the Humber Car Club; long-time VW enthusiast Dean Hosking as well as Rod Davies who with his brother Lloyd wrote and published the excellent book *Volkswagen in Australia: The Forgotten Story*; Mathew McAuley, Peter Wilson, the late Gordon Miller and Mac Chapman for their knowledge of Peugeot; Simon Fitzpatrick for his assistance with Renault and Peugeot details; Virginia Craney and Mark Agnew for their assistance on the rare Ascort; Bill Buckle for his counsel on the equally rare Buckle coupe and John De Ruter on Goggomobils; Peter Elsby, David Evans and Jon Pyle from the Vauxhall Club; Marius Venz for his help where the Lloyd Hartnett was concerned; John Whittaker from the Mercedes-Benz Club of South Australia; Jim Quinn and John Brown from the Simca Car Club; the many members of the Chrysler Restorers Car Club of South Australia and the Chrysler Car Club who assisted with information; Ian Hall for his help with Jeep in Australia and Arthur Garthon where Land Rover was concerned; Graham Tonkin and Don Henley where Ford was concerned; Bob Freeman and David Tuck for their help with the Rambler history.

I am also indebted to Mark Tempe, Jim Quigley and Chris Skinner for help with Studebaker, Kenneth Wright Junior regarding the Lloyd-Hartnett, John Regan and Ted O'Brien on Peugeots and two eminent Australian motoring historians in Pedr Davis and Max Gregory for their assistance with Chapter 11 – it would never have been as comprehensive or as interesting without their input. And then there was Robert Simpson from Sydney who provided me with sasles figures for the decade and Richard Johns from Australian Automotive Intelligence.

The Sporting Car Club of South Australia were a great help in allowing me access to their vast library as was the National Motor Museum at Birdwood. The staff at the GM-Holden archives and at the Ford Motor Company archives were extremely helpful where sourcing of images was concerned.

Beate Frank from the Mercedes-Benz Classic in Stuttgart; Ben Davidson from *Jeep Action* magazine; Maurice Camelleri from the Standard and Triumph Club of Victoria; Steve McNicol from Railmac Publications (Austin, Morris, BMC); and Carl Moll from Club VW of South Australia.

INTRODUCTION

The fifties was a wonderful time in Australia. The war was fast becoming a distant and less painful memory, industrialisation was booming as the country worked its way towards self-sufficiency while wheat and wool exports grew to such an extent that the country was literally being financed 'off the sheep's back'.

For this book I have use 1948 as the starting point because that was the year when so many cars that were to re-establish their manufacturers were released around the world. For example, we had the 48/215 Holden here in Australia while in France the Paris Salon was a stunning affair as Peugeot, Renault and Citroen released their 203, 4CV (known here as the 750) and 2CV respectively, in England there was the Morris Minor, Jowett Javelin and Standard Vanguard while in Germany there were the ubiquitous Volkswagen Beetle, Borgward Hansa (later to become the Isabella) and the pontoon series Mercedes Benz. In the United States by 1948 or at the latest 1949 all manufacturers – GM, Ford, Chrysler, Studebaker, Packard, Nash, Hudson et al – had retooled and were producing their first truly post-war automobiles.

Such was the situation here in Australia that from 1948 through 1950 the Austin A40 Devon was the top-selling car in the country. That was until GM-Holden was able to ramp up production to meet the burgeoning demand from a car-hungry public for its 48-215. When Austin and Morris combined their resources to form the British Motor Corporation of Australia (BMCA) in 1954, between them they commanded a little over 30 per cent of the total new car market in Australia. A decade later that market share had halved and was continuing to slide as Holden became the dominant make – by 1959 it held virtually 50 per cent of the total market with a single-model product range! BMC was beginning to pay the price for refusing to design and build a car that would specifically target Australian conditions and buyers; it continued with its original policy of mildly modifying aspects of its English range of models – the Austin A55 and A95, Morris Minor and Oxford – and refused to acknowledge the needs of local motorists. This haughty arrogance would eventually bring them down.

Ford, meanwhile, had announced in 1958 that it would build a completely new assembly plant at Broadmeadows to manufacture the Zephyr, its challenger to Holden. However, with the release in September 1959 in the USA of the completely new Ford Falcon – it was one of those rare cars from the US industry, a clean-sheet design – those plans were immediately changed and Falcon was committed to Australian production while the Zephyr was left to fade into the sunset.

The other member of the American Big Three, the Chrysler Corporation, stumbled through the Fifties with a range of cars that were out of touch with the market from virtually every point of view – they were big, heavy and expensive to own and run (although they were doggedly reliable) and were mechanically very old fashioned. Badged either as a Plymouth, Dodge or De Soto, these were replaced in mid-1957 by the Chrysler Royal, a move that saw major changes in Chrysler's distribution arrangements. Even by taking Simca on board the company was barely able to make a profit. The Aronde sedan and, later, station wagon, were both very popular with buyers as they were not only thrifty to own and run but had a sparkling turn of performance and excellent handling for the period.

The only other British maker of any significance in Australia was the Rootes Group who began assembling the Hillman Minx and Humber Hawk in a former aircraft factory at Port Melbourne which they had acquired in 1946. As the years passed this facility was expanded and re-equipped to the point where the Hillmans had a reasonably high local content although, like the prestigious and expensive Humbers, they continued to be assembled from CKD packs dispatched from Coventry.

GM-Holden assembled Vauxhall cars, the British arm of General Motors, from CKD kits brought into Australia. They were not volume sellers like the Holden but nevertheless commanded a small-but-consistent share of the market and had a very appreciative clientele who were extremely loyal. From America came various Chevrolet and Pontiac sedans for those who desired the latest and greatest from the world's largest car producing nation.

From Germany we had Volkswagen who established their Beetle as the country's dominant small car and who set up an assembly operation at Clayton, then an outer Melbourne suburb. In 1958 Daimler-Benz negotiated an agreement with Australian Motor Industries (AMI) in Port Melbourne to assemble their 190 and 220 'Ponton' models but the plan was not as successful as both parties had hoped and was discontinued in 1963. Another German company, Borgward, came to an agreement with Lawrence Hartnett, formerly Managing Director of GM-Holden and generally regarded as the 'father of the Holden car', to assemble the small Lloyd cars that were badged as Lloyd-Hartnett from a factory in Brisbane. From the south of Germany, Dingolfing in Bavaria, was Hans Glas GmbH who came to Australia with its Goggomobil cars through the agency of Bill Buckle who bodied the German platform with an Australian-made fibreglass structure and was remarkably successful.

The French were represented by Renault, Peugeot, Simca and Citröen. As with anything French, their history here was never straight forward. Initially Canada Cycle and Motor Company in South Melbourne assembled and distributed Peugeots in Australia beginning with the 203 in 1950, but by the end of the decade they had lost the rights to Continental and General Distributors who had set up a new facility in West Heidelberg where they assembled the 403 and the Citroen ID. In 1954 the Renault Fregate and 750 were being assembled by Ira Berk at a factory in Belmore, Sydney; Renaults were also assembled briefly by Martin and King in Melbourne who had also assembled a small number of Jowett Javelin sedans in the early '50s. Continental and General acquired the rights for Renault in 1962 (beyond the scope of this book) and the West Heidelberg site later became Renault Australia's home.

The Italians never really established a beachhead in Australia in the way that the British, Germans and French did and so never enjoyed quite the sales that the others did although the Fiat 600 and 1100 were reasonably popular.

Fringe dwellers of the local motor industry included Buckle and

Ascort, both GT-style coupes using a fibreglass body which was a new material for the local industry. Both were virtually hand-made in tiny numbers and both lost their creators a lot of money. And there was the Wiles-Thomson from Adelaide that very nearly made production but failed to make the grade.

An Englishman, Reg Shepheard, changed the motoring landscape in 1953 when the first Redex Round Australia trial was announced. Actually, it was only half way around the country at 10,460km (6500mi) but nevertheless was a massive undertaking given the primitive circumstances of the time. Some 192 cars were entered (but only 185 actually started the event) which amazed the pundits. They set off from the Sydney Showgrounds on 30 August and two weeks later a Peugeot 203 crossed the line as the outright winner! People could not believe it – a small four-cylinder French family car had beaten all the favourites!

Further round Australia trials were held in 1954, '55, '56, '57 and '58 with another small European car upsetting the status quo – the ubiquitous VW Beetle. Whenever the cars stopped in a town or city they and their crews were mobbed by an enthusiastic public who were keen to witness what was motoring history. These trials were by far the longest and toughest in the world at the time.

This period of Australia's industrial history was important from the view that our automobile industry would never have prospered like it did without the support of many component manufacturers along with tyre manufacturers like Olympic, Hardie, Dunlop and Goodyear (all now long gone) along with the establishment of several oil refineries around the country (all closed) and companies like Henderson Springs, KLG Sparkplugs, Armstrong York Engineering, W H Wylie, Rubery Owen and of course Repco.

The Fifties was a boom time for Australian industry as the country began to flex its muscles internationally and take the first steps towards the multi-cultural society that we are today. There will never be times like those ever again.

Gavin Farmer
Bridgewater 2022

HOLDEN
GENERAL MOTORS NEW AUSTRALIAN CAR
AUST. 320

CHAPTER 1

GENERAL MOTORS-HOLDEN

Quite possibly the most important single event in the early postwar years of Australia's industrial growth was the re-equipping for the purpose of automobile manufacturing by General Motors-Holden at Fishermen's Bend where on 27 November 1948 the ubiquitous 48/215 model Holden rolled off the assembly line and the then Prime Minister, Ben Chifley, uttered those immortal words, "She's a beauty!" as he announced the car to the nation.

The 48/215 Holden, retrospectively called the FX, was the car that Australian motorists lusted after in those car-starved early postwar years. It possessed a specification that ideally suited what was needed at the time – lazy, torquey six-cylinder engine that provided spirited performance, was reasonably economical and long lasting with good reliability, an interior that was well appointed for the time and capable of carrying six passengers on bench seats front and rear plus a reasonable amount of luggage. It also established a template for the style of car that would evolve into the 'traditional Australian family car', a formula that only Ford (Falcon) and belatedly Chrysler (Valiant) and Leyland (P76) would recognise and adopt.

Designed and engineered in Detroit with considerable input from a group of Holden engineers who travelled to America and spent two years living and working there on the car before bringing the complete project back to Melbourne for production, it was Australia's largest private industrial project at that time. In 1948 Holden had two main plants from which it was operating – Fishermen's Bend which had been built in 1936 and was where all final assembly took place as well as the manufacture of the engine and gearbox using its own foundry and machine shop, and at Woodville in South Australia which dated from 1923 (it was built pre-GM) where the huge press shop was located as well as the toolroom for the manufacture of dies.

Initial production of the 48/215 was carried out at Fishermans Bend. However, once true volume production got underway in 1949 the other GM-H plants around Australia became part of the process. These included Pagewood in Sydney, Fortitude Valley in Brisbane, Birkenhead in Adelaide and Mosman Park in Perth. In 1952 Pagewood was elevated to manufacturing status of the complete car joining Fishermans Bend in this. By 1956 Fishermans Bend had ceased assembly, this role being assumed by the new Dandenong plant where the stamping of bodies and final assembly had been transferred meaning GM-H now had three plants capable of final assembly – Dandenong, Pagewood and Woodville.

In so many ways the 48/215 Holden was a small Chevrolet – its styling was similar to the 1950 Chevrolets, the engine looked to be a smaller version of Chevrolet's famous 'Stove Bolt' OHV six that had been in production for nearly twenty years, and the rest of its specification had that familiar Chev look and feel about it. Like its Chevrolet cousin the Holden had a prominent prow of a bonnet that flowed back to a two-piece split-Vee windscreen with flat glass, an arching roofline with a small rear window and a sloping rear boot line. It was quite different from the Willys-based design that the Australian engineers had been working on during Hartnett's reign.

What was new for Australia was the method of construction of the body. In their advertising and sales brochures GM-Holden described it as 'Aerobilt'. It was a monocoque steel body that was one of the first in the GM world (Vauxhall was first in 1936) and the first for an Australian-made car. It was built on a 2616mm (103-in) wheelbase, was 4368-mm (172-in) long by 1397-mm (55-in) wide and 1270-mm (50-in) high with its kerb weight at 1018kg (2240lb) or one Imperial ton exactly. It was a little lighter than its GM stablemate, the Vauxhall Velox, and was much lighter than the Austin A70 and other similar British cars most of which still had truck-like chassis under them.

For the time, the mechanical specifications were conventional, class average you might say, and certainly not advanced in any way. The front suspension was a simple upper-and-lower wishbone arrangement with brass-bushed kingpins (as was GM's way then) and coil springs with Delco dampers built into the top wishbone pivot; at the rear were five-leaf semi-elliptic leaf springs and lever arm dampers. Steering was by a worm and sector system that required 3.5 turns lock-to-lock for a 11.3-m (37-foot) turning circle while the hydraulic braking system consisted of four cast-iron drums, 228mm (9in) in diameter with the brake lining area being a sparse 95 square inches. Big 15 x 4JJ wheels were specified for decent ground clearance (important then) and shod with 5.50 x 15 cross-ply tyres.

The engine was known colloquially as the 'grey' motor because of the colour it was painted during production. Both the cylinder block and head were made from cast-iron as were the crankshaft and camshaft, the crankshaft being supported by four main bearings and lubricated by a full pressure system with a trochoid pump driven by a shaft off a skew gear on the camshaft. The cylinder dimensions were 76.2 x 79.375mm (3.0 x 3.125in) for a cubic capacity of 2172cc (132.5 cubic inches), and on a compression ratio of 6.5:1 it developed 45kW (60bhp) at 4000rpm and 136Nm (100lb/ft) of torque at just 1200rpm.

As was typical at that time, the drive went to the rear wheels through a three-speed manual gearbox with a non-synchromesh first gear, the gear change lever being on the steering column. As was the custom at the time, seating was by benches front and rear and the dashboard was plain in style and reminiscent of Chevrolets of the period. It consisted of a small binnacle directly in front of the driver that contained a single large dial – speedometer with total odometer – and two small supplementary dials, the one on the left contained the fuel gauge and the one to the right the red warning lights for engine overheating, lack of output from the DC generator and low engine oil pressure. Located either side was the ignition key lock with a separate start button, light switch (dipper switch on the floor) and the switch for the vacuum-operated windscreen wipers; on the Special there was also a cigarette lighter. Provision was made in the centre for a radio and off to the left was a large glovebox. Neat and simple but not very informative.

Initially the 48/215 was available only as a four-door sedan in a limited selection of exterior colours – Gawler Beige, Black, Convoy Grey and Seine Blue (a rare metallic colour) – with either Bedford Cord grey cloth or a red leatherette interior; it was also something of an austerity special insofar as it had only one key operated door lock (driver's door, push down interior buttons locked the other three doors), one taillight, no indicators (not even trafficators) and very little chrome (grille, bumpers, headlight surrounds) although there was a list of Nasco accessories buyers could select from for installation by their dealer. Despite the poverty-pack specification Holden never came close to satisfying demand with production initially set at 100 vehicles a day.

Some fragility in the car's mechanical design became evident from buyers who lived in rural areas. The original differential housing was prone to cracking and was changed to a stronger design with a reinforced ribbed casing in 1949. The following year the front cross member design was altered to a more rounded profile for added strength and the Delco-Remy ignition system was changed to a Bosch system.

This *is* news . . modern all-steel turret-top Aerobilt design

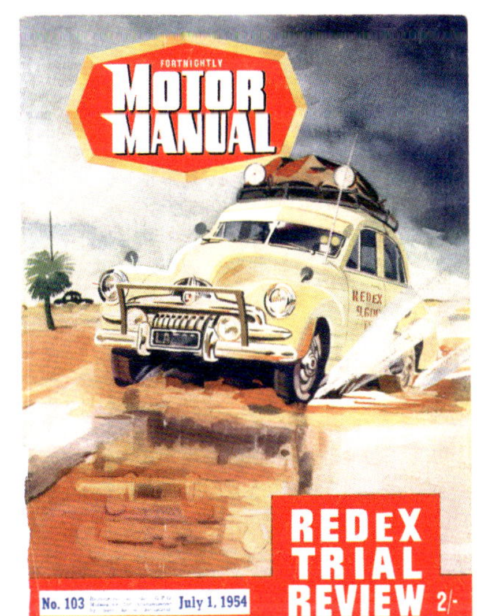

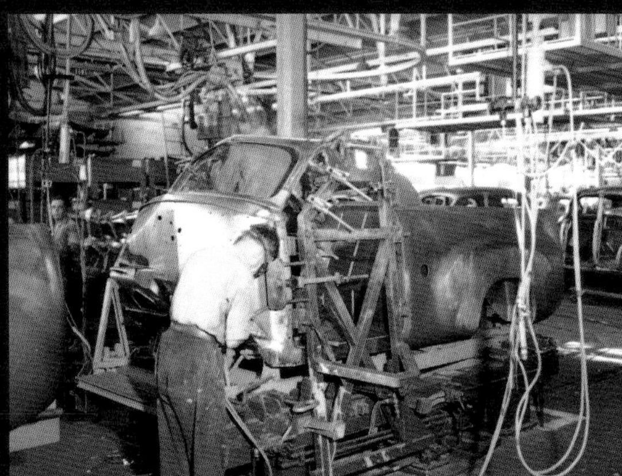

Although no Australian specialist car magazines existed at the time, *The Autocar* from England published a full road test of a UK-registered 48/215 in its 5 October 1951 edition. A caption under the lead photograph gave a clue as to their thinking about the car: “Modern lines with a special character make the Holden an easy car to identify. Good ground clearance and moderate overhangs make it suitable for use in rough country”. Throughout the report they found good points and commented thus: “It should not be thought that because it is light the Holden is flimsy. On the contrary, it gives the impression of a simple, rugged car, built for hard work.” Additionally they wrote, “The power unit is smooth, quiet and flexible and helps give an air of real refinement in running;” to “It cruises happily at any speed between 96 and 112km/h (60 and 70mph) with little noise beyond the swish of the wind;” to “The suspension gives a very comfortable ride over all surfaces, but no anti-roll bar is fitted and some roll is experienced when cornering fast;” and “The seats are generously proportioned and upholstered in real leather; the cushions are not particularly soft, but the seat angles are well-chosen for comfortable riding over long distances.” Even though the Holden was never going to be sold in the UK the report was glowing in every way. As for the car’s performance, they achieved a top speed of 128km/h (80mph) with in-gear acceleration to 80km/h (50mph) in 13.8 secs and 96km/h (60mph) in 20.7 secs, considerably faster than any British 2.2-litre family sedan of the time.

On 29 October 1953 Holden announced the famous FJ, a car that has gone down in Australian motoring folklore; it has been the subject of pop songs and become a cultural icon in a way that the FX mysteriously never achieved. For the first time the car was available in three versions: Standard, Business and Special. The two former versions were aimed at economy conscious buyers, the taxi industry and government fleets while the Special was primarily aimed at family buyers and was referred to in the brochure as “the de-luxe model in the Holden range”.

As with any update of a model, it was easily recognised by its new grille that consisted of a prominent horizontal bar with black-painted accents plus an arched chromed bar above it that culminated in a prominent winged badge embracing the red lion, and a hood ornament.

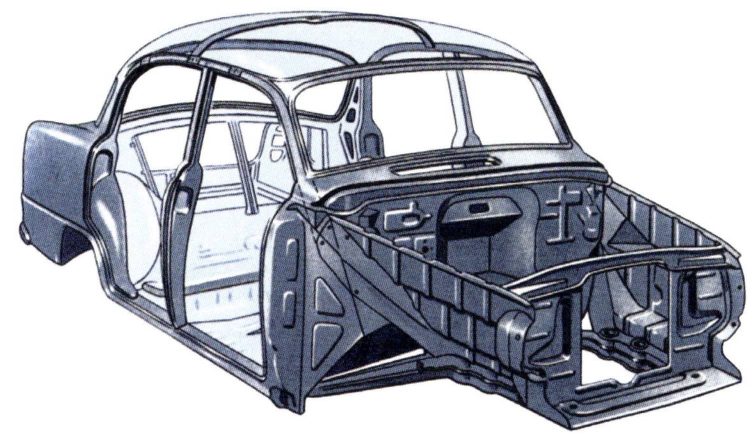

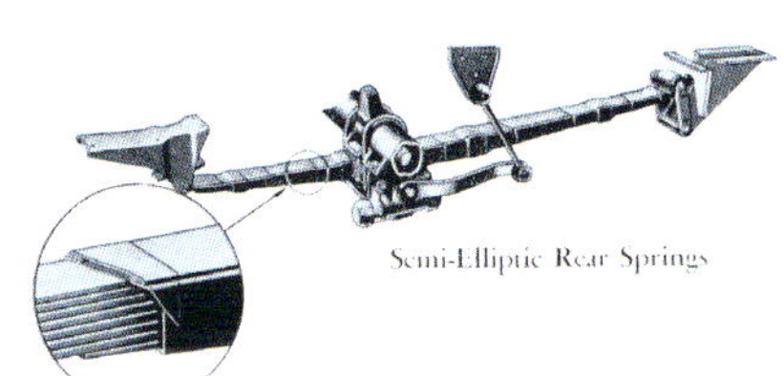

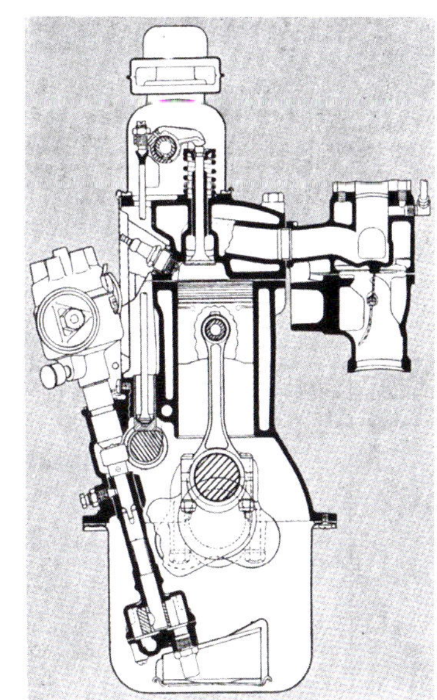

Body panels were unchanged from the 48/215 but the Special, the most popular by far of the three versions, was readily identifiable by its chromed diecast reflector 'fins' on each rear fender plus stainless steel chrome accents around the windows and another that encircled the body at waist level, and larger section 5.90 x 15 tyres. All three had the Holden name in script on either side of the bonnet, back near the shutline with the front door. On the bootlid, above the restyled taillight, again in script, were the words 'Holden Special' or simply 'Holden' on the two lesser models.

Mechanically few changes were made although the most notable was the specifying of telescopic rear dampers that replaced the former lever type that proved to be unable to cope with the harsh conditions, and a revised front subframe made its appearance. After all, if it ain't broke why fix it?

Wheels published a full test of an FJ in its May 1954 issue and said, "The Holden seemed to us to be an eager touring car, well able to maintain high average speeds over any surface. It was comfortable, dust-free and very quiet. We were impressed by its all-round performance and economy and that it has the highest performance in its class." They managed an 132.8km/h (83mph) top speed and a 0–80km/h (0–50mph) time of 12 seconds which was competitive with other similar-sized cars. The price had, however, risen slightly and the Special sedan now retailed for £1093.

During the reign of the FJ, Holden introduced the coupe utility and panel van and again was faced with a sell-out. These two body options were to be an integral part of the Holden range until in the 1990s. Three prototype FJ station wagons were hand-built but with demand far exceeding supply the decision was made not to go ahead with that concept at the time. Meanwhile, buyers had to wait up to five months to take delivery of their new Holden.

By now Holden was holding more than 40 per cent of the total new car market and with buyers still queuing up GM-H released the completely restyled FE model on 19 July 1956 to huge acclaim from the nation's media. The early postwar rounded look was replaced by the pontoon-

145·945

00053·H

9992

sided three-box style that had become the styling fashion earlier in the decade. Included in the rather dramatic styling change were the adoption of a one-piece curved windscreen and a correspondingly large wrap-round rear window, rectangular chromed bar grille, hooded headlights, separate round parking lights under the headlights, new taillights with red and amber lenses, indicator lights, 12-volt electrics, 13 x 4.5-in rims with 6.40 x 13 cross-ply tyres. Carried over were windscreen wipers that retained their clap hands sweep and annoying (and dangerous) vacuum operation. Visibility from the interior was drastically improved as was the general ambience; instruments were still limited to the speedometer and fuel gauge with red warning lights covering all other functions but the style of the cluster was much more modern. In the centre of the dash was again provision for the radio while on the left was a lockable glovebox. Another significant change (for Holden) was the adoption of pendant foot pedals, something that Ford had in their Zephyrs and Consuls for several years, in conjunction with hydraulic operation of the clutch. A major convenience item for the driver was the new combination key-and-starter system that did away with the previously separate ignition key and push button start process.

Available as a four-door sedan or station wagon (released March 1957) with a lift-up rear window and a fold-down lower section, a utility (released March 1957) and panel van (May 1957), the sedans and wagons were available in Standard or Special trim with a Business sedan for taxi purposes. There were virtually no body adornments at all on the Standard – it was plain to the extreme – but the Special had modest amounts of chrome decoration from a strip that encircled the body at waist level and was the natural divider when a two-tone paint scheme was ordered, a chrome spear along the front fenders and onto the front doors, a name badge incorporating the round Lion badge on the rear fender, bumper over-riders and a decorative plinth over the number plates. It was a big step forward for Holden as its main rivals had adopted this slab-sided body styling several years previously.

Under the rear hinged and self-supporting bonnet (and not secured with an internal release) was a slightly more powerful version of the grey motor. Its capacity remained at 2.2 litres but power was now 52kW (70bhp) at 4000rpm and torque 149Nm (110lb/ft) at 1200rpm from a slight rise in compression ratio (from 6.5 to 6.8:1) as well as slightly larger inlet valves and ports. All other mechanical components were carried over basically unchanged although the rear springs were 50.8mm (2in) longer and 6.35mm (¼in) narrower. The wheelbase was stretched by 50.8mm (2in) as was overall length and kerb weight was up by around 45kg (100lb).

Modern Motor and *Wheels* both tested the FE, the latter saying, "The new Holden immediately impresses one as a solid, reliable motor car with up-to-the minute styling and well-proven mechanicals." Both reported top speeds of 131km/h (82mph) and around the 14 second mark for the 0–80km/h (0–50mph) run and 9.5 litres per 100klms (30mpg) economy.

The mildly facelifted FC Holden was announced on 6 May 1958, not quite two years after the FE for which there was still a waiting time for delivery. By far the most noticeable change was to the chrome body mouldings on the Special that made for unusual two-toning. The chrome strip went along the base of the windscreen and around the corner onto the front doors before turning through 90° midway along the rear door, going down about a foot and then turning through another 90° to go straight back to finish under the taillight unit.

At the front the grille was altered only insofar as the bottom edge was made more prominent and extended across to include the now rectangular parking/indicator light units. The steering wheel horn ring was now a half-circle, black plastic 'hoods' were added over the instruments and the texture of the radio grille was different.

Another small increase in compression raised the engine's power output to 54kW (72bhp) at 4400rpm, torque output remaining at 149Nm (110lb/ft) but now at 1400rpm, performance remaining unchanged.

The FC range continued until it was replaced in January 1960 by the restyled FB Holden and that will be covered in the next book in this series, *Australian Cars of the 60s*.

THE **NEW**

KIND OF CAR IS THE NEW KIND OF

FORD

CHAPTER 2

FORD MOTOR COMPANY OF AUSTRALIA

Ford, like GM, was keen to establish a manufacturing facility in Australia as distinct from the assembly operations that it had at Geelong dating from 1925 and the Model T. It was unsuccessful in meeting the federal government's specifications to manufacture a car locally and for a time, therefore, had to be content with marketing a diverse and disparate range of models that were sourced from Dagenham, England and Windsor, Canada.

From England it sourced the Anglia, Prefect, Consul and Zephyr (the bulk of its sales) and for a short time (1948–49) the Pilot V8 while from Canada came the Custom, Customline and Mainline V8 models. Interestingly, the Mainline utility was an Australia-only model continuing the concept initiated and developed by Lew Bandt in 1934.

ANGLIA/PREFECT

The early postwar E93A Anglia and Prefect were carry-overs from 1939 (and earlier) and because of restraints at Ford UK these models were the last to be modernised. In fact they were to retain their upright narrow body style and antiquated mechanical specifications until 1953! Underneath was a simple chassis with a single transverse leaf spring at each end, forged beam axle at the front and torque tube axle at the rear, worm-and-roller steering system and a mechanical rod operated braking system using 228-mm (9-in) diameter cast-iron drums that were dwarfed inside the 17-in wheels shod with skinny 4.50 x 17 tyres. Powering these relics was Ford's long-running side-valve in-line four that in the Anglia had a bore and stroke of 56.6 x 92.5mm for a capacity of 933cc and produced just 17kW (23bhp) at 4000rpm; in the Prefect it had an 1172cc version of the engine – its cylinder bores were out to 63.5mm – that produced 22kW (30bhp) at 4000rpm. It needed the extra power because it had a 101.6mm (4in) longer wheelbase to accommodate the extra rear doors and weighed some 100kg (220lb) more; its gearing was slightly lower because it ran on 5.00 x 16 tyres using the same rear axle ratio. Both models were assembled on the company's Geelong assembly line with a small degree of local content. A utility version unique to Australia was made briefly in collaboration with a Melbourne coachbuilder, believed to have been James Flood.

Performance was not a strong point with either car; acceleration was more a gathering of momentum because getting from a standstill to 80km/h (50mph) took an aching 38–40 seconds in the Anglia while maximum speed on a good day was 88–92km/h (55–58mph).

The biggest change came in 1949 when the model designation

changed to A493A. It was a subtly restyled version of the English car (the first A of the model code); the headlights were moved into the fenders, the dash was painted to give a wood grain effect and the triangular-shaped central instrument pod was made from Bakelite, and the roof was now all-steel. Despite their aged mechanical components, tardy performance, hard ride and unpredictable handling they sold quite well in a car-starved marketplace.

In October 1953 they were replaced in the UK by the 100E series Anglia and Prefect that arrived in Australia a year later. The completely new body was an all-steel monocoque unit that was easier and cheaper to build, and stronger; the wheelbase was 2387mm (94in), length 3860mm (152in), width 1524mm (60in) and height 1473mm (58in), kerb weight was 764kg (1680lb). As before, the Anglia was the cheaper of the two and had a two-door body, the Prefect being a four-door, and they had slightly different textured rectangular-shaped grilles as an exterior recognition point. While it had a boxy look to it, the new style was now in tune with the rest of the industry and was an extension of the thinking that had three years earlier produced the Consul/Zephyr pair. The headlights and separate parking lights were in a bezel attached to the leading edge of the front fender while at the rear there were bolt-on vertical taillight units with a single red triangular-shaped lens. The front windscreen was now a curved single pane of toughened glass swept by parallel action wipers that were operated by a dreadful vacuum system. Unusually, for a Ford, the bonnet was front hinged.

Inside was seating for four people, the front two on small bucket seats with the handbrake between them and the long gear lever coming from the top of the gearbox; the dash was a very simple pressed metal affair that was really an open cubby for all the bits 'n pieces that Mr and Mrs Motorist carry around while the actual instruments were contained in a crescent-shaped plastic moulding mounted on the steering column; it comprised a speedometer, fuel and temperature gauges and warning lights. It could not have been simpler. At the side of the instrument pod

UVX 371

DARD
GOOD YEAR
ROVER
WOLSELEY
HUMBER
MORRIS
SUNBEAM

NXF 597

SWAN
HOTEL
TAYLOR
WALKER
907 EEV

was that most British of switches – the combined ignition and lights while those for the choke and wipers were on the dash and provision was made for the installation of the optional heater/demister. The direction indicators were operated by a small vertical switch on the steering wheel hub. New, too, were pendant-type foot pedals.

The luggage compartment was now far more commodious and had the fuel tank tucked into the left corner and the spare wheel lying under the floor.

In place of the ancient leaf spring front suspension, the 100E now sported the new MacPherson strut system with coil springs, the location of the wheel being by a forged lower transverse link and the front stabiliser did double duty as a drag link against longitudinal forces as well as limiting body lean; it was remarkably simple and effective. At the rear was a live axle suspended by semi-elliptic leaf springs with telescopic hydraulic dampers; drive from the gearbox was by an open propeller shaft, simpler and cheaper to make than the old torque tube arrangements. Braking was new, too, now by 178-mm (7-in) cast-iron drums with full hydraulic operation; the steering was a recirculating ball system; and the electrics were now 12 volts.

While the engine *looked* the same, it had been subjected to a development program that refined it in many details so that very few parts were actually interchangeable with previous iterations. It retained the 63.5 x 92.5mm cylinder dimensions for 1172cc, but had among other things a new and stronger crankshaft. Compression was raised to 7:1, the engine now producing 27kW (36bhp) at 4500rpm and 70Nm (52lb-ft) of torque at 2500rpm. The gearbox was still a three-speed unit and the differential ratio was raised to 4.429:1 because the wheels and tyres were now 4J x 13 and 5.20 x 13 respectively.

Like its predecessors, the 100E Fords were assembled at Geelong using some local content like tyres, trim, glass and paint.

According to *The Autocar* road test carried out in 1954, the Anglia was good for 112km/h (70mph) under favourable conditions, would 'sprint' from 0–96km/h (0–60mph) in 33.2 seconds and return 9.8–8.5 litres per 100km (29–33mpg). Locally the Prefect was timed at 114km/h (71mph) and 19.9 seconds for the 0–80km/h (0–50mph) acceleration run while

returning between 8.5 and 7.5 litres per 100km (32 and 38mpg). A test carried out by *Australian Motor Manual* in the same year recorded very similar results. It was almost universally agreed among motoring critics that the car was hampered in every aspect of its performance by the ancient side-valve engine and 3-speed gearbox and they kept wondering why Ford had not developed a modern OHV unit with a four-speed 'box as had every other manufacturer in the small car class.

For the 1956 model year Ford introduced some running changes. A restyled dash was probably the biggest feature, it now had two round dials – speedometer in one, fuel and temperature gauges plus warning lights in the other – in a broader trapezoidal-shaped panel across the car with an open cubby below that. On the outside new taillight units was the main telltale, each unit now having two sections separated by the round reflector, the top orange lens was for the indicators and the lower red lens was for the tail and brake light functions. Further minor changes arrived in 1958 with the indicator lens now having a flat top (it was no longer triangular) and a rectangular-shaped reflector was now between the two lenses, and a new dashboard was available for the Deluxe model that had a proper glove box and radio speaker grille, the original open cubby dash remaining for the base model.

The completely new 105E Anglia arrived as the decade was closing and will be covered in the next book, *Australian Cars of the 60s*.

CONSUL/ZEPHYR/ZODIAC

Ford of England's first truly modern post-war cars were the Consul/Zephyr twins released at the Earls Court Motor Show in October 1950 and which found their way to Australia a little over a year later. They were the result of an extensive development program that had been initiated in Dearborn and then transferred to Dagenham early in 1948. Neither car replaced any existing model in the Ford UK range; they were totally new, designed from the proverbial clean sheet of paper. There was a slight resemblance between the English Fords and the US Ford Custom V8, not that there should be any surprise there.

From the A-pillar back, the two cars were identical, their forward section differing in length and grille design. The four-cylinder Consul was 203mm (8in) shorter than the six-cylinder Zephyr – their wheelbases

were 2540mm and 2642mm (100in and 104in) respectively with overall lengths of 4166/4368mm (164/172ins), width was 1626mm (64in) and height 1524mm (60in) for both while their tracks were identical at 1270 and 1244mm (50 and 49in) front and rear. The all-steel body was a major departure for Ford as it was the company's first foray into unitary construction. Several other firsts came with these models – new OHV four- and six-cylinder engines that shared their cylinder bore and stroke, 12-volt electrics, boxy pontoon-style bodies, MacPherson strut front suspension, wide panoramic one-piece curved windscreen and pendant foot pedals.

To differentiate between the two models, apart from their size, the stylists gave the Consul a plain rectangular grille with closely spaced vertical chromed bars, and for the Zephyr it was a slightly wider grille with horizontal bars, the centre section raised into the bonnet. For Ford, these cars were in the vanguard of a virtual industrial revolution as the old guard was swept aside in Dearborn by Henry Ford II, his actions having a knock-on effect throughout the entire Ford empire.

The Consul/Zephyr twins were the first mass production cars in the world to be designed around the suspension system devised by Earle MacPherson. Typical of '50s Fords were the suspension towers stamped into the inner wheel arch panel with the upper mounts (and pivot) for the strut clearly visible under the bonnet, and there were two diagonal strengthening beams linking the towers to the bulkhead. The bottom of the strut was connected to a forged transverse I-link by way of a ball joint and the stabiliser bar did double duty as a drag link. What was not forecast at this early stage was that the MacPherson strut suspension system would within a decade be adopted by most of the world's major manufacturers.

Between the suspension towers was, in the Consul, a totally new four-cylinder OHV engine made using cast-iron for the block and head. The forged crankshaft had three main bearings and the low-mounted camshaft (on the right-hand side of the block) was chain-driven off the front of the crank, long pushrods operating the shaft-mounted rockers and valves. For the first time on an English Ford, the cylinder bore – 79.3mm – was greater than the stroke of the piston – 76.2mm; engine capacity was 1508cc, an unusual capacity perhaps but as Ford saw no competition prospects for the Consul it was of no concern. On a compression ratio of 6.8:1 and with a small Zenith carburettor it produced 35kW (47bhp) at 4400rpm and 100Nm (74lb/ft) of torque at 2400rpm. With a kerb weight of 1107kg (2436lb) the Consul was no lightweight.

The Zephyr was powered by a six-cylinder version of the same

A

engine, its cylinder capacity being 2262cc, power was 51kW (68bhp) at 4000rpm and torque was 146Nm (108lb/ft) at 2000rpm; kerb weight was 1196kg (2632lb). The engine was entirely conventional in every respect (although state-of-the-engineer's-art for 1950/51) but it did have a most unusual exhaust arrangement. Rather than the gases being collected in a cast manifold and carried rearwards, they were fed directly into the exhaust pipe which was slotted where it met each port, the pipe being clamped to the left-hand side of the head and curved from the front of the head down and back to the pipe that exited at the rear. The Zephyr ran on 6.40 x 13 cross ply tyres whereas the Consul ran 5.90 x 13 and both used a Burman worm and peg steering box that was never known for its precision or feel; both cars featured a Girling braking system with 228-mm (9-in) cast-iron brake drums all round and 121 square inches of lining area, generous for those days.

From the point of view of passenger accommodation, the Consul and Zephyr were identical. The dash was a flat piece of pressed steel with the instruments – speedometer, fuel and temperature gauges (in Australia an ammeter was optional in place of the temperature gauge) in a flush-mounted insert in front of the driver, its shape mirroring the shape of the Zephyr's grille; the gearchange lever was on the steering column and the handbrake was a pistol grip type under the dash to the left of the steering column. In front of the passenger was a small glove box, its lid being the same shape as the instrument cluster. A bench seat front and rear would take three people each, making both cars true six seaters. At the back was a commodious luggage compartment that had the spare wheel upright at the right and the fuel tank under the floor.

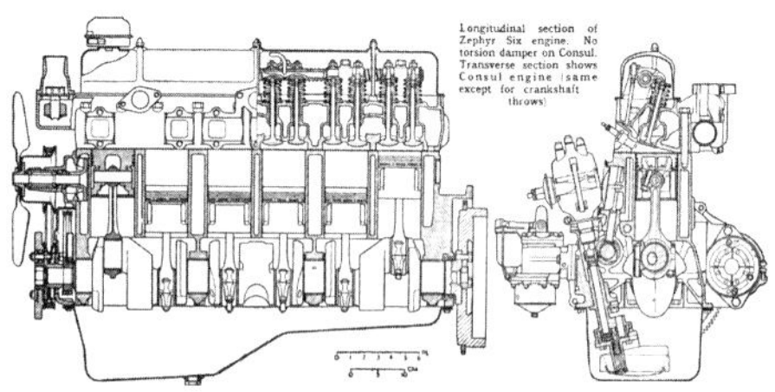

Another first for Ford came with the Consul/Zephyr – vacuum-operated wipers. Under the bonnet was a small tank that stored vacuum generated by the engine and this was used to work the wipers; the trouble was, when under power the engine took all the vacuum and left the wipers stuttering (or still) on the windscreen and the driver with virtually no visibility at all. This diabolical feature lasted until the Mark III range of 1963!

The Autocar tested the Consul in its 13 April 1951 issue and achieved a maximum speed of 120km/h (75mph), a 0–96km/h (0–60mph) time of 31.1 seconds and a fuel consumption of 11.8–10 litres per 100km (24–28mpg) giving a range of around 400km (250mi) from the 42-litre (9-gallon) tank. In Australia *Wheels* published a full test in the January 1954 issue and wrote a very complimentary report and described it as "a very good small family car". From a performance point of view they recorded a top speed of 123.2km/h (77mph, best one-way of 129.6km/h, 81mph) and a time of 16.75 seconds for the 0–80km/h (0–50mph) dash and 25 seconds to 96km/h (60mph), quite a bit quicker than the English car.

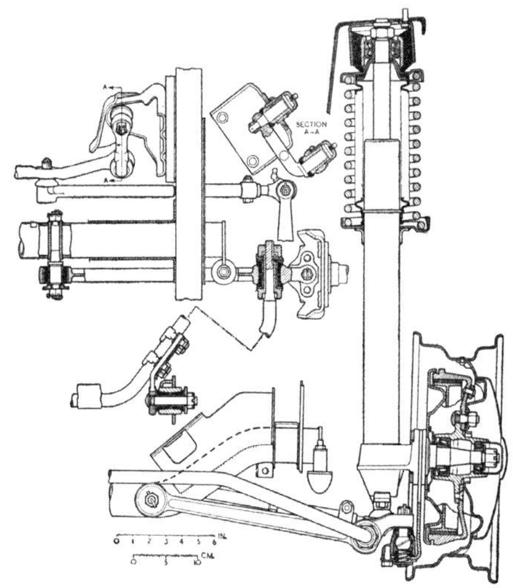

The *Australian Motor Manual* conducted a three-car test in its March 1953 edition, comparing the Zephyr to the 48/215 Holden and Austin A70 Hereford. Amazingly there was very little difference in measured performance between the three cars even though the Zephyr was always regarded by the media as a 'performance' sedan. The Zephyr's maximum speed was recorded at 129.6km/h (81mph), the Holden's was 128km/h (80mph) and the Austin's was 132.8km/h (83mph) while their respective 0–80km/h (0–50mph) dashes were 14.0, 13.5 and 14.5 seconds. The Austin was the heavyweight at 1324kg (2912lb) and the surprise package, the Zephyr weighing in at 1170kg (2576lb) and the Holden at 1069jgs (2352lb). What did come across was the fact that the Zephyr had by far the best handling and roadholding and was the more relaxed long distance touring car. A revised Series II Zephyr was tested in *Wheels* July 1953 – the main change being a new dash – and it recorded a top speed of 128km/h (80mph) and took 13.9 seconds for the dash to 80km/h (50mph). In summary they said, "The Zephyr is roomy and smooth enough in operation to suit the needs of a family; at the same time its performance and design are such that it will satisfy the fastidious driver who wants a thoroughly modern car with a good turn of speed."

It did not take engine tuners long to realise some of the potential in the Zephyr's six-cylinder engine. Probably the first and most popular was the Raymond Mays conversion where the head was skimmed to raise the compression from 6.8:1 up to 7.6:1 and the tiny Zenith carburettor replaced by three SU H4 units, the exhaust manifold remaining unchanged. From tests carried out by *The Autocar*, the 0–96km/h (0–60mph) time was reduced to 16.3 seconds (from 20.4 secs), top speed only increasing marginally. Similarly, it did not take long for the Zephyr to appear in various long distance rallies across England and Europe where it was modestly successful.

In England Ford introduced the Zephyr Zodiac at the 1953 Earls Court Show, the differences being confined to two-tone paint work, whitewall tyres, matched long-range driving lights, two-tone leather upholstery, heater/demister, windscreen washers, clock, reversing lights and more power (53kW/71bhp at 4200rpm) from a slightly higher

RHK 98
RHK 99

1956

compression ratio. This model was never part of Ford's Australian range and neither was the delectable convertible.

For the 1954 model year a series of revisions filtered through to the Geelong assembly line, the most obvious being the repositioning of the instruments into a projecting moulded plastic binnacle on the steering column bringing the same instruments closer to the driver's line of vision, and reshaped taillight units to include rear reflectors. No longer was there a locker in the dash, it was now entirely open with a curved pressed steel panel at the top that incorporated the fittings for the optional heater/demister. Passenger's items were open to view and sliding about while driving.

In August 1956 Ford announced the new Mark II Consul and Zephyr that complied with that oft-used dictum of being longer, wider, lower, larger and more expensive that was common in the 1950s. More interior room was a priority of the redesign and to this end the wheelbase was increased by 101.6mm (4in) on the Consul and 76.2mm (3in) for the Zephyr/Zodiac to 2642mm and 2718mm (104 and 107in); length was increased to 4318mm (170in) for the Consul, 4521mm (178in) for the Zephyr while body width and height were now 1702mm (67in) and 1498mm (59in); wheel tracks were 1346 and 1320mm (53 and 52in) front/rear. Kerb weight had risen slightly. Again, the Consul had the shorter nose and this time its grille was semicircular in shape with a mesh grille while that on the Zephyr was wider and raised in the centre as on the Mark I.

Not only was their new styling clean and attractive, the bodies were relatively unadorned apart from a stainless steel accent line on each side and similar trim around the windows. Inside was a new dashboard that had a semi-circular binnacle atop the dash containing the speedometer plus fuel and amps gauges (a temperature gauge was optional in place of the amps) and some warning lights in a horizontal panel below; provision was made for a radio and heater/demister in a panel under the centre of the dash and there was a lidded glove box in front of the passenger. The lower half of the dash sloped away to give more knee and leg room and although the dash top was covered with vinyl it was not padded.

Both models were far more comfortable six-seaters on their front and rear bench seats and the luggage compartment was more capacious as well with the spare wheel upright on the right, fuel tank in the floor with the filler hidden behind the license plate.

While the MacPherson strut front suspension and live rear axle on leaf springs was carried over as was the steering, the brake drums were widened slightly with the lining area increasing to 147 square inches. The engines, however, underwent far more modifications with their cylinder bores being widened from 79.37mm to 82.55mm and the crankshaft's stroke lengthened from 76.2mm to 79.5mm, capacity of the four-cylinder Consul was now 1702cc and the Zephyr (and Zodiac) 2553cc. Power on a 7.8:1 compression was 44kW (59bhp) and 64kW (86bhp) at 4200rpm respectively.

Wheels magazine tested a Mark II Zephyr in its December 1956 issue and was highly impressed by the car's capabilities from the exterior styling, the roomy and comfortable interior, huge luggage space, its dynamic performance, from the excellent handling and braking to its stability at high speeds. They recorded a maximum speed of 132.8km/h (83mph), 0–80 and 96km/h (0–50 and 0–60mph) times of 11.1 and 18.1 seconds respectively and an economy range of between 14 and 10.8 litres per 100km (20 and 26mpg). They said, "It had a 'right' feel to it and was particularly easy to drive." At £1339 it was £135 more expensive than an FE Holden Special sedan. In the same magazine was also a full test of the Consul about which they opined "It handles extremely well, perhaps even better than the Zephyr, and feels better balanced" and ran the 0–80km/h (0–50mph) dash in 14.9 seconds, on to 96km/h (60mph) in 24.4 seconds and a top speed of 118km/h (74mph). At £1238 it, too, was dearer than the Holden but cheaper than the Zephyr with roominess equal to both and only a minor performance deficit. By way of comparison, *Modern Motor* managed a top speed for the Zephyr of 142km/h (89mph) and 123km/h (77mph) for the Consul and 0–80km/h (0–50mph) times of 11.8 and 14.9 seconds respectively and like their rivals was highly impressed with the cars although they expressed dismay at the dangerous vacuum wipers.

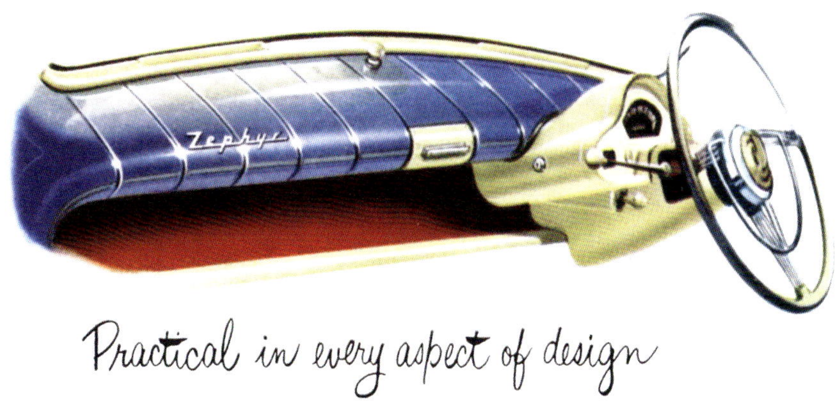

Minor changes came through during the Mark II Zephyr's time with a new grille texture coming in April 1958 that had closer-spaced bars all on one plane and vertical rectangular parking lights (instead of round ones) and a new recirculating ball steering system. In late 1959 another upgrade was announced with a slightly lower and flatter roofline, restyled taillights and a new dashboard. It retained the sharp fall-away for more knee room but now featured a padded dash top and an elongated fan-shaped speedometer again with small fuel and amps gauges (one each end) and warning lights. In February 1959 Ford released the automatic version of the Zephyr. Interestingly, the Consul was not the recipient of any of these changes although it did receive slightly different tail lights and a full-length chrome side strip.

From 1958 Ford Australia introduced the slightly better equipped Zodiac version as well as the Australia-only Zephyr station wagon and utility, the latter two bodies being assembled by James Flood Pty Ltd in Melbourne from Ford-supplied panels before being transported by truck back to Geelong for final assembly. The late Lew Bandt was responsible for their styling.

David McKay tested a Zephyr wagon over 2000mi for *Modern Motor* (December 1959) and found it to be fast, roomy and extremely comfortable and although it was more expensive than the Holden (its price was £1425 compared with £1258) McKay felt it was worth it. He thoroughly enjoyed the drive but had two criticisms – the vacuum wipers he felt were dangerous and the brakes were marginal given the Zephyr's 144km/h (90mph) performance.

Ford Australia had made the decision and investment in a mildly restyled Mark II Zephyr as its challenger to the supremacy of Holden. However, these plans stalled when the then managing director, Charles Smith, saw the clay mock-ups of the forthcoming Falcon, a car that was much more stylish, more modern in every way and, importantly, much lighter and therefore less expensive to manufacture than the Zephyr. The Falcon was immediately chosen as the car to challenge the might of GM-H.

D.&C. AUSTIN
MOUNT GAMBIER
WXC 499

AA-425F

WXC 499

PILOT

The Ford V8 Pilot is possibly the 'forgotten' Ford in the company's Australian post-war history. It was imported in CKD form from England beginning in 1948 and assembled at Geelong to supplement the limited supply of V8-engined cars out of Canada caused by the dollar shortage; it was a postwar development of the pre-war English 22hp model. Pilots remained available until early 1952 and because their chassis numbering was not consecutive it is nearly impossible today to tell one year model from the next.

Its styling was an upgrade of the 1939 model and looked old compared with the brand new 1949 Custom; it was shorter and lighter than the Custom although it offered almost identical accommodation except for the boot which carried the spare tyre in the bootlid which compromised the available space. Also, the headlights were mounted separately on small pedestals on the front guards which made the Pilot one of the few cars remaining in production with its headlights so mounted.

Under the bonnet was the venerable 3622cc side valve V8 (77.8 x 95.3mm) that developed 63kW (85bhp) at 3500rpm, this power going to the rear wheels through a 3-speed manual gearbox with column gearshift; its suspension was Ford's antiquated transverse leaf spring and forged beam axle at the front and torque tube axle and transverse leaf spring at the rear. Braking was by a Girling hydro-mechanical system using cast-iron drums.

As for its size, it rode a 2756-mm (108.5-in) wheelbase, was 4419mm (174in) in overall length by 1765mm (69.5in) wide by 1676mm (66in) in height, its tracks were 1422mm (56in) at the front and 1473mm (58in) at the rear and it was fitted with 6.00 x 16 cross ply tyres.

A road test was published in the *Australian Motor Manual* in 1951 and it recorded a maximum speed of 128km/h (80mph), a 0–80km/h (0–50mph) time of 12.9 seconds and a fuel consumption of 15 litres per 100km (19mpg) on test. These figures were excellent for a sedan weighing the not inconsiderable 1450kg (3190lb) and running on low octane fuel.

Pilot enthusiasts insist the model was a good car – very comfortable, a superb cruiser, relatively quiet and roomy – but it has been tainted by history and judged as being too old fashioned insofar as it was pre-war styling and mechanical components competing in a world that was rapidly modernising as witnessed by the Ford Custom that was being sold off the same Ford showroom floor at the same time. However, as the critics seem to have forgotten, the Pilot was a stop-gap model pending the arrival of more modern post-war designed models.

FORD V8

Following the return of peace Ford began importing CKD kits of the US Ford V8 for assembly at Geelong. This was the 'humpy-back' model that was in effect a revised 1942 model, its styling being characterised by the distinctive fenders over the wheels front and rear and the six-window treatment along with doors that closed on the centre B-pillar, something that was quite common then.

Its engineering was typically Ford – it went back to the Model T in some ways – insofar as there was a separate chassis underneath with the company's traditional transverse leaf spring suspension front and rear, a full hydraulic brake system and of course a 6-volt electrical system. The engine was the 74kW (100bhp) 3.9-litre side-valve V8 that drove the rear wheels through a three-speed manual gearbox with synchromesh on second and top gears.

For the 1947 model year Ford added the Mercury version to its model line-up, the differences being the fine, vertical bar mesh on the Mercury and chromed strips on front and rear fenders plus better quality soft grained leather upholstery and trim inside. Both cars were comfortable six-seaters and could cruise at 96+km/h (60+mph) for hours in quiet comfort. They were, however, interim models as the company awaited the arrival of the new and more modern Custom V8.

The Ford V8 sedan sold for £670 while the Mercury sold for £692, to which sales tax at the rate of 10 per cent had to be added.

CUSTOM

The first truly modern, post-war Ford was the Custom that was released in America in June 1948 in time for the 1949 model year. It represented the proverbial breath of fresh air to the beleaguered corporation that was now being run by a youthful Henry Ford II. While it did retain a separate chassis and the flathead V8, virtually everything else was new. The styling was up-to-date and matched that of Studebaker who had led the industry with its then *avant garde* smooth-sided three-box styling, passengers were seated within the wheelbase for a far more comfortable ride and even though the roofline was inches lower there was still more than ample room inside. The styling was a harbinger of the future at Ford and was copied to some extent for the two British Fords, the Consul and Zephyr. Perhaps unusually, the '49-ers retained a split flat glass windscreen even though Chevrolet, for example, had a split curved glass windscreen.

The 'single spinner' Custom arrived here in September 1949 to replace the 'humpy' Ford V8 Deluxe and was powered by the company's tried and trusted side-valve V8 of 239.4-cid (3.9-litres) displacement that, with improved ignition, induction and a slightly higher compression ratio produced 74kW (100bhp) at 3800rpm and drove the rear wheels through a three-speed manual gearbox with non-synchromesh first gear. The chassis was re-engineered to accept the new coil-and-wishbone independent front suspension that was allied to a Hotchkiss rear suspension, Ford-speak for a live axle and semi-elliptic leaf springs, and the braking system comprised 254-mm (10-in) drums all round with hydraulic actuation. The unit construction all-steel body was mounted to the frame using 22 rubber shims. As a simple means of identifying a Custom, the 49s had the brand name – FORD – spelt out in block letters on the front of the bonnet and had pull-out door handles.

Body length was 5004mm (197in, it certainly did not look that big) on a wheelbase of 2895mm (114in), was 1854-mm (73-in) wide, rode on 16in wheels with a five-bolt stud pattern and the kerb weight was about 1455kg (3200lb).

Unique to the Australian market was the availability from early 1949 of a coupe utility version of the Custom that had a load area of 2184mm (86in) in length by 1562-mm (61.5-in) wide with a load height of 533mm (21in). It would prove to be popular marrying as it did considerable performance with a new style and an ability to carry quite large loads with little complaint.

A minor upgrade came through for the 1950 model year and this included push button exterior door handles, the mounting of the new Ford crest on the bonnet, the main grille bar now wrapped around onto the front fender with the parking lights repositioned below the bar (instead of being in the bar) and the hubcaps were now made from chromed steel.

Ford Australia had by 1950 invested in new press tooling to stamp out some of the body panels as well as other new machinery at Geelong and was manufacturing the side-valve V8 engine plus making the frames and much of the driveline while also sourcing pistons, rings, bearing shells, generators and distributors locally.

Another upgrade arrived in May 1951 and was soon referred to as the 'Twin Spinner' because of that feature in the revised grille. The revision included new broader horizontal taillights made from plastic and no longer glass with a chrome flash on the rear quarter panel to

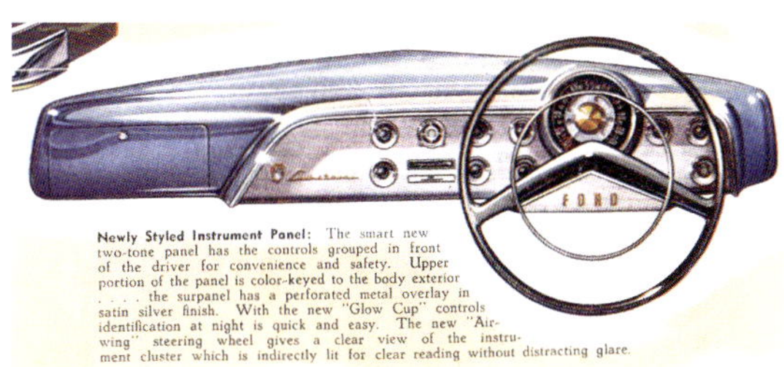

fill in the gap behind the light unit, chromed hubcaps with a stylised 'F' on them, larger rear window, new body mouldings, 15-in wheels for the sedans (the utility retained the 16-in wheels) and a new dashboard. The Custom was a success in Australia and proved popular with the rural community because of their rugged construction, reliability through basically simple mechanical components and an ability to cruise easily at 112–120km/h (70–75mph).

The *Australian Motor Manual* published a report on the twin spinner in its July 1951 issue and reported a top speed of 137.6km/h (86mph), a 0–80km/h (0–50mph) 14.2 acceleration time of 12 seconds and claimed it would return 14.2 litres per 100km (20mpg) at normal driving speeds.

CUSTOMLINE/MAINLINE

In November 1952 the thoroughly revised and slightly larger Ford Customline was released for the '53 model year and is often referred to as the 'Anniversary' model because in 1953 Ford celebrated its 50th anniversary. It retained the separate chassis and running gear from the Custom but with the wheelbase lengthened to 2921mm (115 in), length grew to 5029mm (198ins), width to 1879mm (74ins) and height was 1575mm (62ins); kerb weight increased to 1545kg (3400lb). Under the bonnet was an Australian-made version of the venerable 3.9-litre side-valve V8 that was now developing 82kW (110bhp) at 3800rpm and provided the big saloon with spirited performance. New-for-Customline were pendant foot pedals, dashboard and some nice colours to go with the one-piece curved windscreen glass. The *Australian Motor Manual* published a full test of a 1954 Customline and came back with an 139km/h (87mph) maximum speed, 11.4 seconds for the 0–80km/h (0–50mph) dash and 17.8 litres per 100km (16mpg) with the comment that it was "one of the best and most solid long distance cruising cars available on the Australian market". *Wheels* returned similar performance figures from their test and commented, "The Customline takes six people comfortably over long trips and has an engulfing luggage compartment. There is no effort, no fuss or noise and no outward sign of fast motoring."

As was the way in the '50s, both front and rear seats were benches so accommodation was available for six large adults. Carpets were on the

Customline

Ford

GYR·715

CUS 056

floor and there were door armrests but a heater was listed as an option as was a radio plus there was a wide range of other accessories that buyers could add to their car. Size was regarded as a luxury in the 1950s, not equipment levels as we do today.

From August 1955 came a thoroughly revised Customline. The body styling was clearly based on the passenger section of the previous model but the exterior sheet metal was completely new; it now featured that most '50s of styling icons – the wrap around windscreen complete with knee-bashing vertical A-pillar, and a larger wrap around rear window. The front and rear fenders were slightly longer and culminated in hooded headlights up front and larger round taillights at the rear with a triangular-shaped fake light above them in the subtle fins; the large round red-lens rear lights actually had three functions – one filament was for the tail light, the other (higher wattage) filament had the dual role of brake light and indicator; either side of the wide grille up front were two large round parking/indicator lights. On the side of the body was a full-length straight chrome strip and there were small V8 badges on each front fender. A carry-over from the previous model was the 6-volt electrics.

The Customline was close to being the biggest car on the market, as well as being the biggest in production in Australia, as it continued to be assembled in Geelong from a combination of parts imported from Canada and some that were made locally. Its dimensions increased slightly with the revised body, the wheelbase now being 2933mm (115.5 in), it was 5042-mm (198.5-in) long by 1925-mm (75.8-in) wide and 1549-mm (61-in) high, wheel tracks were 1473 mm (58 in) front and 1422mm (56 in) rear with kerb weight being a hefty 1578kg (3472lb).

While the engineering was mostly carried over there were two major

changes: the arrival of a completely new Y-block overhead valve (OHV) V8 engine in which the block and crankcase were cast as one, and ball joints in the front suspension. The engine's cylinder dimensions were 92 x 83.8mm for a capacity of 4460cc – 3.62 x 3.3 in for 272 cubic inches – that developed 120kW (162bhp) at 4400rpm. After nearly three decades of the old side-valve V8 this was a major step forward for Ford although to be honest it was playing catch-up as most of its rivals in America had OHV V8s in production years previously.

Inside it was much as would have been expected. Bench seats were standard fare making the Customline a full six-seater with good quality washable vinyl as the upholstery and there were carpets on the floor. The instruments – speedometer, fuel and temperature gauges – were in a semi-circular-shaped binnacle on top of the dash (much like that found in the Mark II Consul/Zephyr) with the cute feature of a clear plastic backing. Where the English dash sloped away quite dramatically the American version was flatter with the circular controls for the optional radio – literally an 'around the dial' type – and heater/demister positioned centrally and the big glove box was to the left.

Modern Motor carried out a full road test in its November 1955 issue. The testers were astonished at the performance of this big, heavy sedan that would zip from 0–80km/h (0–50mph) in 8.4 seconds, run to 80km/h (50mph) and 128km/h (80mph) in first and second gears and exceed 160km/h (100mph) in top gear. As they said, "It outperforms all but a few expensive sport cars." Mind you, with only 192 square inches of lining inside 279-mm (11-in) diameter cast-iron drums, stopping when using its performance was always an issue but in those innocent times we simply accepted that without question.

For 1956 Ford in Australia continued with the 1955 Canadian-style body but with a new grille and trim plus 12-volt electrics although the '55 dash was retained. Next year's model continued with the '55 body but was updated using 1956 US Fairlane trim that curved up onto the top of each front fender with a large V8 badge in the grille and chromed headlight bezels. Ford Australia was now out of synch with Canada and so for 1958 it used the 1955 Canadian Meteor grille with the four-pointed star in the centre of the grille – these cars are referred to as the 'Star' model – plus '56 Meteor side trim and round parking lights replaced the former rectangular units. The '58s featured triple paint colour schemes and locally-made Smiths instruments. While the V8 remained Ford introduced the Fordomatic two-speed automatic gearbox in 1957, the selector lever being on the right-hand of the steering column. Bryan Hanrahan wrote in *Modern Motor* after a full test of the new automatic Ford, "As an example of automation the Ford is outstanding and it's the cheapest fully automatic car sold here. Ford can take credit for a fine engineering job." It was slightly slower than the manual tested earlier but nonetheless was timed at 157.3km/h (98.3mph) and 8.8 seconds for the 0–80km/h (0–50mph) run. Its retail price was £2070.

Running in parallel with the Customline sedans was the Mainline half-ton utility that adopted most of the changes along the way.

The same basic body but with revised grille and tail lights was produced through to late 1959 and according to some people the 'Star' model Ford V8s could still be bought new in 1960. However, in November 1959 Ford released the 'tank' Fairlane in three versions: Custom 300, Fairlane 500 and Ranch Wagon. By comparison with previous large Fords in Australia these were gargantuan. Ford described them as "the world's most beautifully proportioned cars" and when displayed at the 1959 Brussels World Trade Fair they were awarded the Gold Medal for exceptional styling by the Comite Francais de l'Elegance. Size must have mattered because every aspect was dominated by its sheer size. The grille was w-i-d-e with five rows of little squares in a rectangular opening that was topped by a broad chromed surround with the enormous bumper below; at either end were huge 'Dagmar-like' housings that contained the indicator lights. Both the bonnet and bootlid had enough surface area to land a Harrier jump-jet and the front windscreen had been increased in area by curving it further around the sides and up into the roof! At the rear were huge round taillights set in large, chromed bezels with the indicator lights above them in a smaller round nacelle on the end of a discreet fin; joining the two indicator lights housings was a broad chrome strip that dipped slightly to a shallow vee in the centre.

The wheelbase had been increased to 2997mm (118in) and overall length stretched to 5283mm (208in) with the ride height at 1422mm (56in); kerb weight was now up to 1634kg (3594lb). Under the bonnet was an enlarged version of the reliable V8 engine, its bore and stroke now being 101.6 x 88.9mm (4.00 x 3.50 in) for a capacity of 5440cc (332 cubic inches). Power was up to 168kW (225bhp) at 4400rpm with torque of 440Nm (325lb/ft) at 2200rpm. Ford listed two gearboxes – a three-speed manual with column shift and a two-speed Fordomatic automatic – with a surprising number being ordered with the manual option. Times were different then.

Racing driver and journalist, the late David McKay, took a Fairlane on an extended drive to one of his race meetings and reported the events in *Modern Motor* magazine (March 1960) saying, "The Fairlane was able to take all our luggage with ease and proved more than able to cruise at high speed in comfort and silence leaving us fresh and relaxed at the end of the journey." When checked against the clock the big sedan returned a 156.8km/h (98mph) top speed, took 11.5 seconds for the 0–80km/h (0–50mph) sprint and returned 19 litres per 100km (15mpg) overall.

The Custom, Fairlane and Ranch Wagon were assembled at Ford's Homebush (Sydney) plant using imported chassis, panels, engine and running gear but local paint, glass, tyres, battery and some trim items.

During the Fifties Ford had by far the widest range of models on offer of any manufacturer competing on the local market but not one was at the top of its market segment. The Prefect was hampered by the ancient engine and three-speed gearbox, the Consul was expensive for what it was as was the Zephyr but at least it had some *brio* and the Customlines were too expensive to own and run for the average buyer so it was limited to a more affluent, mainly rural, clientele. Big changes, however, were just over the horizon …

LLA 810

958 CMO

THE
NEW
CONSUL
CONSUL
Consul

YNO 454

GMR 701

GB

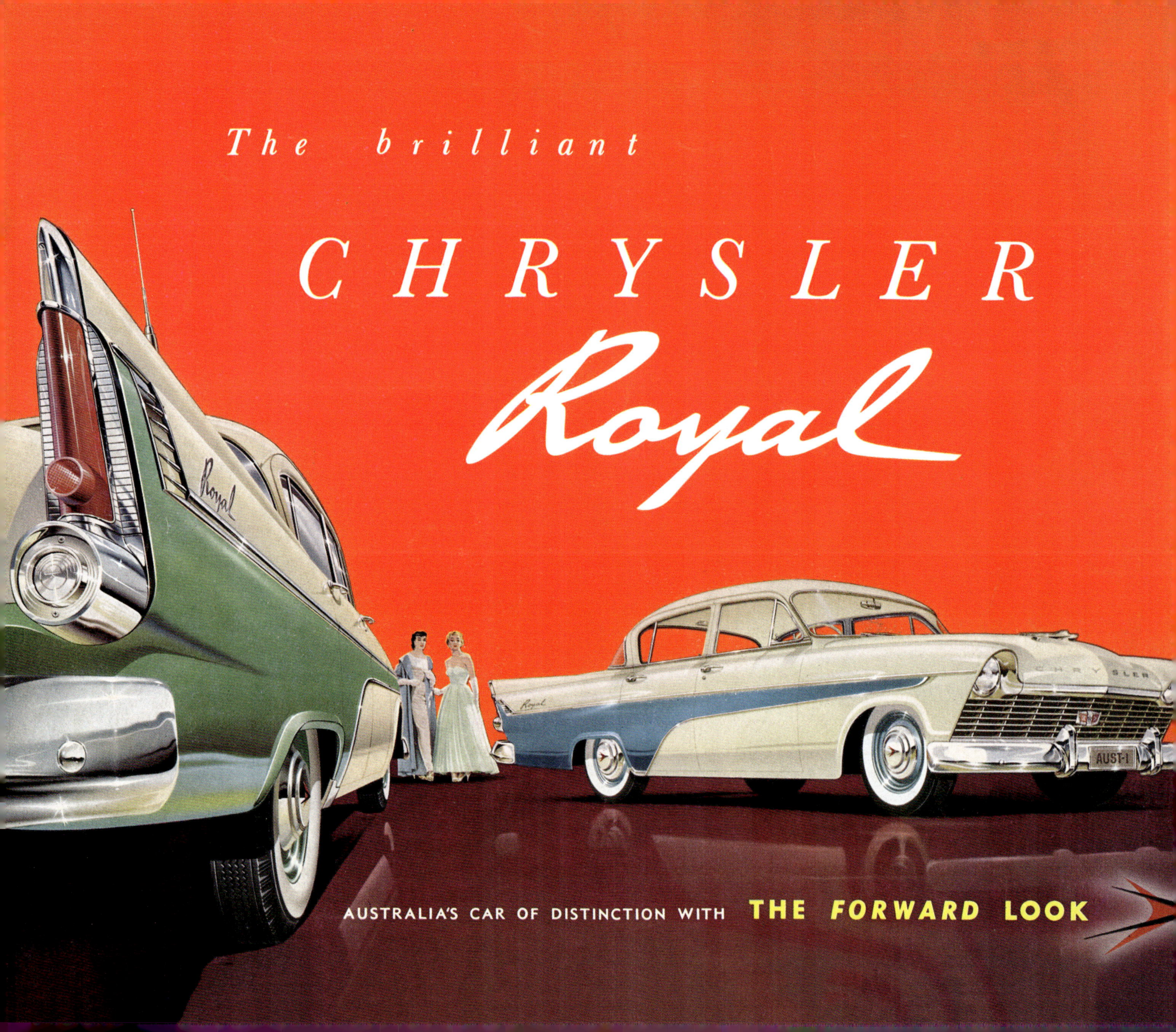

The brilliant
CHRYSLER
Royal
AUSTRALIA'S CAR OF DISTINCTION WITH THE FORWARD LOOK

CHAPTER 3

CHRYSLER IN AUSTRALIA

After the war the Chrysler Corporation was number two to GM in the USA with Ford trailing at number three mainly due to the troubles within the family created by old Henry. In Australia in the immediate postwar years the assembly and distribution of Chrysler products – Plymouth, Dodge and De Soto sedans, Dodge and Fargo trucks – continued under the auspices of Chrysler Dodge De Soto Distributors (Australia) Pty Ltd. This all-Australian company had been established in 1936 when the 18 distributors of Chrysler's cars purchased a controlling interest in T J Richards Ltd, formerly a family-owned coachbuilding company based in Adelaide that built bodies for Chrysler and other companies.

On 6 June 1951 the Chrysler Corporation bought an 85 per cent stake in Chrysler Dodge De Soto Distributors (Australia) Limited which then concentrated solely on Chrysler products. Despite statements made at the time about major investments and an expanded model range, the company appeared to mark time industrially when compared with the rapid expansion of business at GM-Holden and Ford as well as BMC, Volkswagen and to a lesser extent at the Rootes Group.

In line with previous practices, Chrysler Australia Ltd operated three separate dealer networks selling locally-assembled Plymouth, Dodge and De Soto sedans, each being identical to the other with the exception of their grilles and badges. The first postwar Chrysler cars to be made in Adelaide were the fastback sedans with the six-window bodies and their doors closing on the B-pillar. Their styling was based on the company's 1942 models that had been mothballed for the duration of the war and revived for the 1946 model year. Styling differences were confined to the front of the body – the various state distributors imported the rolling chassis from Windsor, Canada to be mated with CDD-stamped, assembled, painted and trimmed (from the A-pillar back) bodies that were transported by rail to each distributor's assembly works. To these were bolted the imported front clip that was slightly different for each make.

The 1946-through-1948 models were carry-over models with a fastback roofline, the Plymouth (P15), Dodge (D24) and De Soto (SP15) being identical in style – there were minor differences in wheelbase/length – and ran a chassis and running gear that had been substantially revised for the 1939 model year to incorporate an independent coil-and-wishbone front suspension for the first time on a Chrysler product. What was new for 1947 was the availability of the company's new break-through in gearbox engineering, the famous Fluid Drive.

In 1949 came the first new post-war design that saw a return to the three-box body style; it was very conservative in comparison with its GM and Ford rivals and mechanically was a continuation of the old components. While sales dipped significantly in the USA, they held up well in Australia because of the burgeoning wealth of the country and the car's reputation for indestructibility. However, where the various GM divisions managed to give the styling of their ranges some character and flair, Chrysler's efforts looked dowdy and lacking in sparkle which in many ways mirrored the personality of its CEO, Kaufman T Keller. It was he who insisted that he be able to wear his hat while seated in the back seat, for example. The vee-windscreen was split with two flat panes of glass and there were vestiges of fenders at the rear where the international trend was clearly towards slab sides. There were four doors all hinged at their forward edge leading to a very roomy interior and the dashboard continued to house the speedometer and four supplementary gauges – oil pressure, fuel, temperature and amps – under a slightly raised binnacle directly in front of the driver. Provision for a radio and heater/demister was in the centre and the glovebox was off to the left.

Mechanically the 49-ers were carry-over 48s with only minor revisions. The side-valve six now produced 72kW (97bhp) at 3600rpm and the separate chassis had a 2819-mm (111-in) wheelbase.

The next model change came in 1953 with the arrival of a much more modern design – but not mechanicals – Plymouth P24/Dodge D43/De Soto SP24 that brought a wider and lower look along with a curved one-piece windscreen. This third post-war generation of cars from Chrysler again did not follow the lead from GM and Chrysler paid the price in market terms. Where all five GM divisions (and Ford) went for longer, lower, wider and more powerful cars with the release of their 1953 models, Chrysler went the other way! Keller again decreed that the cars be more compact and taller so he could sit and drive with his hat on. The end result of this goof was that Chrysler dropped sales volume dramatically and was no longer second to GM but third behind an emerging and re-energised Ford. Not even the release of the virile performance-leading Hemi V8 engine or the delightful pillarless hardtop coupes was able to stem the flow of defections away from Chrysler products.

For the 1955 model year the *American* De Soto and Chrysler ranges sported completely new styling that emphasised the longer, wider, lower themes. In Australia Chrysler retained the original 1953 body for all three marques until mid-1957 because it had tooled to press the panels and could not afford to change.

Under the bonnet was Chrysler's ageing side-valve in-line six-cylinder engine that was assembled at the Mile End factory using a combination of imported major components and smaller items that were sourced locally. The engine had a bore and stroke of 86 x 108mm (3.38 x 4.25 in) for a cubic capacity of 3764cc (230 cubic inches) and produced 75kW (101bhp) at 3600rpm; its power was considered more than acceptable for the time but it was its torque that buyers were more impressed with – 243Nm (179lb/ft) at just 1400rpm – that allowed the car to be dropped into top gear at not much more than 13–16km/h (8–10mph) and left there. It made driving simpler even if it is was a lazy way of driving.

Drive went to the rear wheels through a single-plate clutch and a three-speed manual gearbox with the obligatory steering column gearshift. As an option buyers could order an overdrive unit. The mechanical components were mounted on a robust separate box-section chassis with an X-cross member in the centre; at the front was an

XSW 279

XSW 279

Royal

CHRYSLER
DLU 816

independent suspension comprising upper-and-lower wishbones, a coil spring with concentric hydraulic telescopic damper; at the rear was a live banjo axle supported by semi-elliptic leaf springs; braking was by small 254mm (10in) cast-iron drums for each wheel with hydraulic action, the handbrake being a drum on the output shaft from the gearbox. Much of the mechanical components were carried over from well-proven parts that had been in production for many years. The only mechanical item that was new was the optional two-speed Powerflite automatic transmission that arrived for the 1956 models.

Wheels tested a Plymouth Cranbrook in its February 1954 edition and said, "The Cranbrook is a very good automobile, soundly built and well-finished. It exhibits a pleasant character on the road and will take six people and a mountain of luggage effortlessly from one place to another." They liked its easy-going manner and handling, especially on dirt roads; they managed a top speed of 144km/h (90mph) and found it would cruise comfortably for hours at 112–120km/h (70–75mph). These comments could equally apply to the Dodge Kingsway and De Soto Diplomat as the three cars were close siblings. In fact, in the

July 1955 issue they tested a De Soto Diplomat Plaza equipped with the Powerflite two-speed automatic and described the car as a 'revelation'. They further said, "The De Soto has a big, lazy slow revving engine which has obviously been designed to give a large torque output over its whole range."

Differences between the 1953 and 1957 versions of these cars were minimal. For example, the '53 De Soto had an 11 bar grille and short stainless steel strips over the flared wheel arches, for 1954–55 the grille had only nine bars and the chromed strips stretched along the full body side while for 1956–57 it reverted back to two short strips over the wheel arches and the headlights were now hooded. The Dodge and Plymouths all went through the same minimalist cycle; the '56 models are easily recognisable because they all had chromed hooded headlight bezels.

In Australia, these cars continued to be marketed through separate sales channels but try as Chrysler might, sales declined in the face of the exploding demand for the mid-sized Holden 48/215, FJ and FE that succeeded it. The Australian motoring public had decided that the Holden was what they wanted, not the larger, heavier and thirstier

VBY·202

SA 1073

P
ANGLE
DODGE
UJL·213

RAM·056

Chrysler products. Where the American versions included the V8 engine and neat looking hardtop sedans and coupes, the Australian market had to settle for the increasingly ancient side-valve six and the single four-door body offering. A single station wagon prototype was built but not produced.

Although considered compact by US standards, here in Australia these sedans were larger than the big selling Holden 48/215 but smaller than the Ford Customline. They all sat on a wheelbase of 2895mm (114in), were 4851mm (191in) overall, 1854-mm (73-in) wide by 1574-mm (62-in) high and weighed 1428kg (3136 lb) although this depended on what gearbox was fitted. In 1956 each make was available in three versions: for example, the P25 Plymouth came as the Cranbrook with the three-speed manual gearbox and 75kW (101bhp) engine for £1778, as the Savoy if it was ordered with the manual gearbox with overdrive and 83kW (112bhp) engine for £1878, and the 83kW (112bhp) Powerflite automatic cost £2028.

If a buyer decided a Dodge (D49) was what he wanted the choice was from the £1787 Kingsway Custom with 75kW (101bhp) and three-speed manual gearbox, the Kingsway Crusader that came with the 83kW (112bhp) engine and overdrive gearbox for £1886 and the top Dodge was the automatic Kingsway Coronet that cost £2036. And in the De Soto (SP25) showroom the choice was from the Diplomat with the small 75kW (101bhp) engine and manual gearbox for £1800, the Diplomat Regent with 83kW (112bhp) and the overdrive gearbox for £1898 and then the Diplomat Plaza automatic at £2036. Power assisted steering and brakes were new options to the local market and came in 1956.

In May 1957 the AP1 (Australian Production Number 1) Chrysler Royal was announced, this one model replacing the three previous offerings from the company. In the beginning it had been intended that there would be Plymouth (AP1), Dodge (AD1) and De Soto (AS1) versions but at the last minute a board decision created a change of model policy. Within a short time there was mayhem among the former Chrysler dealers as the company sacked distributors in each state (except Queensland) and many dealers.

Managing director W D Ferguson stated at the time, "It is easier and cheaper to build one make of car than three. Chrysler Royal combines the dependability of Dodge, the flashing performance of Plymouth and the distinction of De Soto." What that meant, of course, was the end of the line for those three famous marque names although they would reappear unexpectedly later in another guise.

The Royal comprised the passenger cabin section of the P25 Plymouth with new sheet metal based largely on the '55 and '56 US Plymouths grafted on front and rear. The interior was furnished with a new dashboard comprising round dials with, on automatic versions, *push buttons* to control the Powerflite two-speed automatic transmission in the far right bezel. There were only four buttons: N for neutral, D for drive, R for reverse and L for low gear. A huge glove box was in the centre of the dash and there was a circular radio speaker on the far left; seats were massive benches and the boot was huge – 35-cubic feet – with the spare upright on the right for easy access.

Built with a local content of more than 90 per cent, most of the mechanical components were carried over from the P25 – separate X-braced chassis, coil and wishbone front suspension, live axle and leaf springs at the rear and the comparatively small 254-mm (10-in) cast-iron drum brakes. The venerable side-valve six-cylinder engine that dated from 1930 continued in two capacities – 82.55 x 117.5mm for a capacity of 3769cc (3.25 x 4.625 in, 230 cid) and 87.31 x 114.3mm for 4096cc, (3.4375 x 4.5 in for 250 cid). As before, if you ordered a manual gearbox it came with the smaller six that now produced 85kW (115bhp) and 263Nm (194lb/ft) of torque, all automatics having the bigger Kew-sourced engine that gave 87kW (117bhp) and 278Nm (205lb/ft). Several interesting options came with the Royal, items like vacuum assisted power brakes, power steering (actually available a year earlier), automatic overdrive plus comfort items like a heater/demister, deep pile carpets and radio.

Priced at £1697 for the manual version and £1883 for the six-cylinder automatic, the pricing was slightly less than previously which was a nice surprise for buyers. A full test was conducted by *Wheels* in its August 1957 issue, the test car being covered in camouflage because at

the time it had not yet been released. The roominess of the Royal was never in question and neither was its ability to take the family's luggage in the vast boot. Allowing for the different standards that we accept today, the writer praised the car for its stability over varying surfaces travelled at high speed (higher than 112km/h/70mph) and found it a relaxing long distance cruiser. The Powerflite transmission came in for high praise, too. Only the brakes came in for any real criticism which should have surprised nobody. Against the clock the heavy – slightly over 1954kg (4300lb(!) ready for the road – Royal managed a top speed of 136km/h (85mph), 0–80km/h (0–50mph) in 12.5 seconds, 0–96km/h (0–60mph) in 19.2 seconds and the fuel consumption varied from 23.5 litres per 100km (12.5mpg) on full-bore testing to 15.5 litres per 100km (18.2mpg) when touring.

Six months after the AP1 sedan was placed on the market Chrysler surprised everybody with the release of the Plainsman station wagon and Wayfarer utility. Neither was a sales success and both were discontinued after less than two years in production. And as if that was not enough, the engineers at Keswick managed to squeeze the wide poly-head 313 cid V8 (out of the Canadian Plymouth Fury) into the Royal's engine bay, a task that was not as straight forward as it might have seemed. Now the Royal had 164kW (220bhp) at its disposal taking its maximum speed to around 160km/h (100mph) with much quicker acceleration. Sales of the Royal saloon increased markedly following the availability of the V8 engine because it made long distance country travelling that much more enjoyable. Mind you, there were still those tiny 254-mm (10-in) brake drums at each wheel trying to stop the big and now heavier Royal …

In 1959 Chrysler released the AP2 Royal that was unchanged except for a garish and bold new grille and unusual fin-upon-a-fin at the rear. Technically those extra fins were an option but it is doubtful if an AP2 left the assembly lines without them!

Wheels managed one of the few road tests of the AP2 V8 and published it in the September 1959 issue. They liked the firm suspension and the vast amount of room in the interior and the boot but lamented the brakes and headlights as not being up to the car's storming performance. As they commented, "It will knock the spots off anything the opposition can offer and considering its bulk it goes around corners very well" and further said, "It is tasteful and comfortable inside." Despite its bulk it was not nearly as large as its recently re-introduced Detroit relations and the magazine's testers felt it was a better car in tough going. Against the clock it registered a top speed of 155km/h (97mph) and 0–80 and 96km/h (0–50 and 60mph) times of 8.2 and 11.6 seconds respectively while returning between 19 and 13.5 litres per 100km (15 and 21mpg).

SA 441·702

ADULTS
PIONEER SPRINGS
PLYMOUTH

Mobil
ROUND AUSTRALIA
PLYMOUTH

DODGE-DE SOTO-PLYMOUTH RETURN

With the gradual decline of sales of the Royal – it was failing to meet expectations of a changing buyer profile – Chrysler made the perhaps inevitable decision beginning with the 1958 model year to re-expand their big car range by importing from Detroit small numbers of the then current Plymouth Belvedere (in four-door hardtop form), Dodge Custom Royal and De Soto Firesweep in CKD kits that were assembled at the company's Mile End facility. These sedans featured the long, low and wide style that had swept the studios at the Chrysler Corporation since the arrival of stylist extraordinaire Virgil M Exner. He transformed the appearance of all Chrysler products and was the man behind the 'Forward Look' that came to be one of the Corporation's advertising mantras at the time.

The editions imported were, by comparison with the Royal, light years ahead in style. They were perhaps no roomier and only marginally faster but they did what they did in style and that was important to people paying upwards of £3000 for their car. All three famous names were V8-powered, as you would have expected. Plymouth's power came from a 5211cc (318-cid) 'poly' engine driving the rear wheels through the excellent new Torqueflite 3-speed automatic gearbox. New to these Chryslers was the Corporation's superb wishbone front suspension with longitudinal torsion bars that imparted a sense of tightness and handling precision that the Chevrolets and Fords did not have. Mind you, they still had drum brakes (279-mm/11-in diameter) with power boost and power steering that felt somehow disconnected. Despite having 168kW (225bhp) on tap the Plymouth was not a sports sedan even though it was good for 172–180km/h (108–112mph) with 96km/h (60mph) coming up in 9.8 seconds from rest. In a straight line it was quick – quicker than the 313-cid V8 powered Royal – for a sedan sitting on a 3098-mm (122-in) wheelbase, stretching some 5435mm (214in) overall and weighing a hefty 1727kg (3800lb).

Both the Dodge and De Soto were powered by the bigger 350- and 361-cid 'poly' head V8s respectively that pumped out 186kW (250bhp) and 205kW (275bhp), would push the sedans to 80km/h (50mph) in 7.2 seconds and run to 172.8km/h (108mph) plus while consuming fuel at the rate of 19 litres per 100km (15mpg). Like all American sedans of the period, acceleration both from a standstill and for passing was their forte, top speed being somewhat incidental which was perhaps just as well given the vehicle dynamics.

All three retailed at more than £3000 – the Dodge Custom Royal, for example, cost £3275 – but that was no impediment to demand or sales. Part of the much higher price compared with Ford and Chevrolet was attributable to the fact that they were Detroit-sourced and not from Windsor which meant that there were no Empire import duty concessions.

After testing a Custom Royal in its August 1958 issue, *Modern Motor's* tester Bryan Hanrahan said, "I personally like the styling and the vast interior as well as the surprisingly good roadholding and it's a fantastic cruiser over the long Australian distances."

The trio lasted until the 1960 model year when they were replaced by the Dodge Phoenix about which more details will be found in the second volume in this series, *Australian Cars of the 60s.*

FINS-58

SIMCA

In 1958 the Chrysler Corporation took a controlling interest in Simca, the fourth largest (and youngest) of the major French automobile manufacturers. Until 1951 the company's business had been successfully built on license-built French editions of Fiats, mostly the 500 and 1100. Then the company announced the Aronde sedan that was entirely its own design although it must be said that the design of the engine, gearbox and front suspension bore remarkable similarities to those from the Fiat 1100. From around 1954 small numbers of the Aronde found their way to Australia and were assembled by Northern Engineering for Canada Cycle and Motor Company in Melbourne with individual distributors in each state being responsible for sales.

With the takeover in France consummated, Chrysler in Australia was quick to add the Aronde late in 1958 to their local range of products to supplement the Royal that was selling in very small numbers. The Aronde soon became the company's most popular model and was number three behind the ubiquitous VW Beetle and Morris Major in the small car sales stakes.

Its mechanical specification was pretty much standard fare for the times with the 1290cc OHV water-cooled in-line four-cylinder engine (bore and stroke 74 x 75mm) driving the rear wheels through a four-speed manual gearbox (non-synchromesh first gear) with a column gearchange. The front suspension comprised upper-and-lower wishbones with coil springs and concentric dampers while at the rear was a live axle and semi-elliptic leaf springs; braking was by big 254-mm (10-in) cast-iron drums all round and the steering was a worm and roller system. The Aronde's wheelbase was 2438mm (96in), overall length 4114mm (162in), width 1575mm (62in) and height 1498mm (59in) making it the physically biggest small car on the market. One of the bugbears of the car in Australian conditions was the extensive use of plastics in the interior. At that time it was the simple and cheap way to design and make a nice interior but the art of making plastics was in its infancy in the 1950s so after a couple of summers some of the plastics would lose their shape or become brittle and crack or break. Owners soon learned to be very careful in using any switches or opening the glove box especially in summer.

Most newspapers and magazines road tested the Aronde and each gave a glowing report. *Wheels* featured an Aronde on the front cover of its April 1957 issue and a full test inside. Aside from praising its performance for its neat combination of briskness – maximum speed of 125km/h (78mph), 0–80km/h (0–50mph) in 14.7 seconds and 8 litres per 100km (35mpg) economy – the testers were full of praise for the interior's ambience, roominess and its equipment although in comparison with today's cars it was a little sparse (it had a heater/demister as standard which was a big deal in 1957, especially in a car costing £1195) and its road dynamics. A little more than a year later the Aronde was rolling off the assembly line at Chrysler's Mile End factory.

In late 1959 Chrysler began assembling the Simca Vedette V8 Beaulieu sedan on its Mile End line from CKD packs sent from Poissy, France. This move saw the retail price of the sedan drop dramatically from £1799 to £1395, less than £100 more than the Mark II Ford Zephyr to which it was closely related, having been designed in Dearborn at the same time. The version Chrysler assembled at their Mile End plant was the heavily updated model that replaced the Ford Zephyr Mark II clone; its styling was where most of the effort was directed with new sheet metal at the front – re-profiled guards, new bonnet and grille – and at the rear where the tail overhang was extended by 254mm (10 in) and

"C'est Magnifique!"
VEDETTE
VEDETTE
V8 Vedette
FROM CHRYSLER - SIMCA

GZD·555

VACUUM
AGENT
SMB 555

SIMCA 1

SIMCA 1

CH·9116

CH·9116

given small fins *à la* American cars of the era. Mechanically the wheels and tyres went from 13in and 6.40 x 13 to 15in and 6.50 x 15 and the finned brake drums were enlarged to 279mm (11 in) in diameter with a huge 197 square inches of lining area. What remained the same was under the bonnet – the 2.3-litre side-valve V8 engine derived from the Ford V8-60 from pre-war days.

Wheels and *Australian Motor Sports* magazines carried out full road tests of the Vedette V8 Beaulieu and both were highly impressed with it. The *Wheels* story was headed 'Simca's Virile Vedette' and began with a brief dissertation on the car's unusual genesis and went on to give the reader a positive impression of it, its fittings and the general quality of its construction. As for its dynamics, the writer (Ian Fraser) was highly impressed saying it was "outstandingly good" where its roadholding and handling was concerned; he went on to say "pressed hard into tight corners the Vedette just sails around happily and does not wash off speed in front end drifts". He recorded a fine set of performance figures, figures that belied the size of the engine and put the FB Holden to shame. The Vedette's top speed was 148.9km/h (93.1mph) with 54km/h and 94km/h (34mph and 59mph) available in first and second gears respectively while the times for the 0–80, 96 and 112km/h (0–50mph, 60mph and 70mph) acceleration runs were 11.9, 17.7 and 24.4 seconds, fuel economy was 14.8 litres per 100km (19.2mpg) for the full test and 11.2 litres per 100km (25.3mpg) when touring so the cruising range from the tank was more than adequate for our big country.

Assembly of the Vedette ran until late 1961 and it quickly vanished from the scene. Finding one today is more down to luck.

AUS50

CHAPTER 4

AUSTIN

Austin, under the dictatorial leadership of Leonard Percy Lord, got off to a flying start in the early postwar years, initially with the warmed over 10, 12 and 16hp models that gave way to a completely new range in 1947 beginning with the ubiquitous Austin A40 Devon. This was followed a year later by the Austin A70 Hampshire. These were exported all around the world, primarily to former Empire countries, although Lord targeted the USA with its huge hunger for new automobiles, and was successful at first with the A40 but sales fell as Detroit geared production up to meet the enormous demand. In Australia the Austin A40 Devon was top of the sales charts from its release here in 1948 until late 1950 because it was priced right, had an acceptable specification, reasonable performance and, vitally, was readily available. From 1951 it faded after GM had ramped up production of the 48/215 Holden that soon headed the charts and was never challenged until the end of the decade when the Ford Falcon was announced.

Where Rootes and Nuffield elected to use their meagre resources to design and mass produce monocoque bodies for their new postwar ranges of family cars and retain their ancient side-valve engines, Austin went the other way. They retained the separate chassis method of body construction and went ahead and developed a completely new overhead valve 1.2-litre four-cylinder engine that had a bore and stroke of 65.5 x 88.9mm. Actually it was the second OHV engine because the first was the 2.2-litre four fitted to the postwar Austin 16, it being a derivation of an Austin truck engine developed for the war effort. The second engine was similar in broad concept – narrow bore x long stroke, cast-iron block and head – and would form the basis of the later B series engines. It developed 30kW (40bhp, hence the model name) at 4300rpm and drove the rear wheels through a four-speed manual gearbox with a non-synchromesh first gear; for the first time on an Austin came an independent front suspension by upper-and-lower wishbones and coil springs, the dampers being incorporated in the upper wishbone pivot; braking was by a Girling hydro-mechanical system that had the front drums operated hydraulically and the rears by mechanical linkages.

The body was an interesting mix of new ideas and a longing not to go too far forward from what was known and understood; it was not a proper full-width body but retained definite signs of the old mudguards and vestiges of running boards between the wheels, the bootlid folded down as a ledge for added carrying capacity and the windscreen, while one piece of glass, was flat and not curved like that on the Hillman Minx and Jowett Javelin. Interior room was fine for four – two up front, two in back – seated on individual front seats and rear bench, the upholstery being leather; the pressed steel dash had Smiths instruments in a symmetrical housing in front of the driver and comprised a speedometer flanked on either side by minor gauges for fuel, amps and oil pressure (no temperature gauge!) and there were a variety of pull-push switches in the centre including that most English of switches in the middle, the Lucas combined ignition and light switch. On the left was a lidded glovebox for odds and sods. Trafficators were operated from a switch on the steering wheel hub and the hand brake was a pistol grip type under the dash. A long wand of a gearlever sprouted from the floor and the foot pedals also came up through the floor; a heater was an optional extra.

Dimensionally the A40 was spot-on for the family car market in

England but was too narrow for most of the export markets it was forced to compete in. Built on a wheelbase of 2349mm (92.5in), it was 3886mm (153in) in length by 1549-mm (61-in) wide and 1626-mm (64-in tall); weight was a solid 968kg (2130lb).

For its time the A40 was regarded as spirited in its performance being capable of 111km/h (69.5mph) according to *The Autocar*, the 0–80km/h (0–50mph) sprint taking 26.9 seconds. On the showroom floor the A40 was available at the reasonable price of £697 which is why it sold so well.

Coming a year later was the A40's big brother, the A70 Hampshire. The lines were simply scaled up and there it was, the body bolted to a substantial chassis derived from the Austin 16 but with a heavier, stronger version of the upper-and-lower wishbone independent coil spring front suspension, leaf spring rear suspension and Girling hydro-mechanical braking system. Also taken from the 16 was the A70's big four-cylinder engine, a long stroke design – 79.4 x 111.1mm, 2199cc – that developed 51kW (68bhp) at 3800rpm and mountains of torque; drive went through a four-speed manual gearbox with the expected column lever but with a difference insofar as first gear (non-synchromesh) was away from the wheel and up making the H of the gearshift back-to-front compared with most others, reverse required pulling out the end of the gear lever, pushing away and down. For its time and type it was satisfactory although gear movements were long. Such was the car's gearing that first gear need only to be used on hills or in an emergency, second being more than capable for starting in normal conditions. As with the A40, the pedals were pivoted through the floor. The A70 had a 2514-mm (99-in) wheelbase and was 4242mm (167 in) long, kerb weight being a hefty 1222kg (2688lb).

Accommodation in the A70 was superior to the A40 but the fittings were not special, even by the standards of postwar England. Typically of most British cars in those early postwar years, the A70 had its instruments grouped in the centre of the dashboard with lidded cubbies at either end. There were two large round dials, one for the speedometer and other housing the minor gauges (fuel, amps and oil pressure) with the pull-push switches and the ignition/lights in a line below. Space was provided for the radio in the centre and heater/demister controls underneath when fitted – surprisingly it was not a standard fitting. In front were individual seats that could be aligned to form a bench for carrying three people with a wide bench seat in back also capable of taking three passengers; the front seats featured pull-down armrests on either side, an early version of the so-called 'captain's chair' that some makers have touted as being unique and special in more recent times.

The ride was good (for the time) although it did not take long for the front dampers to lose their effectiveness and set up the well-remembered 'Austin bounce'. Performance was pretty strong from the A70, it being capable of 128km/h (80mph) which made it quick for the day and would run the 0–80 and 96km/h (0–50 and 0–60mph) dashes in 14.9 and 22.3 seconds respectively and return 13.5 and 11.8 litres per 100km (21–24mpg).

From the viewpoint of Australian motorists, the A40 and A70 were locally assembled by Ruskin Motor Bodies in Dudley Street, North Melbourne and Larke Hoskins in Riley Street, Sydney before moving to Enfield in 1952 and changing the company's name to Pressed Metal Corporation. Pressed Metal was a company established by Larke Hoskins in the late 1930s to build motor bodies. The connection here is that Larke Hoskins was a long-time Austin distributor in NSW. Ruskin's history dated from 1903 when it was established as the Melbourne Motor Body Works and built bodies for a wide variety of manufacturers. Also located in Melbourne was the Autocraft factory and with the amalgamation of Austin and Morris in 1952 in England, 1954 in Australia, consideration

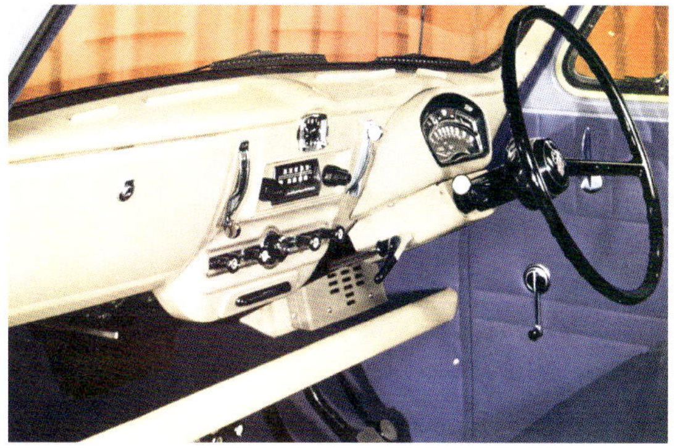

AUS 7

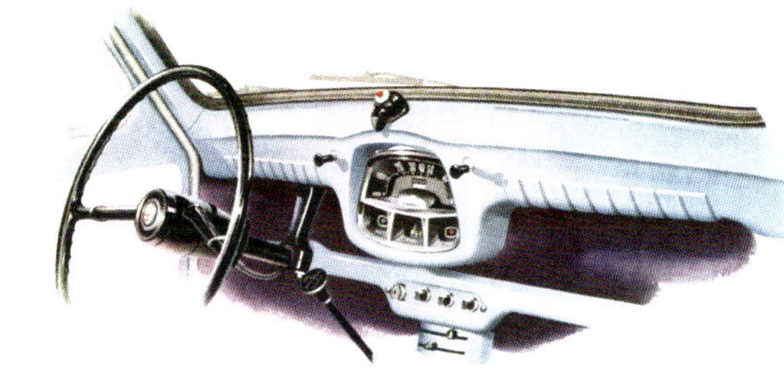

was given by management to using and indeed extending the Autocraft factory, but George Lloyd, the first Managing Director, closed both assembly plants in 1958.

Ruskin Motor Bodies remained independent until 1 August 1948 when the company name was changed to the Austin Motor Company of Australia Limited and it continued to operate as that until 9 April 1954 when the Austin Motor Company Limited of Longbridge, England, took it over and gradually operations were wound down as all production and assembly was gradually transferred during the mid-to-late 1950s to the new Waterloo (Sydney) factory established by the Nuffield Group in 1950.

The A70 Hampshire was replaced in 1950 after barely two years' production by the A70 Hereford, this new model being the harbinger of a major styling change that would find its way to the forthcoming A40 Somerset and baby A30. This new styling would be described today as bulbous, particularly on the A70 which was the first Austin to feature a one-piece curved windscreen; when compared with the equally new Ford Zephyr from the same period, the Austin looked big, bloated even, and still retained vestiges of separate mudguards despite the fact that internationally the industry was clearly moving to full-width slab-sided bodies. And the Zephyr came with a smooth six-cylinder engine and not a thumping big four of similar capacity plus pendant foot pedals that had yet to find their way to Austins. Did Austin zig when the rest of the world zagged? Maybe so …

Mechanically everything was carried over from the Hampshire with one exception – the braking system was now a Girling full-hydraulic system – so this model change was really a body thing. Interior fittings were the same but different insofar as the instruments were still in the centre of the dash – there was now a large central speedometer with rectangular minor gauges in a row underneath – and the various switches were still lined across the centre as before. The front seats were individual that could be lined up to form a bench if necessary. Like its predecessor the A70 Hereford was an 128km/h (80mph) saloon and more than able to cover the vast distances in Australia with ease. *Wheels* magazine said of the A70, "It is a most practical family saloon that is well-suited for long, hard work. It is comfortable and performs well and with good ground clearance would make it a useful car in the country." At £1179 for the standard version and £1227 for the Deluxe the A70 was not inexpensive.

During 1950 the A40 Devon underwent a minor upgrade, the most significant changes being the adoption of a column gearshift and revised instruments that were now in the centre of the dash. Then, in early 1952 the A40 Somerset arrived as a direct replacement for the Devon; again it was a styling change as all mechanical components were carried straight over with the exception of the brakes which were now full hydraulic in their operation.

Wheels tested an A40 Somerset in its February 1954 issue and said, "The A40 Somerset is a comfortable 4–5 seater to drive and ride in. It has a moderate performance with a 70mph top speed and is well-suited to family and business use." They coaxed 116.8km/h (73mph) out of it and ran the 0–80 and 96km/h (0–50 and 60mph) sprints in 16.0 and 25.3 seconds while getting more than 8 litres per 100km (35mpg). We would expect far more from a 1.2-litre saloon today but in the early '50s the A40's performance was considered more than acceptable. Two editions were sold – a full import for £1040 and a locally assembled version for £1012.

The Achilles' heel for the A40 in particular was a penchant for blowing cylinder head gaskets if pushed hard on a long distance journey and all this generation suffered from poor damping of the front suspension.

In 1952 came the A30 that was Austin's delayed response to the Morris Minor, this being the first Austin to have a monocoque body and the first to be powered by the new A-Series four-cylinder engine.

AUSTIN A55 Saloon
VOB 278

'40'

100 SIX

NOJ 389

JDT 328

ORU 434

LGF 99

MYH 27

Its Australian release was at the Melbourne Motor Show in March 1953 with local assembly of the 4-door version commencing in May.

The styling of the A30 shared a common theme with its two larger siblings, the bodies being rounded in appearance with a small rear window, the retention of outlines of the rear guards and a small hatch-type bonnet that made accessibility to the engine bay for maintenance and repairs rather difficult. Where the front windscreens on the A40 and A70 were one-piece with curved glass, that on the A30 was flat for cost reasons. The interiors also were similar, particularly the A40 and 70 that shared the same dashboard design, while the A30's was much simpler, having a large single dial in the centre of the dash that contained the speedometer with a fuel gauge in the lower part of it with switches for lights and wipers, the horn and high beam switch being on an arm projecting from the steering column. A revised version arrived in 1954 that had a new dashboard with all gauges and warning lights contained under the one glass, a full-width parcel tray replaced the open cubbies either side, the fuel tank was moved and its filler repositioned, the spare wheel was relocated to the side and stored vertically and the door handles were now conventional. The biggest difference was in the gearshifts – the A30 had a floor shifter while the two larger Austins had column shifts.

Built on a short 2019-mm (79.5-in) wheelbase and spanning just 3454mm (136in) overall, the A30 was the smallest Austin in a long time and in so many ways was the post-war equivalent in the range to the original Austin 7. The 803cc engine developed 21kW (28bhp) at 4800rpm and was able to push the sedan along at up to 100km/h (62mph, in-gear maxima were 24, 44.8 and 72km/h (15, 28 and 45mph) and accelerate it from 0–80km/h (0–50mph) in 30 seconds. A performance sedan it was not but that was never its designer's intention. As an economical and easy-to-drive family saloon it certainly was a success while one writer was moved to say because it had an 'orthodox specification' in would have a long life. The showroom price for the A30 was £758 for the locally assembled version and £797 for the imported one.

CKD packs arrived from the UK around April 1953 for assembly at the Autocraft factory owned by Austin Distributors (who also owned the old Ruskin Motor Bodies) and which was located at Fisherman's Bend, opposite the General Motors-Holden site. As Craig Watson noted in *The BMC Experience* magazine, "The factory had been built in 1933 to assemble Morris, MG, Hillman, Sunbeam and Humber cars, and was bought by Austin in 1948." He continued by adding, "With the formation of BMC Australia in 1954, plans were drawn up for the expansion of the factory to be capable of producing 1000 cars a week on the 20-acre site. However, with the expansion of the Zetland factory in Sydney, Fisherman's Bend was closed down in 1958."

The A30 in four-door form continued to be assembled in small numbers in Australia – it was totally overshadowed by the Morris Minor – until late 1957 but it took until early 1959 for the last one was sold. Within a few months it was replaced by the Farina-designed Austin A40.

From an Australian perspective these Austins showed their designer's and engineer's lack of understanding of export conditions and requirements. They had quite clearly been designed and built with English conditions in mind where the owners would toddle off to the shops in the village on narrow lanes and at speeds of not much more than 48km/h (30mph). Their shortcomings were obvious – low gearing in particular which made them unsuited to long distance travel in Australia (except the A70) – and these were amplified when the Holden became available.

While the A30, A40 and A70 were Austin designs, as were their successors, they were the last Austin-built Austins because in March 1952 Leonard Lord pulled off his long-sought merger – or was it a takeover? – of Austin with Morris (or more correctly the Nuffield Group) to create the biggest British car company ever until then. It was the British Motor Corporation (BMC).

the
MORRIS
MINOR
1000
Now better than ever
IMPROVED PERFORMANCE · INCREASED SAFETY ·

CHAPTER 5

THE NUFFIELD CARS

Morris's world was changed overnight with the release at the 1948 London Motor Show of the ubiquitous Morris Minor created largely by one man, Alex Issigonis, later to be knighted for his services to the automobile industry. It was the perfect car for that time in England's motoring history; it was also a landmark car for Morris as a company even though its owner, Lord Nuffield, tried very hard to prevent its manufacture! Amazing but true.

Shown at the same London Motor Show was the MO series Oxford sedan that in many ways looked like a scaled-up Minor but was in fact quite differently engineered, particularly in the body. The following year saw the release of the Morris MS Six, Wolseley 4/50 and 6/80, the Wolseleys being based on the Morris Oxford from the A-pillar back but featured Wolseley-specific front sheet metal, in particular the famous grille with that cute oval-shaped badge that lit up at night, and they had a better quality interior.

The Morris Six was a clone of the Wolseley 6/80 that featured the expensive-to-build 2.2-litre single overhead camshaft six-cylinder engine, a four-cylinder version of which powered the 4/50. Small numbers of both the Six and 6/80 were sold in Australia and are rare finds today. The Minor and Oxford, however, were sold in significant numbers and were assembled locally by Nuffield at their new Sydney plant that had been established on the 113-acre site of the former Victoria Park horse racing track which had been bought by Lord Nuffield during his visit in 1947. These were the last Nuffield Morris cars because following the merger/takeover of the Nuffield Group with the Austin Motor Company, there was some immediate sharing of components that gradually diluted the character of all marques involved.

George Lloyd was the first managing director followed shortly after by the appointment of John Buckley who had a vision of the company being a full manufacturer like Holden. In 1953 the Unit factory began operations making engines, transmissions and other components.

MORRIS MINOR

The Minor was the car that put the Nuffield Group on the world map in the postwar years. Originally intended by its creator to be powered by a horizontally opposed side-valve four-cylinder engine of around 900cc capacity, with an optional 1100cc unit, it reverted to an existing engine when Lord Nuffield refused to sanction the investment needed for the new family of engines. When it went into production it was powered (if that was the right word!) by the old Morris E Series side-valve engine that dated from the early 1930s. It was an engine that was already old long before it ended up under the bonnet of the new Minor.

It was a typically British engine, long in stroke and narrow in bore – 57 x 90mm – with a capacity of 918cc; it had been updated in 1939 to include shell bearings for the crankshaft although it never gained a water pump, another peculiarly British thing. Power was a dismal 20kW (27bhp) at 4400rpm gained from a compression ratio of 6.6:1 (Pool petrol remember) and a single side-draft SU carburettor. On the engine compartment bulkhead was mounted an SU electric petrol pump that is remembered by mature aged owners with disdain. A small hammer was usually part of the tool kit for 'emergencies!'

Technically the Minor was considered to be quite advanced for its time; certainly it was by the standards of the British motor industry. Issigonis had devised and designed in collaboration with skilled draftsman Jack Daniels a light-weight monocoque body construction with vestigial chassis rails underneath the floorpan to support the weight of the engine, gearbox and the running gear. It was built using a wheelbase of just 2184mm (86in) and had an overall length of 3759mm (148in); weight was 790kg (1740lb).

At the front there was an independent suspension system comprising fabricated upper and lower wishbones – they were each made as two pressed steel parts bolted together – with the longitudinal torsion bar splined to the lower one and anchored half way along the underbody beneath the front seats; the lever dampers were integrated into the upper pivots. At the rear was a conventional live axle on semi-elliptic leaf springs. Seven-in (178mm) cast-iron brake drums with full hydraulic operation proved to be more than adequate for the Minor's meagre performance and, in a first for a British saloon car, it had a delightfully direct rack and pinion steering system.

Seating consisted of two small buckets in front that in the two-door versions tipped (there were no safety catches) for access to the rear bench seat, all of them being upholstered in leather. The dash was unusual in that it was asymmetrical and therefore easily suited to right-hand or left-hand drive depending on the export market; in front of the driver was the speedometer flanked by two small rectangular gauges, one for fuel and the other for temperature. In the centre was a grille for the optional radio speaker and under that were the pull-push switches for ignition, lights, choke and wipers, and at the left was the glovebox, the lid of which was identically-shaped to the panel containing the instruments. On the floor was the long wand of a gear lever, the pull-up handbrake and the small closely-spaced foot pedals poked up through the floor.

Initially available as a two-door saloon and convertible, its doors were front hinged with an adjustable front quarter window for ventilation, the rear window was quite small and the front windscreen was split and vee-d, the glass being flat. Under the floor of the small luggage compartment was the spare wheel and the 23-litre (5-gallon) fuel tank that was painfully slow to fill without blow-back. The grille was plain and painted body colour with the headlights alongside – today we refer to this arrangement as the 'Low-lite'.

The Autocar carried out a full test of a two-door Minor in its 26 November 1948 issue and achieved a maximum speed of 100km/h (62mph), with the 0–80km/h (0–50mph) acceleration taking forever at 36.5 seconds and its economy worked out at 7 litres per 100km (40.5mpg). As they said at the end of their test, "The new Minor can without hesitation be awarded full marks, especially for suspension, steering, stability and general roadworthiness." No mention, you note, of performance! *Australian Motor Manual* tested a fully imported Minor in April 1949 and recorded the same 100km/h (62mph) top speed and 0–80km/h (0–50mph) time.

In 1951 Morris added a four-door body but this option was at first limited to export markets only. To comply with legal requirements in some export markets – remember this was the 'export or die' period of British history – the headlights were re-positioned at the top of the front wings, such models now being referred to as the 'Hi-lite' models. Within a very short time the lights on the two-door saloon and convertible were also raised.

With the amalgamation of Nuffield and Austin, for the 1953 model year the Minor adopted the 803cc OHV A-series four-cylinder engine developed by Austin for its A30. This raised the power slightly, to 22kW (30bhp), but a reduction in overall gearing meant that the engine was noisy and intrusive when touring, especially so in a big country like Australia. Interestingly, the Morris Minor sedan was not only assembled at Zetland but also at the Autocraft factory in Fisherman's Bend, Melbourne such was demand for it while commercial versions – panel van and utility – were made at Pressed Metal at Enfield.

MINOR 4

18424
MPH

MORRIS OXFORD

Announced at the same time as its famous little brother, although completely overshadowed by it, was the MO series Oxford saloon. It was designed and developed in parallel with the Minor which is why it shared so many styling cues although it always had its headlights mounted up in the front guards. However, the construction of its monocoque body was different insofar as it had to cope with far greater weight than the Minor's and was gusseted and strengthened accordingly.

Under the rounded bonnet was a new *side*-valve in-line four-cylinder engine that, with a bore and stroke of 73.5 x 87mm, had a capacity of 1476cc. Like its smaller sibling, its cylinder block and head were cast-iron and the three main bearing crankshaft was forged with steel connecting rods. Using a single SU side-draft carburettor and a 6.8:1 compression, the power output was 30kW (40.5bhp) at 4200rpm. Drive went through a four-speed manual gearbox (synchromesh on the top three gears only) with a steering column change to the rear wheels. Again mirroring the Minor, the Oxford's suspension consisted of wishbones and longitudinal torsion bars up front, live axle and semi-elliptic leaf springs at the rear, rack and pinion steering and 203-mm (8-in) Lockheed hydraulic brakes.

The Oxford sat on a wheelbase of 2464mm (97in) and it was 4204mm (165.5in) in length while weight was listed at 1089kg (2396lb).

No road tests appear to have been carried out on the MO Oxford in Australia – *Wheels* and *Modern Motor* did not arrive until 1953 – but *The Autocar* did publish a full test, one in 1948 and another in 1951 when a very slightly revised model went into production. The major difference was a lowering(!) of the car's gearing from 4.55:1 to 4.875:1 in the interests of top gear acceleration. The Oxford's size as an ideal family car impressed as did its fittings and quality of finish. They wrote, "The Oxford is entirely up to date in design, having among its features integral chassisless construction and independent front suspension by torsion bars. One soon feels that it is a robust, go-anywhere kind of car. It is not too big for the average private garage and is handy in narrow lanes."

Performance was claimed to be acceptable but standards were far different then compared with now. Top speed was measured at 107km/h (67mph) with 30/51/75km/h (19/32/47mph) available in the intermediate gears, the 0–80km/h (0–50mph) 'sprint' taking 27.4 seconds.

Take a look—at the new look
MORRIS OXFORD
"Quality First" all the way through

WOLSELEY

The structure of the MO Oxford was cleverly used to broaden the model range within the Nuffield Group with a minimum of expense. The upmarket Wolseley brand took the Oxford body from the A-pillar back and bolted unique front panels on it to create the four-cylinder 4/50 that retained the Oxford's wheelbase, and the longer wheelbase six-cylinder 6/80. Where the Oxford's nose sloped down and was smoothly rounded, the Wolseley variants had a much straighter, almost horizontal bonnet line that culminated in the traditional upright Wolseley grille complete with its oval-shaped badge that lit up at night. Only the front door exterior panels were different from the Oxford, the Wolseley having a squared-off line for the fender where the Oxford's was rounded.

Inside there was the usual British club atmosphere of deep pile carpet on the floor, walnut woodwork and real leather upholstery, fold down armrest in the back seat and further armrests on each door and fog lamps on the front bumper; in the centre of the dash were the round Smiths instruments that gave the driver full information about what was going on under the bonnet as well as how fast he was travelling, and the time.

The Wolseley engine shared cylinder dimensions with the Oxford although the actual blocks were slightly different – the Morris was a side-valve unit, the Wolseley had a single overhead camshaft with shaft-and-bevel drive – which meant that many machining operations could be carried out on the same production tooling. The 4/50 engine shared the complex bevel shaft drive mechanism with its larger sibling, the 6/80, with the cam lobes running on a finger rocker to operate the valves. When properly set up it was a good system but like so many good ideas it was at the mercy of poorly trained (or just plain dumb) mechanics who invariably set it up incorrectly and it was not long before expensive trouble raised its ugly head. A correctly set up 4/50 (and 6/80) engine was a delight to drive behind. Power output of the 4/50's engine was up to 38kW (51bhp) at 4400rpm, an increase of 7.5kW (10bhp) over the Oxford while its maximum speed was clocked at 124.8km/h (78mph, plus 16km/h/10mph) and the 0–80km/h (0–50mph) acceleration run took only 17.8 seconds (10 seconds quicker). It not only got you to your destination quicker but it cosseted you more on the way.

Big brother 6/80 rode a wheelbase that was stretched from 2590mm (102in) to 2794mm (110in) with a corresponding increase in length to 4496mm (177in) and weight increased to 1222kg (2688lb) The 6/80's SOHC six-cylinder engine shared the 73.5 x 87mm cylinder dimensions (for a capacity of 2215cc) with the 4/50 and Oxford but with dual SU carburettors developed 54kW (72bhp) at 4600rpm. Drive went to the rear wheels via a four-speed manual gearbox (non-synchro first gear) with a column shift, the suspension was typically Nuffield of the day insofar as at the front were longitudinal torsion bars with upper and lower wishbones, the upper wishbone pivot having the damper built-in, and at the rear was a live axle on semi-elliptic leaf springs, braking was by Lockheead 254-mm (10-in) drums all round with a Bishop cam and peg steering box. During 1950 a major running change took place where the in-built front dampers were replaced by twin telescopic units each side to better control body movement.

For its day the 6/80 was regarded as something of a sporting saloon, so much so that Scotland Yard and many other police forces in England used them as patrol and pursuit cars. Various road tests from the day suggested a top speed of 125km/h (78mph) and acceleration times from zero to 80km/h (50mph) in 17.1 seconds and to 96km/h (60mph) in 24.4 seconds.

Naturally the 6/80 featured a walnut dashboard with central Smiths instruments and lidded cubbies either end, leather upholstery over Dunlopillo foam rubber seating, floor carpets, a reach adjustable steering wheel with a full circle horn ring, twin roof lights in the rear compartment, boot light and reversing light plus a rear window blind. For its time it was a quite luxuriously equipped car and in conjunction with its regal upright grille and long bonnet oozed class.

With the return to the fold of Gerald Palmer, back from his sojourn at Jowett, design and engineering on the next generation Wolseley, MG and Riley cars commenced in mid-to-late-1949. What was not known for certain when these were under development was that these cars – the Wolseley 4/44 and 6/90, MG Magnette and Riley Pathfinder – would be the last of their genre. These cars were in two pairs – the four-seater 4/44 and Magnette, and the six-seater 6/90 and Pathfinder – and shared a great many ideas that began when Palmer saw a Farina-bodied Bentley coupe at the 1948 Paris Motor Show. Each had the slab-sided look that was coming into vogue, each had their vertical chromed grille (a given at the time for every British car!) standing proud at the front with the lines sloping gently and elegantly back to the rear.

The first to be released, in late 1953, was the Wolseley 4/44 that was initially powered by the old XPAG 1250cc MG four-cylinder OHV engine and the gearbox was from the Oxford complete with column gearshift; the front suspension was an all-new upper-and-lower wishbone system with coil springs and tubular dampers. Within a year the XPAG engine had been consigned to history and was replaced by the new 1489cc BMC B-series engine (73 x 88.9mm) that later went into a whole raft of BMC cars. Palmer had designed both the 4/44 and Magnette to accept the B-series engine because the merger was "a possibility" during the design period. By the time the 4/44 was in the dealerships Austin and Nuffield had amalgamated.

In keeping with the image of Wolseley the interior of the 4/44 was a nice place in which to travel with its walnut dash, centre instruments (another tradition), loop pile carpets, leather upholstery and a heater/demister was a standard fitting.

Nuffield assembled small numbers of the 4/50 during the period from 1950 through 1953 and the Australian arm of the company continued with the 4/44 and the 15/50 through to 1957, now with 37kW (50bhp) at 4200rpm and a floor gearshift lever replacing the former column shift lever. The model name was in script by the bonnet opening and there were now chrome wing flashes to help distinguish the new from the old.

All four of the Palmer-designed cars came to Australia, the Magnette, Pathfinder and 6/90 all being fully imported. And they are all very collectable today.

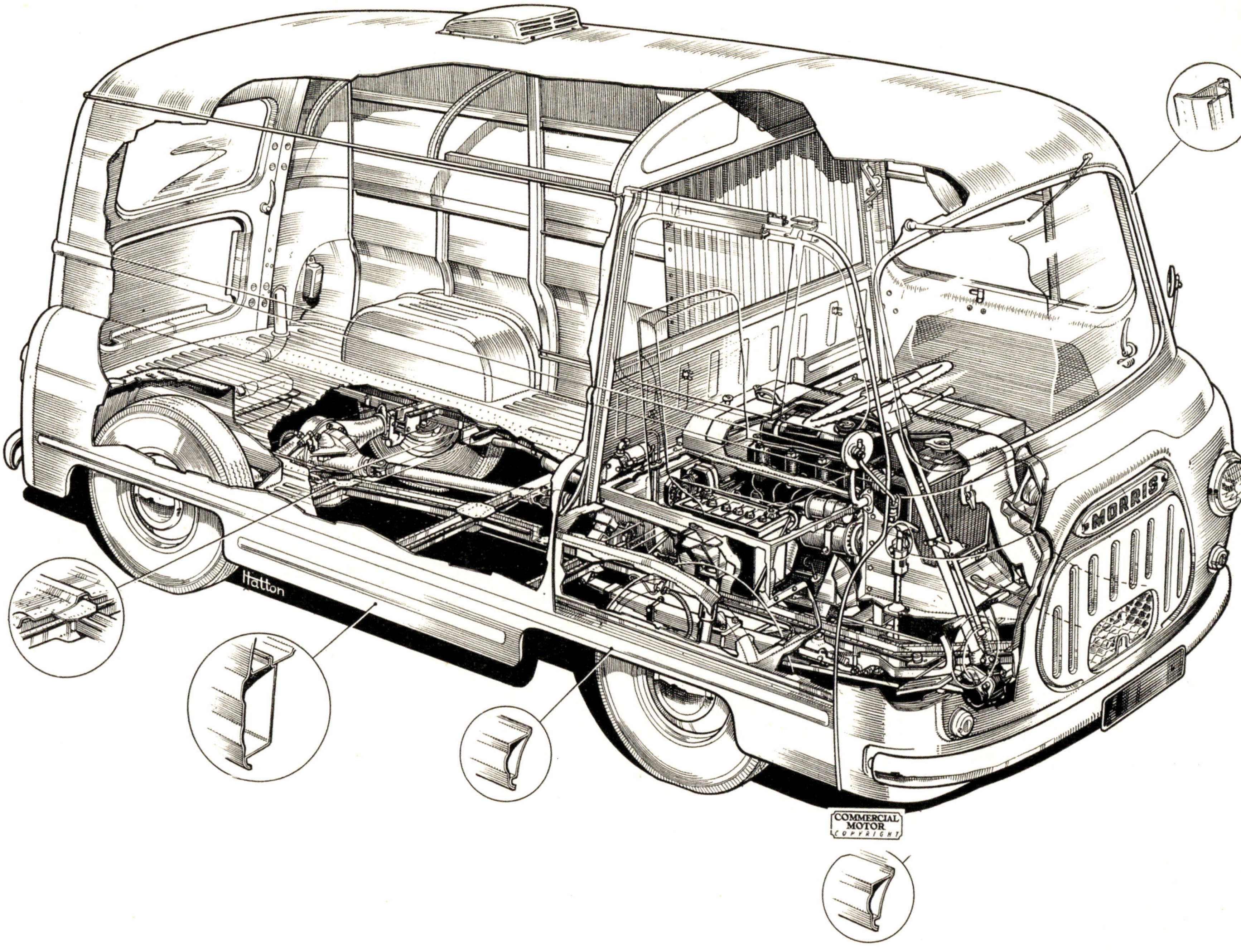
MORRIS
Hatton
COMMERCIAL
MOTOR
COPYRIGHT

CHAPTER 6

THE BRITISH MOTOR CORPORATION IN AUSTRALIA

One of the most significant events in British industrial history occurred with the merging of the Nuffield Group and the Austin Motor Company, the deal being driven by the ego of the managing director of Austin, the acerbic and autocratic Leonard Lord. He was a man on a mission from the time he acrimoniously departed Nuffield in 1936 after being refused an increase in salary by Lord Nuffield – he reputedly told Nuffield he would "pull the factory down, brick by bloody brick!" That process which had begun in 1936 culminated in the formal announcement of the merger on 31 March 1952.

In Australia, the assembly of Austin cars was gradually transferred from the old Ruskin Motor Bodies (renamed the Austin Motor Company of Australia in 1948) and Autocraft in Melbourne beginning some time in 1956 to join the Morris and Wolseley cars on the line at the new facility Nuffield had constructed on the site of the former Victoria Park race course 5mi (8km) south of the Sydney CBD. This meant that the factory was now assembling from CKD kits the following models: Morris Minor, Morris Oxford and Wolseley 4/44 from the former Nuffield Group, and the Austin A40 Somerset and A70 Hereford from the Austin side of the business. At this early stage of the factory's operations, and in the life of the British Motor Corporation of Australia (BMCA), the local content consisted primarily of paint, various trim items and upholstery, wheels and tyres, glass and some Lucas electrical items. However, managing director John Buckley envisaged a full manufacture operation and to this end began recruiting new people, mostly from Holden. His first recruit was Bill Abbott who was followed by Bill Serjeantson, Reg Fulford, Graham Hardy and many others. The idea was to establish a production engineering department at Zetland.

Meanwhile, back in Cowley and Longbridge, head quarters of the Nuffield Group and Austin respectively, the new model development program was going ahead as many were long past the point of no return. The only proviso given the Nuffield engineers at this early stage of the merger was that Austin engines and driveline components were mandatory. This made sense because the Nuffield engines were either out-dated old side-valve or expensive to manufacture SOHC designs while the Austin engines were new OHV designs. At Cowley a restyled Morris Oxford, the Series II, was under development as were new MG, Wolseley and Riley models that appeared beginning from late 1953 as the MG Magnette saloon (ZA), Wolseley 4/44 and 6/90 and the Riley Pathfinder, these cars being the work of a small team led by Gerald Palmer. The MG Magnette was announced in England in early 1954 and was powered by a 60bhp version (twin SU carburettors, higher compression) of the new B series engine. The Pathfinder and Wolseley 6/90 were also styled alike although remarkably there were very few actual interchangeable panels between the pairings. All MG Magnettes, Wolseley 6/90 and Riley Pathfinders that were sold in Australia were fully imported.

The Morris Minor was an early recipient of the new rationalisation process. Having been upgraded to 'Hi-lite' status in early 1952 in Australia it was further upgraded during late 1953 and early 1954 to receive the BMC A Series OHV 803cc engine and gearbox from the Austin A30. Accompanying this change was a new horizontally slatted grille and during 1954 a new dashboard was phased-in, the new one having a single large centre-positioned dial containing the speedometer, fuel and temperature gauges and open cubbies either side.

Further changes arrived in 1956 when the Minor was significantly improved. Its styling was enhanced by the adoption of a deep one-piece curved windscreen swept by electric wipers with a clap hands sweep pattern, an enlarged rear window and bolder taillights; inside was a shorter, remote gearshift lever, dished sprung-spoke steering wheel and lids for the two dashboard lockers. Under the bonnet was the 948cc A Series engine mated to the new close ratio A35 gearbox, the Minor now had a whole 27.5kW (37bhp) to play with that pushed its top speed up to 116.8km/h (73mph), although despite sporty pretensions acceleration from 0–80km/h (0–50mph) took 18.0 seconds. Many believe the Morris Minor 1000, as it was now badged, was the definitive Minor and its specification remained basically unchanged for the rest of the decade. A member of the media was moved to write, "The new 1000 is the fastest, most economical, most improved, best-performing Minor to date." He must have been British!

In late 1954 the MO Oxford was replaced by the new Series II Oxford which was also an Issigonis design. It was a completely new car from the point of view of the body design, although much of the running gear was carried over, but under the bonnet was the BMC B series OHV four-cylinder 1.5-litre engine and gearbox. It was another step towards the sharing of major components that would continue through the decade.

The new body retained the monocoque construction that had been developed for the MO but was now a full-width style with just the faintest suggestion of a fender at the rear; what was new was a single-piece curved windscreen swept by electric wipers with clap hands sweep pattern. A neat touch from the past was the retention of a starting handle, the access point for it being concealed behind a lift-up flap in the centre of the front bumper, complete with the letter 'M'.

It had a 2515-mm (99-in) wheelbase, was 4343-mm (171-in) long and was the same width and height (as the MO) although the rounded nature of the design gave the impression it was much larger; weight was up slightly, to 1118kg (2460lb). Inside were front and rear bench seats upholstered in leather and able to seat six passengers, the steering column was slightly offset in relation to the car's centre-line and the two large round Smiths instrument – speedometer in the one nearest the driver, the four minor gauges in the other plus warning lights – were in the centre of the dashboard, some distance away from the driver. There was a neat lineup of switches under the dials that were hard to reach and if a heater was fitted its controls were down there too.

Continuing the Nuffield tradition was the torsion bar front suspension and rack and pinion steering gear. On the road the Series II was good for 120–123km/h (75–77mph) and could accelerate from 0–80km/h (0–50mph) in 16.4 seconds which was class average for 1954. *Wheels* magazine wrote of the Oxford, "It impressed us as being the ideal family car. It is roomy, easy on petrol, handles better than most saloons, and above all is comfortable and quiet." They thought that at £1046 it was excellent value for money. *Modern Motor* said of it, "It is an entirely new car with lively performance, has a roomy body and top-grade finish."

In 1957 an updated Oxford appeared – the Series III – with a new grille, new bonnet and re-profiled rear quarter panels that now included sublime 'fins' and new two-unit taillights in a chromed surround, and there was an extra 3kW (5bhp) from the 1.5-litre engine and it now had a full-flow oil filter replacing the earlier by-pass unit; little else was changed as BMC did not feel the need because the model was selling well. Incidentally, the locally-produced version lacked the heater/demister and under-dash ventilation and substituted Karhyde (a tough synthetic material) for the previous leather, but gained front and rear seat armrests and a dished steering wheel, padding on the upper leading edge of the dashboard and there were now drop down lids on the cubbies either side of the instruments whose binnacle had been raised to give the driver a better view. It continued in production until 1959 when BMC adopted the new Farina look for all its mid-range cars which meant that when the new Oxford appeared it had lost its distinctive styling and both its torsion bar front suspension and rack and pinion steering as part of the BMC-isation of the range. Following a full test of a Series III *Modern Motor* said, "The Oxford is a good-looking if a little conservative design that will undoubtedly prove a popular 'bigger car' in the 1500cc field. It has generous accommodation, is lively on the road and economical." Actual performance was near-identical with the previous model but the price had risen to £1230.

Arriving in 1955 was the Morris Isis, a longer-nosed six-cylinder version of the Oxford. It was powered by the new C series 2.6-litre engine. The wheelbase was extended an amazing 26.7mm (10.5in), all forward of the bulkhead, and the front of the bodyshell was strengthened by the addition of two full-length box-section side rails; the delightfully accurate rack and pinion steering was replaced by a cam-and-lever system from the Austin parts bin. Apart from larger section 15in tyres, all other aspects of the Oxford and Isis were the same. It had, after all, been hastily cobbled together to appease the Morris dealers in the UK who wanted a large saloon to sell against the Austin A95, Ford Zephyr and Vauxhall Velox.

Performance, however, was in a different league with the Isis capable of running to 136–144km/h (85–90mph) – a 112km/h (70mph) highway cruise was a doddle – and accelerating from 0–96km/h (0–60mph) in 16.4 seconds, fuel economy varying from 15.8–11.2 litres per 100km (18–25mpg). On test by *Wheels* it was discovered that the C series engine had so much torque and flexibility that it would pull smoothly from 8km/h (5mph) in top gear and would tackle top gear starts without hesitation or shudder. At £1335 the Isis was not inexpensive but certainly the *Wheels* people were captivated by its wide range of abilities. For BMC in Australia and its Morris dealers it was a sales dud, buyers in this price bracket being more interested in the Austin A90 and A95.

Despite the failure of the Isis the desire for an Australia-only big Morris did not fade away. On 28 October 1957 BMC announced the Morris Marshall that was a badge engineered Austin A95 with both cars being assembled initially at Charles Hope Ltd in Brisbane under contract, assembly being transferred to Zetland in 1959. The differences were absolutely minimal and confined to a new bonnet pressing, grille with a so-called boomerang shaped name bar and model badges. It had the 63kW (85bhp) 2.6-litre C Series six-cylinder engine and four-speed gearbox from the A95 so its performance was superior to the Holden at which it was supposedly aimed but at £1459 was never in the hunt. Its performance not surprisingly paralleled that of the A95 with its top speed of 144km/h (90mph) and 0–96km/h (0–60mph) time of 17.2 seconds but this did not impress potential buyers. In 1959, for example, BMC sold a mere 359 examples and by mid-1960 it had quietly faded into history. A single example of a proposed Marshall 105 – a cousin to the Austin A105 – was built but production never followed. Does that car exist today I wonder?

MORRIS MAJOR / AUSTIN LANCER / WOLSELEY 1500

The first cars to be manufactured (as distinct from being assembled) by BMC Australia were derivatives of the Wolseley 1500 and badged as the Morris Major and Austin Lancer, all three being based very closely on the Morris Minor. The original intention of the model's program back in Longbridge had been to develop a replacement for the Minor which by then was more than 6 years old but demand for it remained at levels high enough to justify keeping it in production and so the decision was made to focus on a slightly larger model. Curiously these models shared their major dimensions – wheelbase and wheel tracks, for example – with the Minor that included the entire floorpan and running gear; this made them a fairly tight squeeze as family four-seaters. Where they differed was in their squarer, more modern exterior styling and interior appointments which were better, luggage carrying capacity that was almost doubled in size and the engine which was the corporation's 1489cc B series unit tuned for 41kW (55bhp) at 4400rpm.

Journalists from all over Australia were summoned to Zetland in July 1957 for a major announcement from BMC Australia. Actually it turned out to be three – the production of the 50,000th Morris Minor, the release of the new Morris Major and its badge-engineered siblings, and the completion of a £13-million expansion program that the Corporation's executives said would take BMC into direct competition with GM-Holden. The corporation now had its own full press shop capabilities plus a new machine shop equipped with automatic transfer machines (designed and built by Austin in the UK) that would allow them to manufacture the B series engine locally. It was asserted by management at BMCA that the Austin-Morris twins had the highest percentage of local content of *any* car made in Australia. The first car of the new family was produced in December 1957 with the first actual production car coming off the line in January 1958; the 1000th car arrived a month later.

All three models were basically identical, the only differences being at the front where the Morris had its own bonnet pressing and because of the way the body was pressed a separate exchangeable clip was pressed for each version – the Morris had an almost square grille with its badge in the centre, the Austin had a modern rendition of the vertical grille used years earlier with small side grilles and the flying A on top, while the Wolseley had its traditional upright grille with two small side grilles and the oval-shaped Wolseley badge (that lit up when the lights were turned on) at the top. Inside each had its own dashboard although most of the components were already in the parts bin; the Morris's dash featured a large single instrument binnacle that contained the speedometer, fuel and temperature gauges positioned in the centre with a padded dashtop; the Lancer had the same single unit positioned in front of the driver while the Wolseley had just what you would have expected – walnut veneer panel with two large round Smiths dials in the centre, on the right (nearest the driver) the speedometer and on the left, separated by the radio speaker grille, the minor instruments comprising fuel, temperature and oil pressure. As would have been expected, the Wolseley 1500 came with a heater/demister as standard equipment and carpets on the floor; it was a mini-luxury saloon in the marque's long tradition.

Modern Motor put a Lancer through a full test program (May 1958) and came away with the figures of 126km/h (79mph) for its top speed, 14.5 seconds for the 0–80km/h (0–50mph) dash and found it returned anywhere between 8.3 and 6.8 litres per 100km (34 and 42mpg) depending on driving circumstances. They wrote, "The Lancer has a nice driving position, good front room but was tight in the back seat, and with a relatively roomy boot." Steering and braking came in for praise, too. The lack of a standard heater/demister and a toolkit were thought to be penny-pinching on BMC's part. *Wheels* said, "It is an engaging little car with loads of sting, has good handling and a moderate thirst. There are one or two oversights but it has a great deal of charm and is pure fun to drive." The magazine had earlier tested the Wolseley 1500 and achieved similar performance results from the £1100 saloon and said, "The Wolseley's suspension is magnificent absorbing all bumps, and the steering is blissfully positive allowing the car to be flung into skids on dirt roads with ease and safety."

In July 1959 BMC released the Series II versions of the Major and Lancer, the pleasant Wolseley 1500 being unfortunately discontinued with no explanation. Significant changes were made to counter the one criticism of the cars – the lack of interior room. To achieve this, the wheelbase was extended by 152mm (6in) and overall length was up by 228mm (9in); this extension gave more legroom for rear seat passengers and boot space was increased to 13½ cubic feet, all of it useable. Long box-sections were added to the locally pressed floorpan (it was unique to these Australia-only cars) to strengthen it and make it more suited to local conditions – less than 15 per cent of our highways were sealed at the time so it was imperative that BMC's cars be attuned to our conditions, something the Longbridge overlords consistently failed to understand.

Weight was up by 27kg (60lb) over the Series I – now 968kg (2130lb) – and the rear axle ratio was lowered from 3.7 to 4.22:1 to compensate and give the Series II slightly better in-gear acceleration and flexibility. This complete re-engineering included a host of smaller but important improvements, improvements that were important only to Australian buyers and included better dust sealing using double rubbers around all doors and the boot lid, a fuel tank increased in capacity from 32- to 41-litres (7- to 9-gallons) and protected by a pressed steel stone shield; the moving of the handbrake from the centre tunnel to the outside of the new bench front seat; far stronger and bigger capacity dampers; wider wheel rims with 5.20 x 14 tyres; new dashboard with a moulded plastic binnacle positioned directly in front of the driver with two dials – speedometer, combination with actual gauges – and an open cubby to the left; key start ignition (yes, really!); a crude ventilation system that admitted lots of air to either the base of the windscreen or to the footwells (a heater/demister was optional) and windscreen washers were fitted. A thorough job that carried a retail price of £997, a bargain for those looking for four-cylinder motoring.

Wheels January 1960 carried a full road test of the Austin Lancer and found it something of a curate's egg. Its interior was nicely roomy but the seats were poorly designed and became uncomfortable on long journeys, the dashboard was cheap-looking although the actual instruments were clear and easy to read, the plastic floor material looked cheap and they thought that some of the styling details were handled rather clumsily. Its performance was barely class average at 117km/h (73mph) maximum speed with the 0–80km/h (0–50mph) sprint taking a comparatively slow 16.8 seconds, but fuel consumption worked out at 7.6 litres per 100km (36.8mpg) cruising. The same comments would have applied to the Morris Major as the two were identical apart from their grilles.

	Morris Minor 1000	**Morris Major, Austin Lancer, Wolseley 1500**	**Morris Major Series II, Morris Major Elite**
Wheelbase mm (inches)	2184mm (86in)	2184mm (86in)	2336mm (92in)
Overall length mm (inches)	3759mm (148in)	3860mm (152in)	4089mm (161in)
Engine	948cc A Series	1489cc B Series	1489cc B Series 1622cc B Series
Power kW (bhp)	27.5kW (37bhp)/4750	37kW (50bhp)/4200	37kW (50bhp)/4200 43kW (58bhp)/4250
Weight kg (lb)	764kg/1680lb	940kg/2070lb	967kg/2128lb
Top speed km/h (mph)	116.8km/h (73 mph)	126.4km/h (79 mph)	116.8km/h (73 mph) 121.6km/h (75.9mph)

AUSTIN

Austin, the senior 'partner' in BMC, had relatively quickly changed its models in the post-war years, the Devon being replaced by the Somerset and the Hampshire by the Hereford all before 1954 when the completely restyled Austin A50 Cambridge appeared continuing the company's tradition of naming its cars after counties or cities in England. The Cambridge was the first senior Austin to feature monocoque body construction – only the A30 had this feature up until then – and also featured a new engine, the B-series four-cylinder OHV engine that would subsequently be manufactured for the next two decades. Whether in a Morris or an Austin it had the cylinder dimensions of 73.0 x 88.9mm bore and stroke for a capacity of 1489cc; on a 7.2:1 compression and using a single Zenith carburettor it produced 37kW (50bhp) at 4400rpm. At the time, if the engine was mounted in a Morris, it would be fitted with an SU carburettor although that would later change.

Styling was now up-to-date with its contemporaries insofar as it now had the popular slab-sided look with a character line sweeping along the side of the body dipping down to the rear wheel arch and over it to the rear fender. At the front was a simple flat-bottomed semi-circular grille, the Austin badge displayed prominently just above it, the headlights at the head of the front fenders and the famous 'Flying A' mounted on the prow of the bonnet. At the rear were two pairs of round lights, one pair each side, positioned vertically. Where many manufacturers had gone to the fashionably small 13-in rims, Austin (like Morris and Hillman) stayed with 15-in rims shod with 5.60 x 15 cross-ply tyres in Australia.

Built on a wheelbase of 2520mm (99.25in) and with an overall length of 4114mm (162in) the new Cambridge was a roomier car inside than the Somerset it replaced and as a bonus had a much more useable boot and accessible engine compartment.

For the first time on a post-war Austin the instruments were positioned in front of the driver in a curved rectangular binnacle perched on the steering column cover; it consisted of a fan-shaped speedometer plus gauges for fuel and temperature plus a bunch of warning lights. In the centre of the dash was provision for a radio flanked by vertical slides for the optional heater/demister with the controls for lights, wipers and choke below. There was, of course, the obligatory column gearshift that continued to work the reverse way to others – first was away from the wheel and up, second straight down from there with the two most used gears, third and fourth, closest to the steering wheel rim; in daily use it made eminent sense. As seemed to be an Austin trait at the time, the A50 could be driven in normal traffic as a three-speed car by taking off in second gear such was the torque at low revs and the low gearing. New with the A50 were pendant foot pedals, at last.

Wheels conducted a full test of an A50 (March 1955) and came away impressed; the B Series engine endowed it with good performance, top speed being 120km/h (75mph), 0–80km/h (0–50mph) acceleration taking 17.5 seconds with economy in the 11.3–9.4 litres per 100km (25–30mpg) range. They liked the uncluttered and roomy interior and the stability of the car at speed whether on the highway or gravel roads. They concluded by writing, "The Cambridge gives the customers plenty for their money, particularly in the deluxe version. It is a great improvement over the earlier model and has just about enough to please most people."

Within weeks BMC released the A90 Westminster that continued the Austin tradition of having its two main models looking similar to each other by sharing styling themes, although the A90 was considerably larger than the A50. It was longer in the wheelbase (2635mm/103.75in vs 2520mm/99.25in) and overall length (4318mm/170in vs 4114mm/162in), wider (1625mm/64in vs 1549mm/61in), taller (1600mm/63in vs 1549mm/61in) and heavier by more than 250kg (550lb). Inside the dash carried over the same themes but instead of a simple instrument binnacle the more upmarket A90 had twin round Smiths dials, one for speed and the other carrying the minor gauges and warning lights all positioned in a binnacle on the steering column.

Under the bonnet was a completely new OHV engine, the BMC C-series six-cylinder unit of 2639cc from a bore and stroke of 79.4 x 88.9mm; intriguingly it was designed and developed at the Morris Engines Branch in Coventry. Like its siblings, the A and B series, it used cast-iron castings for all major components although the crankshaft was forged; on a 7.3:1 compression and using a single small Zenith carburettor it produced 63kW (85bhp) at 4000rpm, enough to push the 1272kg (2800lb) sedan to 136km/h (85mph) with ease, 0–96km/h (0–60mph) coming up in 18.9 seconds. Allied to this performance were huge 279-mm (11-in) brake drums with 180 square inches of lining, considerably more than Ford, Vauxhall or Holden had for sedans of similar capabilities.

Both the four-cylinder and six-cylinder cars were upgraded in late 1956 for the 1957 model year to become the A55 Cambridge and A95 Westminster, assembly of the A55 taking place at both Zetland and Fisherman's Bend with the A95 being assembled at the UK and Dominion Motors facility in Fortitude Valley, Brisbane. As the badge names might suggest, power of the B and C series engines was raised but the major differences had more to do with the styling. Both sported completely new sheet metal at the rear with it being lengthened by 101mm (4in) on the Cambridge and 254mm (10in) on the Westminster, the bootlid now went down to bumper level for added convenience and there were new taillight units, new side mouldings, bigger 72-litre (16-gallon) fuel tank (A95) and minor trim changes. Other improvements included a wheelbase increased by 50mm (2in) and an optional high compression (8.25:1) cylinder head that raised power to 68kW (92bhp) for the A95 and there was a new grille for that model whose extremities embraced the indicator lights.

Bryan Hanrahan, writing in *Modern Motor* November 1957, tested the A95 and achieved a maximum speed of 153.6km/h (96mph), 0–80km/h (0–50mph) in 11.2 seconds, 0–96km/h (0–60mph) in 17.1 seconds and a fuel economy figure of 10.9 litres per 100km (26mpg), all for £1447. Although touted as the Australian A95, it was definitely not a Holden competitor which was £250 cheaper, a big price difference at the time.

Available for those who valued status was the much better equipped A105 Westminster. It had two-tone paint work, stainless steel wheel trims, chromed hooded headlights, twin spot lamps, twin wing mirrors and whitewall tyres as its exterior distinguishing features. Inside there were new front split-bench seats upholstered in leather, half horn ring(!) and a padded dashtop. Under the bonnet was a twin-carburettor (unusually, they were SUs) version of the six-cylinder engine with an 8.25:1 compression, reworked exhaust system and double valve springs all of which combined to produce 76kW (102bhp) at 4600rpm.

These big Austins, in so many ways the last real Austins, carried on in production at Waterloo until late in 1959 when they were replaced for the 1960 model year by the Farina-designed Austin A99 sedan that was considerably more expensive and not assembled locally but rather fully imported. The A99 was nowhere near as popular as the A95 it replaced;

in fact it was something of a commercial failure for BMC and proved to be the end for BMC in the middle-class family saloon market, leaving it to Ford and Vauxhall.

The A55 Cambridge gave way to the Farina-designed A60 Cambridge in November 1959, and it was made in Australia with more than 90 per cent local content. The square(ish) edgy style that Farina developed and sold to several European manufacturers – Fiat and Peugeot, for example – was quite distinctive, the BMC version even moreso because of the pronounced pointy fins at the rear on the first generation cars. Much of the under-structure and floorpan was carried over from the A55 so the A60 had a 2514-mm (99-in) wheelbase but the rear overhang was slightly longer making its overall length 4521mm (178in); the wishbone and coil spring front suspension and semi-elliptic leaf spring and live axle rear end, too, were basically unchanged. The Australian A60 was different from its English counterpart in a number of ways, the most important being a larger capacity B Series engine. England stayed with the 1489cc version but the Australian engineers worked out a way of recasting the cylinder block with siamesed bores of slightly greater diameter – 76.2mm instead of 73mm – to give a capacity of 1622cc. Power output was quoted by BMCA at 41kW (55bhp) at 4250rpm and torque at 117Nm (86.5 lb/ft) at 2100rpm.

Modern Motor said of the A60 in its October 1959 issue: "It is quite an exceptional car; except for lacking 2 extra cylinders it has everything the Holden offers plus a few distinct advantages of its own and is priced £12 below the Holden Special." They felt its (column) gearchange was excellent, the brakes powerful, it was good looking and very comfortable; maximum speed was 124.8km/h (78mph), 0–80kkm/h (0–50mph) took 15.5 seconds, and its economy range was 9.8–7.8 litres per 100km (29–36mpg).

Released shortly before the A60 was the Austin A40, a Farina-designed two-box two-door economy car based on the A35 platform. In many ways the A40 established a new genre of small family cars but many in the industry felt that BMC missed a golden opportunity to pioneer a truly new style of car but the innate conservatism of the corporation prevented it. The A40 had a conventional bootlid hinged at the bottom (like the original A40) for access to a box-shaped compartment where many felt a lift-up hatch would have been a better solution. The hatch did eventually happen along with proper wind-up windows and reclining front seats but not until 1962 and that model was sold in Australia for a brief period prior to the arrival of the Mini. Being based on the A35, the A40 carried over its predecessor's mechanical components and so had a wheelbase of 2133mm (84in) and an overall length of 3657mm (144in); the 948cc A Series engine developed 25kW (34bhp) at 4750rpm and in a *Wheels* road test pushed the car to 107km/h (67mph), ran the 0–80km/h (0–50mph) sprint in 19.5 seconds and returned 8.6 litres per 100km (33mpg) under all test conditions. The test crew were impressed with its nippy performance around the suburbs, the capacious loading arrangements and the ease of driving and at £915 they felt it was good value. *Modern Motor* tested the A40 Countryman and came away with a maximum speed of 108km/h (73.4mph), 0–80km/h (0–50mph) in 18.9 seconds and 7.8 litres per 100km (36mpg) fuel economy on test, all for £925. A bargain!

MG

What is amazing is the fact that BMC UK management turned down the MGA when it was presented to them because the boss, Leonard Lord, wanted to build only the new Austin Healey. What became the MGA had its origins in rather special TD that was coded EX172 at Abingdon. Its aerodynamic design was intended to compete at Le Mans in 1951. With refined styling a running prototype was built and began testing in November 1952 without Longbridge being aware of its existence! Initial work was with the car powered by the ancient XPAG engine and it was not until late in 1953 that the engineers at Abingdon received their first B-series engine with a 1489cc capacity.

With MG losing market share rapidly in the vital US market, it took until June 1954 before Lord relented and okayed the MGA for production with the final version displayed at the Earls Court Motor Show in 1955. It was a total break with what purists regarded as an MG sports car – think of the upright grille, anaemic 1250cc engine, crude creature comforts, hard ride and so on – and so it was not welcomed by the MG fraternity with any eagerness. When production ended in 1962 it has become an icon of the marque!

Under the sleek styling of the MGA was a separate chassis (can you believe it?) with upper-and-lower wishbone coil spring front suspension allied to a live rear axle suspended by semi-elliptic leaf springs, the steering was a delightful rack and pinion setup, braking was by four-wheel drums while power came from the new B Series four-cylinder OHV engine that was BMC's staple unit. In the MGA it developed 54kW (72bhp) at 5500rpm on an 8.3:1 compression and using two SU 1½ in carburettors. The standard gearbox was a four-speed manual with synchromesh on the top three gears, the gearshift being a stubby lever on the floor.

Demand was such, especially from the USA, that Australian dealers did not see the MGA until early 1956, the first locally assembled example coming off the Pressed Metal Corporation's line at the end of October 1957 from components sent out from Abingdon in CKD packs. It sounds amazing today in our high pressure, high volume world but PMC were producing the MGA at the rate of only three cars a day! As was the custom, at first most of the A was sourced from Abingdon but quickly BMCA arranged for interior trim, electrical components and some mechanical parts as well as paint to be sourced locally. Many industry experts questioned BMC's wisdom of local assembly but gradually volume built as sales improved.

The Pressed Metal Corporation had a business liaison with BMCA through its assembly of Austin cars during the early '50s. With Zetland working at capacity BMCA retained the services of PMC and contracted them to assemble the MGA. PMC was a versatile company with some 33 different models rolling off their production lines ranging from the MGA through to large Leyland commercials and including Land Rovers.

PUBLICATION No. 55.95 H.E.
First of a new line
THE COMPLETELY NEW
MG
SERIES MGA

Initially supplies of the MGA coming into Australia were fully imported and in its July 1956 issue *Modern Motor* carried a full test of a privately owned A because a press car was not available from BMCA! Under the heading of "As Good As It Looks…" the magazine proceeded to run the sports car to a maximum speed of 155km/h (97mph) with 0–80, 96 and 112km/h (0–50, 60 and 70mph) acceleration times taking 9.9, 12.6 and 18.9 seconds respectively which was pretty darn quick for a 1500cc sports car that weighed just over 864kg (1900lb). The tester loved the car's accurate steering, sharp responsive roadholding and excellent brakes. Its retail price was £1256.

Interestingly, in the same magazine was a full test of the Triumph TR3 that, with a 2-litre engine producing 74kW (100bhp) at 5000rpm and although some 100kg (220lb) heavier was able to run to a maximum speed of 168km/h (105mph) and dash from 0–96km/h (0–60mph) in 11.1 seconds; it was quicker than the A, nowhere near as stylish – the TR3 was a brutish looking machine by comparison – and retailed at £1630 which meant that it was chasing a different buyer profile.

A few months earlier *Modern Motor* had published a full test of an Austin-Healey 100 (May 1955). It was powered by the 2660cc four-cylinder engine from the ill-fated Austin Atlantic and had only 67kW (90bhp) at its disposal so its top speed was not as quick as the TR3 at 163km/h (102mph) and a time of 11.2 seconds for the 0–96km/h (0–60mph) dash. The tester loved the car and felt that at £1390 it was very good value for money. Within two years the Healey was the recipient of the new C series 2.6-litre six-cylinder engine that gave it a power boost to 76kW (102bhp) at 4600rpm but very little by way of a performance boost. Its price rose significantly to £1811 making it far more expensive than the MGA but with no more performance. No wonder the A was so popular!

Sports Car World carried out a full road test of an early example in its June 1959 issue and came away with a top speed of 147km/h (92mph) for a two-way average, the fastest one-way being an impressive 154km/h (96.4mph) – pretty damn good for an unsophisticated sports car of the time. At 5500rpm it pulled 44.8km/h (28mph) in first gear, 72km/h (45mph) in second and 123km/h (77mph) in third while acceleration from 0–890 and 96km/h (0–50 and 60mph) took 10.3 and 15.5 seconds respectively. A mundane hot hatch today would outpace the MGA but that was never the point then, or now. At £1367 it was significantly cheaper than the Austin Healey 100-6 which now cost £2098 while the Triumph TR3 with overdrive cost £1695. Both would outperform the MGA but that was never really a negative issue on the showroom floor.

The journalist who tested the A was none other than Doug Blain, one of the stalwarts of the era and now owner of *The Automobile* magazine in England. He loved the driving position, once he was seated, with good support from the dished seats, gearshift in exactly the right position, well-placed steering wheel, nicely calibrated instruments and the fly-off handbrake but he was not pleased with the positioning of the foot pedals because they were not placed for heel-and-toe downchanges. That said, the roadholding and handling qualities impressed as did the brakes.

In its seven year production run very few changes were made to the MGA. Attempts were made to update the styling but nothing they tried in the studio looked right and so the shape was untouched apart from new taillights for the 1600 MkII and a recessed grille. Engine capacity went to 1600cc in two stages – firstly to 1588cc which was the same as the Twin Cam and then to 1622cc after the Australian engineers showed Longbridge there was life in the old block yet! Disc front brakes came with the 1600 engine and wire wheels were a popular option. The MGA continued being assembled at PMC's Enfield factory until 1962 when it was replaced by the MGB. That story will be covered in *Australian Cars of the 60s*.

A BETTER BUY – BECAUSE IT'S BETTER BUILT

CHAPTER 7

THE ROOTES GROUP IN AUSTRALIA

The Rootes Group came about through the endeavours of two brothers, William and Reginald Rootes, who were major retailers of cars in England in the 1920s and who invested their money in the industry by buying bankrupt companies like Hillman, Humber, Commer, Sunbeam-Talbot and, later, Singer. By the mid-30s they had rationalised their production processes and model range across the whole spectrum and built quite a successful business. Critics would say that they destroyed the character and blood lines of the companies that they took over but at least they survived where extinction was the only other alternative. They were quick to get their pre-war cars back into production and exported to parts of the Empire, like Australia for instance.

Rootes was the first British company to establish an assembly operation in Australia after the Second World War when they purchased a factory built in Salmon Street, Fishermen's Bend by the Commonwealth government during the war to assemble aircraft. Assembly of cars from CKD kits did not begin until late 1947 – it took more than a year to convert the plant to automotive use – when more than 2800 vehicles were produced, rising to more than 3800 in 1948, the 50,000th coming off the line in 1954. Gradually the percentage of locally-sourced materials increased although the company never established a press shop like BMC did nor were the major engine castings locally produced or sourced even though the company purchased a parcel of land near Dandenong for expansion needs.

The first cars assembled locally were Hillman Minx Phase IIs and they were followed by the Humber Hawk, Super Snipe and small numbers of Commer commercials.

By far the most significant Minx was the Mark III released at the Earls Court Show in September 1948. Of monocoque construction, the newly styled body's design was something of a half-way house between the retention of fenders and the coming pontoon-style that was beginning to sweep the world. It was a full-width body that retained the outlines of fenders, especially at the rear, the front fender line flowing back to meet with the rear; at the front was a rectangular grille made up of six horizontal chromed bars with the thicker top one carrying the Hillman name. The Mark III Minx was the second mass produced English family car to feature a curved one-piece windscreen, the first being the Jowett Javelin. For the era, the glass area of the Mark III was large. Compared with its Austin A40, Morris Oxford and Vauxhall Wyvern rivals it was generally a far more modern design that was destined to have a long production life with several facelifts, a strategy that Rootes was to adopt with all its models.

It was a comfortable four-seater, the two bench seats having cloth upholstery with leather edgings. At a pinch six-people could be carried although because of the 2362-mm (93-in) wheelbase the rear wheel arches did intrude considerably on the available rear seat space. Like most British cars of the time, the dashboard featured a central instrument panel comprising a round Smiths speedometer on the right (the driver's side) and a gauge for fuel contents, all other functions being monitored by warning lights. Blinking indicator lights had yet to arrive on a Rootes car, direction changes being shown by quaint trafficator arms located in the B-pillar.

Mechanically the Minx was pre-war, Hillman (like Morris) opting to spend its development budget on the new monocoque body technology rather than a new overhead valve engine – that would come later. The Mark III was powered by the long-serving side-valve in-line four that had first powered a Minx back in 1932. Its bore and stroke were 63 x 95mm for a capacity of 1185cc; compression ratio was 6.3:1 and the engine produced just 26kW (35bhp) at 4100rpm. A carry-over four-speed manual gearbox with a steering column gearshift lever and synchromesh on the top three ratios transmitted the drive to the 5.22:1 rear axle.

The new front suspension comprised upper-and-lower wishbones with coil springs and telescopic dampers, the assembly being mounted on a substantial subframe bolted up to the underside of the body. At the rear were traditional semi-elliptic leaf springs and a sway bar together with a live axle. A Burman worm and nut steering box was used and a Lockheed full hydraulic system with small 203-mm (8-in) diameter cast-iron drums comprised the braking system.

Performance was on a par generally with its Austin, Morris and Ford rivals at around 104km/h (65mph) maximum and a 0–96km/h (0–60mph) time of 40+ seconds. Buyers at the time cared little for performance in the way we are obsessed today, they considered themselves lucky to be able to buy a new car and were far more interested in fuel economy, ease of driving and reliability.

In 1949 Rootes announced a two-door convertible Minx Mark III followed six months later by the Minx Mark IV that was notable only for its larger capacity side-valve engine, now 1265cc with a cylinder bore of 65mm. The new engine looked exactly like its predecessor but in fact had a new block casting – it was an attempt to cure overheating problems that were being experienced by owners in hot climates – and also featured a stronger and fully counter-balanced crankshaft, a new water pump and the generator was now positioned on the side of the engine block. With the compression ratio increased fractionally to 6.6:1 the revised engine produced 28kW (37.5bhp) at 4200rpm. Any performance increase was marginal, *Wheels* managing to coax just 113.6km/h (71mph) out of a Minx and timed the 0–80km/h (0–50mph) run at 17.0 seconds; economy was, however, excellent at 8.6 litres per 100km (33mpg) for all tests. It was still a slow car by today's standards but that was of little consequence then.

Nearly two years later, in October 1951, came the Mark V where again only details were changed; for example, there was a new Burman steering box, the radiator cap on the cooling system raised the pressure to 7lb/sq inch and chromed stone guards appeared on the leading edge of the rear fenders. There was a chrome strip fitted along the front fender and vertical chromed bars on either end of the grille.

Rootes celebrated the 21st anniversary of the Minx name badge with the release of the Mark VI in February 1953. It was pretty much the same car with the exception of a completely new grille and bonnet pressing and a larger boot; the grille was rectangular in shape with a bold, wide chromed border, nine horizontal bars and the Hillman name etched into the centre of the top part of the border, and the round taillights were flared into the rear fenders. What was really new was the release of the Hillman Californian, a two-door hardtop coupe that had an unusual three-piece rear window that curved around the sides. As you could possibly tell by its name, it resulted from a visit to America by Billy Rootes who noted that hardtop coupes were gaining in popularity

1956 Hillman Minx Series I Brad & Janet Flockhart

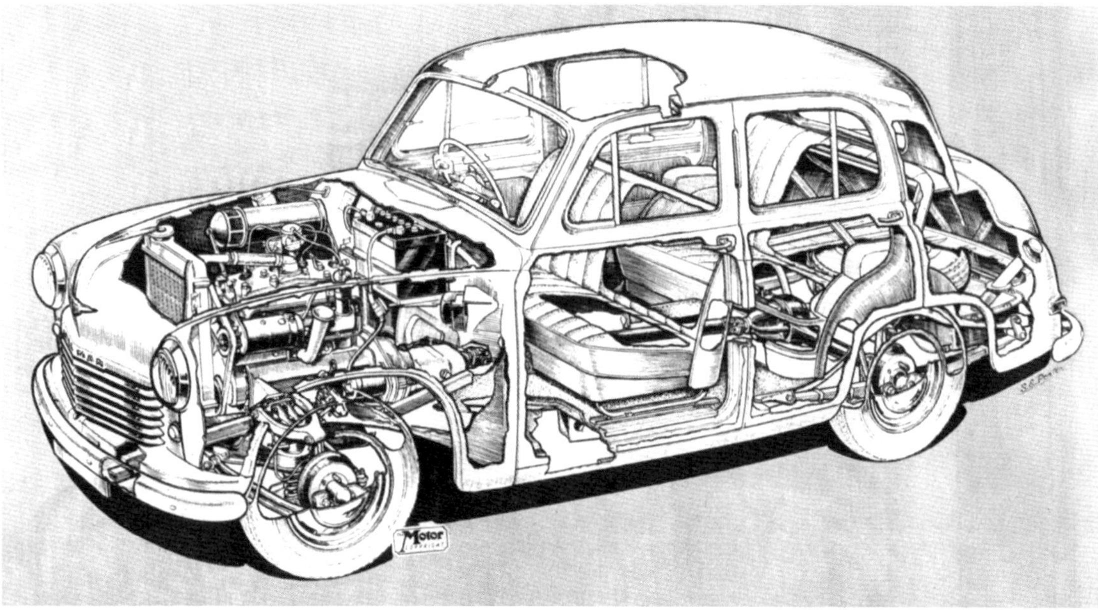

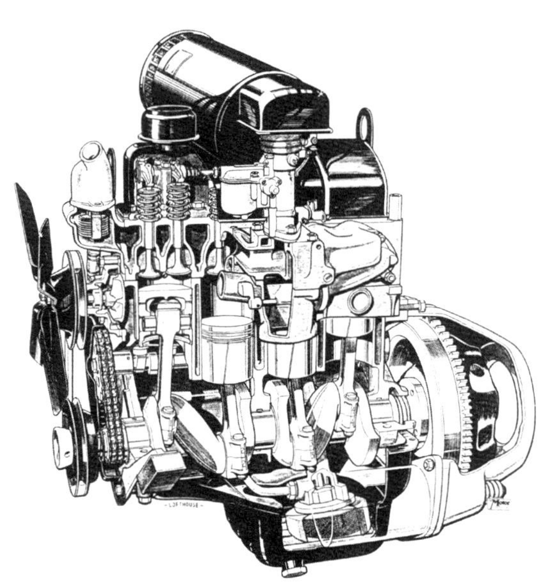

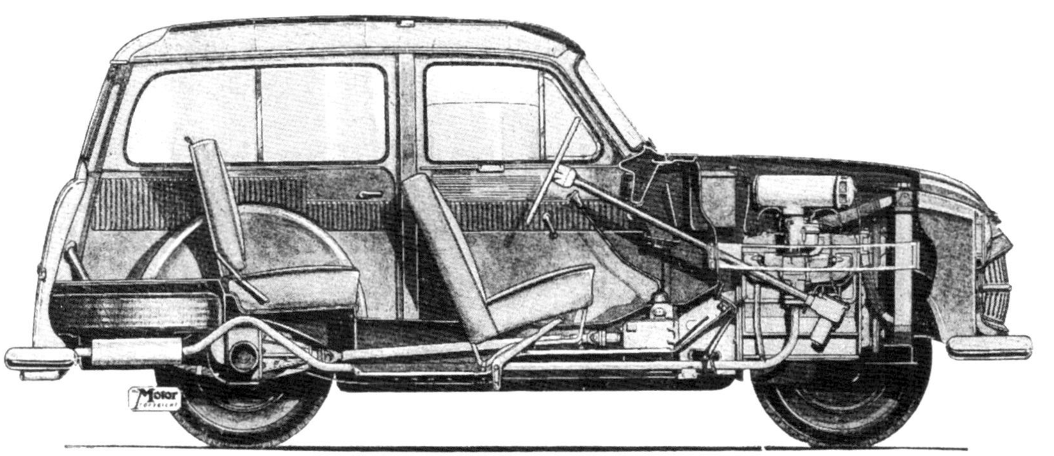

and so he instructed his chief engineer Bernhard Winter and the team to build a production version, based on the convertible, to sell in their biggest market. It was sold in Australia but numbers were small. Where the Minx sedan sold for £994, the Californian cost £1130.

For the 1955 model year with the release of the Mark VIII, the Hillman Minx gained what it had needed all along, a completely new engine. In typical Rootes manner, and reflecting the character of its chief engineer, it was a conservative design and was a relatively heavy, if rugged, engine. Its bore and stroke were 76.2mm each for a capacity of 1390cc; with a tiny Zenith carburettor and a compression ratio of 7:1 it produced 32kW (43bhp) at 4400rpm. According to *Wheels* magazine (August 1955) its maximum speed was 111.5km/h (69.7mph) (some other sources quoted up to 116km/h/73mph) with the 0–96km/h (0–60mph) sprint taking 29.0 seconds. It was no faster in outright speed but it was quicker off the mark and was more economical. At £1008 it was considered good value and to be a well-made and roomy family car although it was by then well off the pace from a styling perspective.

To distinguish it from its predecessors it had a vertical bar grille with a prominent single horizontal bar across the centre. The quaintly named 'Gay Look' Minx arrived as a Mark VIIIa in 1956 and was notable for its two-tone paint job that was something special in those days. This iteration was the last of the line for that body shape.

Running parallel with the Minx from 1955 was the utilitarian Hillman Husky, a station wagon-cum-small panel van that shared much of its componentry with the Minx. Built on a floorpan that had a 228mm (9in) shorter wheelbase and an overall length that was 356mm (14in) less, it had two side doors and a rear door that opened to give access to the load area. It was available as a panel van with no side windows and as a four-seater station wagon in which the rear seats folded to give a surprisingly capacious load area.

The front body panels were from the Minx so there was a shared family resemblance but it was different from the A-pillar back. Under the bonnet was the Minx's side-valve four detuned slightly – down to 26kW (35bhp) from 28kW (37.5bhp) that makes you wonder why they bothered. Where the Minx had a column gearshift, the Husky featured a floor lever – more utilitarian? Performance was class average at 104km/h (65mph) maximum, 24.3 seconds for the 0–80km/h (0–50mph) run and fuel economy in the region of 7 litres per 100km (40mpg). Where the Minx adopted the totally new OHV engine in 1955, the Husky retained the side-valve unit until the complete model change that came along in 1959.

In late 1956 for the 1957 model year a completely new Minx was released, the Series I. The new body was built on a wheelbase of 2438mm (96in), was 4114mm (162in) in overall length, 1524-mm (60-in) wide and 1498-mm (59-in) high and weighed just over 909kg (2000lb) which, for the size of the car, was considered heavy. It was, however, extremely rugged and able to withstand most of the abuse handed out by the tough Australian conditions. The new Minx was a big step forward in styling terms having had input from the American consultancy Raymond Loewy and Associates; gone were the plain sides and tumble-home roofline to be replaced by larger areas of glass, the rear window curving around into the C-pillar and the body sides were plain apart from a full-length character line just below waist level. At the front was a broad grille with vertically positioned closely spaced bars and a single horizontal bar with the parking/side lights at its extremities, a chromed surround and hooded headlights, at the rear small vertical light units with amber/red lens and the license plate recess in the bootlid that opened down to the bumper. Inside was a new dashboard that retained the central positioning of the instruments – three round dials – with a central binnacle also containing the heater/demister controls (when fitted) and radio plus cubbies either side, bench seats and the ubiquitous column gearchange lever. New was the hand brake positioned between the seat and driver's door. Like the previous model, Rootes would stay with this body for much of the next decade making small changes to it on almost an annual basis.

Mechanically it carried forward the 1390cc engine and four-speed gearbox, independent front suspension now with ball joints, drum brakes and 15-in wheels from its predecessor but now with four wheel studs instead of three.

Bryan Hanrahan, road tester at *Modern Motor* wrote in a January 1957 test of the new Hillman, "The best all-round motor car Rootes have ever made, I think, is the current Humber Hawk. Apart from a few shortcomings in roadholding the Minx has the same functional qualities and charm as the Hawk." He managed to record a top speed of 122.4km/h (76.5mph) from the Minx that took 16.0 seconds to go from 0–80km/h (0–50mph), not quick but more than acceptable by the standards of the day.

In the same body but with a different front end styling treatment – a pressed steel filler panel was used to fill in the space where the chromed bar grille was on the Hillman and a traditional upright Singer grille was there instead – Rootes offered buyers the Singer Gazelle. This was a hurriedly cobbled response to Rootes taking over the moribund Singer Motor Company in England and consisted of the Minx body unchanged (apart from the grille) but with a mildly reworked version of Singer's SOHC four-cylinder engine under the bonnet; it had previously powered the Singer Hunter, the last of the real Singers. With a bore and stroke of 73 x 89.4mm its capacity was 1496cc and with a 7.5:1 compression it developed 39kW (52.5bhp) at 4500rpm. Performance was superior to the Minx, the top speed being measured at 134.4km/h (84mph) and the 0–80km/h (0–50mph) run taking 13.9 seconds. Inside there were the expected polished wood dashboard and door cappings, carpet on the floor and a heater as befitted an English small sporting sedan that sold for £1331.

A year later Rootes released the Series II that was their Jubilee Minx celebrating 50 years of Hillman and 25 years of Minx. It was distinguished from the Series I by a slightly different grille featuring a gold plated Hillman badge on the right-hand side. How many have survived I wonder?

The Series III of 1959 was an improved car having a larger 1494cc engine achieved by widening the cylinder bore to 79mm; power rose to 38kW (51.5bhp) at a lower 4200rpm and top speed was now 121.6km/h (76mph). Mechanically it had a larger clutch and the gearbox ratios had been changed with mixed success. *Wheels* road testers thought the ratios were naff, first gear being so close to second as to be useless in real terms – in-gear maxima were 48-, 59- and 94km/h (30-, 37- and 59-mph) while the 0-80km/h (0-50mph) time was 15.3 seconds, not quick even by the standards of the day. Rootes listed four Minx models in their 1959 range: the Special at £999 with no creature comforts but a centre-floor gearshift lever, Deluxe at £1099, station wagon at £1182 and an estate van at £1075. Included in the Series III was a full-length chrome strip on each side that formed the divider for the two-tone paint finish.

The Series IIIA rolled into showrooms from late 1959 and this will be covered in *Australian Cars of the 60s*.

The second generation Husky had a 2184-mm (86-in) wheelbase (50.8mm/2in longer), was 3784mm (149in) overall (25.4mm/1in extra), 1524-mm (60in) wide by 1575-mm (62-in) tall, weight was a solid 1093kg (2405lb), ready for the road. Under the bonnet now was the 33kW (43bhp) 1390cc OHV engine allied to a floor shift. Again much of its mechanical specifications were shared with the Minx as were its front body panels. On the test track *Wheels* achieved a maximum of 112km/h (70mph), 0–80km/h (0–50mph) in 16.6 seconds and fuel economy in the 9.5–7.8 litres per 100km (30–36mpg) region. At a recommended retail price of £890 for the van, £978 for the wagon, they reckoned it was something of a bargain. It sold steadily through its model life although it was never a big seller like the Minx on which it was based.

HUMBER

Further up the social and price scale was the conservative Humber range of cars, the four-cylinder Hawk and six-cylinder Super Snipe. Bought out of insolvency by the Rootes brothers in 1928, they merged Humber with Hillman and Commer (who made commercial vehicles in Dunstable) and began a program of model and parts rationalisation that at first created quite a stir amongst the traditionalist establishment British. Within two years of the Rootes brothers assuming control the combine was profitable.

After the war the first Humber assembled and released in Australia was the Hawk Mk I that was really the pre-war Humber Snipe body over the pre-war 14HP Hillman chassis brought back to satisfy demand. Already old in style and specification, few were built until the arrival of the thoroughly revised Mark III in early 1948. This model had a full-width body and a new coil-spring upper-and-lower wishbone front suspension system. Power came from the ancient 1944cc side-valve four-cylinder engine that also powered the Sunbeam-Talbot 2-Litre saloon. Built on a robust separate chassis that had a wheelbase of 2667mm (105in), an overall length of 4420mm (174in) and kerb weight of more than 1227kg (2700lb), the 42kW (56bhp) engine struggled to move the luxury saloon to 112km/h (70mph) and needed an egg-timer for the any of the acceleration runs. Its interior featured leather upholstered bench seats front and rear, cellulosed metal panels and, surprisingly, a heater/demister was an option, even in the UK. Instruments consisted of a semi-circular central speedometer flanked by fuel and temperature gauges, some warning lights and switches, all in a centrally-mounted binnacle. On the windscreen header rail above the rear view mirror was a clock, interesting.

For the 1950 model year the Mark IV Hawk received a larger capacity version of the engine whose cylinder bores were widened by 6mm (now 81 x 110mm, 2267cc) and that yielded 1.5kW (2bhp) extra! Performance figures were marginally better, *The Autocar* timing a maximum speed of 112km/h (70mph) and the 0–80km/h (0–50mph) run now took 'only' 19.3 seconds. As they said, the engineers were more concerned with providing excellent torque characteristics and an easy loping performance rather than going for more speed. "A sensible compromise," they opined.

Minor improvements came in 1952 with the Mark V having new more rounded side grilles with vertical bars, the thick outer edges incorporating the round parking lights, heavier wrap around bumpers,

YGH 499

YGH
499

MRK 455

chrome sill moulding and spats on the leading edge of the rear fender. There was more of this fine detail modifying coming for 1954 in the Mark VI that included the name badge on top of the grille, a chrome strip on the front fenders that extended onto the doors, flashing indicators, new raised rear wings with narrow, vertical tail lights but importantly with the much-needed OHV conversion of the engine that had been fitted to the Sunbeam-Talbot 90 since 1950. Now with 52kW (70bhp) at 4000rpm, speed was up to 128km/h (80mph), acceleration from rest to 80km/h (50mph) now was a comparatively spritely 15.3 seconds. Overdrive was an option for buyers who wanted it. The Mark VIa came in 1956 and that was the final flutter for this Hawk.

This body, now getting on for 8 years in production, was replaced by the completely new Series I Humber Hawk saloon in July 1957 in England, the following year in Australia. It was a whole new ball game for the arch-conservative Humber division of the Rootes Group. Gone was the old-technology heavy and cumbersome separate chassis to be replaced by a larger version of the unitary construction body that the Rootes engineers had developed for the Minx. There had been suggestions that the new Humber styling was influenced by Raymond Loewy's people but that is now in question as more credence is being given to the work of Ted White and Ted Green who simply adopted some of the American styling cues that were flooding the world and, with the American market still taking large numbers of their cars, the Rootes brothers wanted the new models to have a style that would appeal in that market. Dimensionally the new Hawk was slightly larger – wheelbase was increased to 2794mm (110in, a 127-mm/5-in stretch), overall length to 4699mm (185in) (+76.2mm/3in) and while it was slightly narrower on the outside (but wider inside, the seats were a full 1524mm (60in) across, it was also lower and slightly lighter.

The new body had eliminated all vestiges of fenders and was full-width in every way with the hooded headlights at the top of the front fenders, rectangular grille with chrome border and neat horizontal bars, rectangular parking lights, a wrap around windscreen that was nowhere near as extreme as some, wrap around rear window and reasonably deep side windows, and vertical taillight units alongside a bootlid that opened down to the rear bumper level for easy loading and unloading. The only body adornment was a chrome strip just below waist level that began behind the headlight and at the rear dipped down before it reached the taillights; it was an ideal demarcation line for two-tone paintwork. An interesting touch was the location of the fuel filler – behind the right-hand reflector!

Inside it could only have been British – an attractive well-padded dash with a mottled fake wood finish over pressed metal, deep pile carpet on the floor and pleated leather over Dunlopillo foam on the seats. Gone was the centre dash instruments that the Brits had hung onto for so long and in their place was a symmetrical facia that had a raised hump each side – in front of the driver were the main Smiths instruments comprising speedometer with trip/total on the right, separate fuel gauge in the middle and combination dial to the left with only a temperature gauge (oil pressure and amps were optional) – and in front of the passenger was a lockable glove compartment; in the centre were the rotary heater/demister controls and provision for a clock and a radio. Suddenly the Humber Hawk was very contemporary.

Under the bonnet was the same long-stroke in-line four-cylinder

OHV engine that was now producing 58kW (78bhp) at 4400rpm with the aid of a new Zenith downdraft carburettor and a higher 7.5:1 compression ratio. Power went to the rear wheels through a four-speed manual gearbox although buyers had two further options from which to choose – four-speed manual with a Laycock de Normanville overdrive unit or the Studebaker-designed Borg Warner DG150 three-speed automatic, all with a steering column change lever. Because of the longer wheelbase, a two-piece tail shaft was used for added driving refinement. The Lockheed hydraulic drum braking system was carried over although uprated with 279-mm (11-in) cast-iron drums and a huge 181 square inches of lining area, as was the Burman Douglas steering system and while the suspension specifications read the same, the front suspension was now part of a detachable sub-frame that was heavily rubber bushed to the underbody to minimise the transfer of road vibrations to the interior.

On the road it was a vastly improved mid-sized luxury saloon. Gordon Wilkins, the doyen of British motoring journalists, wrote a detailed article following the car's release in England and was highly impressed making comments like "there's an exceptional freedom from both engine noise and vibration", "driving vision is fine, all four wings are visible and the screen pillars are set well back", to "the engine is powerful and oh-so-smooth". He was able to exceed 144km/h (90mph) on one run although Rootes claimed 140km/h (88mph) as the Hawk's top speed and the 0–80 and 112km/h (0–50mph and 0–70mph) times were 15.25secs and 31.5secs respectively.

Some months after its Australian release *Wheels* carried out a full test (February 1959) of a locally-assembled Hawk and were, like Wilkins, most impressed. They compared the manual-with-overdrive with the automatic and found the automatic to be slightly slower – 0–80km/h and 0–96km/h (0–50mph and 0–60mph) in 12.3 and 17.9 seconds for the manual, 14.2 and 18.8 seconds for the auto – with the manual running to 136km/h (85mph) and the auto to 129.6km/h (81mph). The testers appreciated the deep seats that were soft and well upholstered, the full carpeting and the way the doors went 'kerthunk' when closed. They preferred the abilities and ease of driving of the automatic to the manual, particularly in stop-start city traffic and thought the extra cost – £1873 compared with £1698 for the manual, £1795 for the manual with overdrive – was worth every pound.

Further up the socio-economic scale Rootes were catering for those for whom running costs were of little consequence with the Super Snipe models. The first after the war was the Mark I, basically the same as the 1939 model but with the addition of a boot. Separate chromed headlight surrounds distinguished this model from later Mark II and III models that introduced a new style by using the Mark I bodyshell and adding new front guards and a very long, slender 'beak' bonnet and short tail; the nose needed to be long to house the physically huge 4.1-litre side-valve six-cylinder engine that powered it. This engine – called 'Dynamax' – had seen sterling service in various Humber staff cars during the war as well as under the bonnet of a range of Commer commercial vehicles. Typically it was a long stroke design – 85 x 120mm, 4086cc – that produced 74kW (100bhp) at a low 3400rpm but was an extremely torquey unit. Built on a 2896-mm (114-in) wheelbase and 4572mm (180in) overall, the Super Snipe was a roomy and comfortable place in which to travel with acres of space in the back seat for three large passengers. Like the Hawk, the interior was trimmed to high standards with supple leather on the seats, pile carpet on the floor, heater/demister and so on but unlike the Hawk and against the usual practice for the British motor industry, the instruments were in front of the driver with the necessary switches in the centre of the timber veneered dashboard. In front of the passenger was a glove box with an inlaid clock.

Underneath was a massive separate chassis that proved to be virtually unbreakable even in tough Australian conditions, the Super Snipe being a car favoured by wealthy farmers; the front suspension was independent by a massive transverse leaf spring and the live rear axle had wide semi-elliptic leaf springs. Kerb weight of this behemoth was over 1590kg (3500lb)! Given its head a Super Snipe could run to 128km/h (80mph) if you could keep it supplied with fuel (23–17.5 litres per 100km/12–16mpg was the norm!) but it would cruise the highways of the '50s at 88–96km/h (55–60mph) with some ease.

Very little change took place until 1952 when the Mark IV was

THE NEW

released, this model being a clever combination of the existing Hawk cabin section with a new, longer bonnet and larger boot complete with the more rounded and stylish grille, vertical taillights and a lack of running boards gave it a much more modern appearance. Because the Super Snipe used the Hawk body, the instruments returned to the centre of the dashboard, the semi-circular speedometer being flanked by temperature, fuel, amps and oil pressure dials.

Under the long bonnet was a new OHV six-cylinder engine, called the 'Blue Riband', still with commercial vehicle origins, that displaced 4139cc (88.9 x 111.1mm) and now produced 84kW (113bhp) at 3400rpm, good enough to push it to 144km/h (90mph) making it one of the fastest luxury saloons on the market at the time. Wheelbase had grown to 2946mm (116in) and its overall length to 5004mm (197in), weight escalated to just over 1820kg (4000lb). While it was thirsty (17.5 litres per 100km/16mpg), it was also a most comfortable place in which to travel the huge distances in Australia and it was no surprise to find that the Rootes dealers in rural areas sold many Super Snipes to the local farmers who were doing very nicely with their wheat and wool exports. If you purchased a locally assembled Snipe the price was £1849 while an imported one would cost £1948. A road test in *Wheels* October 1953 revealed the big saloon capable of 144km/h (90mph) and able to run from a standstill to 80km/h (50mph) in 9.1 seconds and to 96km/h (60mph) in 14.9 seconds. The tester admired the serene way in which the Snipe quietly and without stress covered long distances and cosseted the occupants from the outside world.

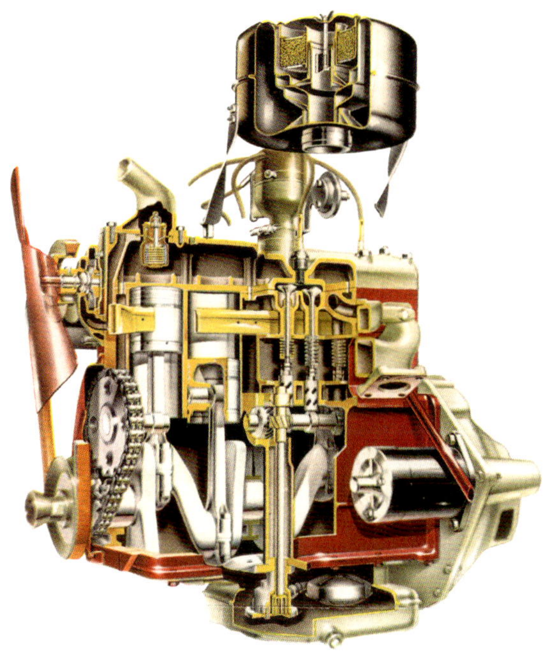

The Mark IVA – just to confuse things it retained the Mark IV designation in Australia – brought wider brake drums, more engine power (up to 86.5kW/116bhp) and timber veneer dashboard although locally assembled cars retained the moulded bakelite dashboard that Rootes Australia felt was better suited to local conditions. The Mark IVB (Mark IVA in Australia) brought a chromed waist band, blinking indicators in lieu of the earlier trafficators, 90kW (121bhp), and choice of gearboxes – manual, manual with overdrive or the Borg Warner DG200 automatic. *Wheels* carried out a test of a Super Snipe exactly four years after the previous one and produced an almost identical set of figures and still admired the way in which the car went about its business.

Modern Motor tested a Super Snipe in the May 1957 issue, this car being one of the last batch of CKD Snipes to be locally assembled. There were several improvements that came through as running updates – engine power increased to 97kW (130bhp) at 3600rpm, higher 7.36:1 compression, redesigned exhaust manifold, strengthened chassis suspension points and an increase in brake lining area from 191 to 200 square inches. Tester Hanrahan could find little to complain about such was his admiration for Humber cars; he coaxed 163.2km/h (102mph) out of the Snipe and ran the 0–80 and 96km/h (0–50 and 60mph) runs in 9.9 and 14 seconds, fuel consumption was a hefty 17 litres per 100km (16.9mpg)!

As with the Hawk, the big change for the Super Snipe came with the Series I that arrived in December 1958, a year after the Hawk. The delay was due to the fact that the production engineers in Coventry wanted to make sure that all the bugs had been eradicated from their new production system. Rootes had collaborated with their Coventry neighbours Armstrong Siddeley on the design, development and production of the totally new six-cylinder engine that would power the Super Snipe. Both the cylinder block and head were cast-iron and the forged crankshaft ran on four wide main bearings so while it was no lightweight design, it was a breath of fresh air from Rootes. The cylinder head utilised cross-over pushrod and rockers, overhead valves and central spark plugs in a hemispherical combustion chamber like the Sapphire engine on which it was clearly based, and with a single Stromberg carburettor power output was 78kW (105bhp) at 4800rpm from the 2651cc (82.55 x 82.55mm) unit.

The actual body of the Series I Super Snipe was shared with the Hawk – no longer did the Snipe versions have an extended nose – and so all dimensions were the same as were accommodations. The most obvious visual difference (apart from the name badges) was the grille which had a mesh insert 'floating' within a wide chromed border that swept around into the fenders and embraced the rectangular parking/indicator lights. Only the weight was more, now 1558kg (3248lb). Three gearboxes were on offer: three-speed manual, three-speed manual with Laycock de Normanville overdrive (special order in Australia), and most commonly a Borg Warner DG250 three-speed automatic, all with a column shift lever. Braking was by an all-drum system with a vacuum booster.

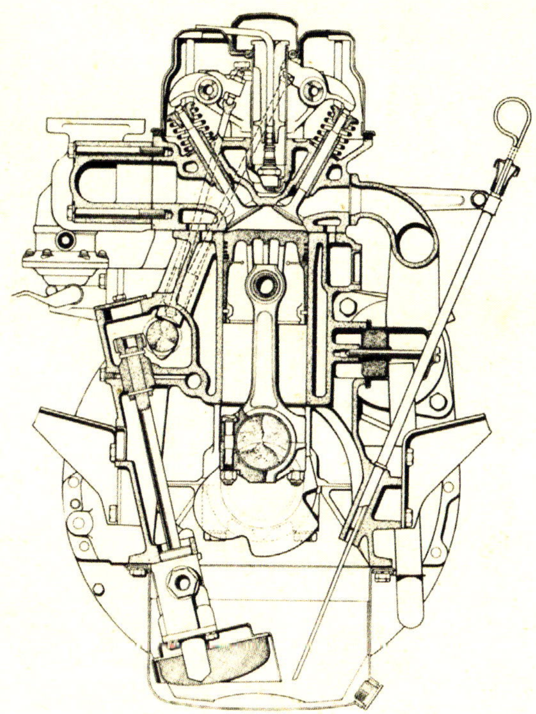

Inside was a typical Rootes interior that cosseted the driver and passengers as was expected of a top-of-the-range Humber saloon; polished walnut wood on the dash and door cappings, leather upholstery (Rootes made this an extra cost option in Australia), deep pile carpets, heater/demister with fan, armrests all round and so forth. Actually, items like the heater/demister were technically options (as was the automatic gearbox) but Rootes Australia ordered packs from the UK that included such items as standard equipment to maximise their unit profits. When announced in Australia the Series I Super Snipe was regarded as not just a luxury saloon but as something of a sporting saloon; after all, its maximum speed was in the mid-140km/h (90mph) range and it was able to cruise at a relaxed 112km/h (70mph) for as long as the conditions allowed. Fuel economy was far better than its predecessor – better than 14 litres per 100km (20mpg) now – and the levels of refinement with respect to ride and handling were a revelation. When compared with other 'luxury' British cars the Series I Humber Super Snipe set a new benchmark, especially at a showroom price of £1974 for an automatic, £1825 for the manual.

Wheels carried out a full test (May 1959) of the new Snipe with writer Ian Fraser heading the article with the words, "This is Humber's first entirely new model for quite a few years – and it is the best Super Snipe ever. It will become one of Australia's best selling big cars. It should. It's a beauty." He wrote most favourably on its dynamic abilities with comments like "there was a definite, but completely stable tendency to understeer on fast corners", to "the Snipe is the sort of vehicle which inspires confidence regardless of the conditions", and "performance was excellent and, thanks to the car's good shape, it could comfortably keep up with its direct competitors, some of whom have twice the engine capacity". He summed up by saying, "If Australians don't buy the Humber Super Snipe in large quantities, there is definitely something radically wrong with our population." The road test was written in a hugely positive way all the way through and must have been like pennies from heaven for the PR people at Rootes in Port Melbourne.

Against the clock the Super Snipe ran to 147.2km/h (92mph), did the 0–96km/h (0–60mph) sprint in 18.2 seconds, the standing quarter mile in 21.2 seconds and at normal highway cruising returned 11.8 litres per 100km (24mpg). *Modern Motor*, too, tested the new Super Snipe and wrote a similarly glowing report; they achieved an average of 153.6km/h (96mph) top speed (best one-way was 163.2km/h/102mph), 15.1 seconds for the dash to 96km/h (60mph) and returned 13.5 litres per 100km (21mpg) on test. Rootes with its recently refreshed Humber range and comparatively young Hillman Minxes and Singer Gazelles continued unabated into the next decade.

857

CHAPTER 8

STANDARD MOTOR COMPANY

Like its rivals Austin and Morris, the cars from the Standard Motor Company in the early post-war years were warmed over pre-war offerings. Not very exciting and really not up to the 'export or die' mentality that pervaded the British industry at the time. Sir John Black, managing director of the company, had enthusiastically embraced the one-model program as espoused by the Attlee Labour Government and in late 1947 the company released the Standard Vanguard. It was an immediate sales success internationally, especially so in Australia where its rugged separate chassis and wet liner engine had instant appeal.

The Standard Motor Company of England continued its association with Standard Motor Products Ltd in Australia with the assembly of the essentially pre-war Standard Eight saloon beginning in 1946, with most of the body panels being pressed by outside contractors like James Flood and T J Richards, later to become Chrysler Australia Limited. Sales of Standard and Triumph cars exceeded all expectations in a car-starved market with the numbers being assembled and sold increasing dramatically each year. Between 1948 and 1952 when a completely new factory was purpose-built in Bertie Street, Port Melbourne by Standard Motor Products Ltd, Vanguards and the smaller Standards were assembled in A'Beckett Street in Melbourne as well as by T J Richards in Adelaide. The new factory was erected to not only build the Vanguard but also the new small Standard 8 saloon and the TR series Triumph sports cars that had had been added to the range in 1954. In the same year the plant's area was expanded from 16 acres to 33 acres. A subsidiary company was assembling the famous 'grey' Ferguson tractor for which there was a huge demand. In 1959 the Triumph Herald succeeded the Standard Ten as the company's small car market representative. However, by November 1958 the company's name had been changed (again), this time to Australian Motor Industries Ltd.

Australian Motor Industries evolved out of Eclipse Motors that held the Victorian distributorship for Talbot and Clement-Bayard cars in the mid-1920s. Later the company successfully negotiated the franchise for Standard cars for Victoria, the first examples arriving in 1929 when the company changed its name to Standard-Talbot Distributors. By 1931, with the world still in the grip of the Depression, two important new Standards arrived, the Big 9 and Little 9. Some were imported while others had locally produced bodies. The Little 9, renamed the Popular 9 in Australia, was assembled on the first floor of the company's premises at 568 Elizabeth Street in Melbourne. Standard Cars was formed in 1938 and an assembly operation commenced at Port Melbourne.

Having successfully launched the Vanguard in Australia early in 1949 the company's greatest problem was being able to purchase sufficient CKD packs from Coventry to satisfy demand. The Vanguard was the result of a two-year gestation period, short even by the standards of the day, and was a curious mix of British and American influences that ultimately worked well for the car which had quite a long production life. Its styling was clearly based on the last of the pre-war American cars (a 1942 Plymouth in fact) that had adopted the rounded, hunchback style as espoused by Ford and Chrysler products; the Vanguard included the six-window look as did several other English manufacturers at the time and had a split, flat glass windscreen. It featured the coming 'pontoon' look with slab sides that were devoid of any suggestion of fenders or decoration. The grille comprised 15 horizontal chromed bars, closely spaced and with the upper six shorter than those below and there were substantial chromed bumpers both ends.

Built on a relatively short 2387-mm (94-in) wheelbase (and 4166mm/164in overall), the doors were not as wide as perhaps you would expect and so getting into the car, particularly the back seat, was not as easy as it could have been. There were bench seats front and back, the front being wide enough to seat three abreast but the rear seat was really only comfortable for two people because it was placed over the rear axle and so the wheel arches encroached conspicuously. A flat dashboard was symmetrical in design making left- and right-hand drive manufacture easy; the instruments comprised a fan-shaped speedometer plus fuel and temperature gauges and some warning lights in a console directly in front of the driver, a matching section in front of the passenger housing the glovebox. On the early cars (the '49 models) the gearshift for the three-speed manual gearbox was on the right of the steering column (for right-hand drive cars) to facilitate the three-abreast seating that was an important sales point back then, and the steering wheel was that most British of wheels with three sprung metal bars per spoke set in the shape of the letter T and with the trafficator switch positioned on the hub.

Like most cars at the time the Vanguard was built upon a sturdy channel section steel chassis with centre cross-bracing and the body mounted onto that by way of rubber insulated bolts. Up front there was an independent suspension system comprising upper-and-lower wishbones with a coil spring and telescopic damper each side, at the rear was a live Salisbury axle suspended by semi-elliptic leaf springs. Stopping the car were comparatively small 228mm (9in) cast-iron brake drums – they were inside big 16in wheels with 6.00 x 16 tyres – with full hydraulic action and the steering was a Bishop cam and roller system.

The Vanguard was powered by what became one of the most respected, versatile and famous four-cylinder engines of its time. It was built around a rugged cast-iron cylinder block that was open at the top and into which were inserted 'wet' cylinder liners that greatly simplified engine rebuilds, and a cast-iron cylinder head was bolted down by ten long bolts. The forged steel crankshaft was supported by three main bearings, and the camshaft was driven by a chain from the front of the crankshaft; long pushrods with mechanical tappets on a rocker shaft operated the two overhead valves per cylinder. The intake mixture was supplied by a Solex carburettor and a cast-iron exhaust manifold led the gases away. The car displayed at the 1948 Earls Court motor show had an 1849cc version of the new engine – 80 x 92mm bore and stroke – but shortly after production began the capacity was raised to 2088cc through an increase in the cylinder bore to 85mm. On a compression ratio of 6.7:1 the engine developed 51kW (68bhp) at 4200rpm and 146Nm (108lb-ft) of torque at 2000rpm. It was an engine that would have a long and varied life powering not only the Vanguard but also the Triumph Renown saloon, Ferguson tractors (albeit with a slightly modified block casting), Triumph sports cars and an assortment of small-scale British makes, particularly Morgans.

The first Vanguards arrived in Australia in late 1948 and were immediately popular even though they were priced at £829 if imported (the imported ones had a Fisher & Ludlow UK plate affixed on the bulkhead) or £797 if locally assembled, more than the Holden 48/215 although to be fair the Vanguard was never seen as nor intended to be a Holden competitor. It was more a middle-class car designed to compete with the Ford Zephyr, Vauxhall Velox and Austin A70. *The Autocar* carried out a full test in 1951 of the slightly revised model that also featured the optional Laycock de Normanville overdrive. The revisions amounted to separate side lights positioned under the headlights, the gear lever positioned on the conventional left side of the column and the door pressings were modified to close above the sill panel and not below it. Maximum speed was measured at 128km/h (80mph) with the 0–96km/h (0–60mph) sprint taking 27.7 seconds; fuel economy was in the 12.5–11.3 litres per 100km (23–25mpg) range. For a four-cylinder saloon weighing more than 1272kg (2800lb) and with only a three-speed gearbox the performance was considered to be more than acceptable.

The ruggedness of the Vanguard's construction soon became evident and appreciated in regional Australia where after its sterling performances in the rugged round Australia Redex Trials in 1953, '54 and '55 it was voted by the motor magazines of the day as the best performing car in those trials. In many rural towns Vanguards outsold the Holden even though it was considerably more expensive!

By 1952 further upgrades had taken place – a new and much simpler grille design with a prominent top bar which was where the large Standard badge was now positioned, chromed surround around the circumference of the front opening and then a rather thick bar (also chromed) horizontally across the centre; new bumpers; concealed fuel filler cap and a larger rear window.

In 1953 the styling was dramatically updated by Walter Belgrove and the small team of stylists at Standard. Known in England as the Phase II but in Australia as the Spacemaster, the redesign involved only the rear half of the body and added a sizeable boot to the car, now making it a traditional three-box design. The hunchback look was gone as was the six-window arrangement. The new roof pressing curved down to the waist of the body and included a wider rear window; the rear door pressings were new as were the rear fenders and bootlid. Interestingly, despite Belgrove's desire to increase the wheelbase he was denied it, with the result that interior room was no better than before. The dash was new but familiar having the same instrument pod mounted in front of the driver and a glove box over on the left; what was different was the centre section that had a neater appearance and more symmetrical placement of the six unlabelled switches (including that most British of switches, the Lucas combination light-and-ignition switch) plus room for the optional radio and heater. Bench seating continued front and rear, the upholstery material was leather and each door had an armrest. The enlarged boot space was a tremendous fillip for sales in Australia along with the car's reputation for ruggedness.

Because mechanically it was a continuation of the well-proved components from before, although the operation of the clutch was now hydraulic, *The Autocar* road test of the Phase II returned very similar results – 124–128km/h (78–80mph) top speed and a 0–96km/h (0–60mph) time of 20.8 seconds with 14–11 litres per 100km (20–26mpg) economy. The improvement in acceleration was because of the need for low octane Pool fuel in the original test due to restrictions. By comparison *Wheels* achieved a top speed of 132.8km/h (83mph) and times of 12 and 18 seconds for the 0–80 and 96km/h (0–50 and 60mph) acceleration runs in a locally assembled example.

After almost eight years in production, the original Vanguard was replaced by a completely new Phase III model in 1956 that brought a new style to the brand. Designed in-house by Walter Belgrove's team, it brought the modern three-box style to Coventry in a package that challenged Ford with their Mark II Zephyr. New were such niceties as a one-piece curved front windscreen and a similarly large curved rear window, comparatively thin cabin pillars and door frames, headlights at the top of the front fenders and large taillights also at the top of the (rear) fenders. The engine air intake was a large rectangular opening with a chromed surround and a wide body-coloured horizontal bar across it with the parking lights (that also were the direction indicators) at each end. There was even a hole for the standard crank handle between the bumper and lower rim of the grille. How many cars had retained this feature by the mid-50s?

What was new for Standard was the unitary body construction that was heavier than its contemporaries and retained vestiges of the old chassis by way of reinforcing members at the front and rear bulkheads. The new body reduced the car's kerb weight by about 100kg (220lb). The wheelbase grew from 2387mm (94in) to 2590mm (102in) which dramatically increased interior roominess, particularly for those seated in the rear; the luggage boot also was a much more useable shape with the spare wheel in a wind-down tray outside and underneath the body. The tools were housed in a panel above the 56-litre (12.5-gallon) fuel tank that was positioned behind the back seat.

Along with the new exterior styling came a new dashboard that, like the Mark II Ford Consul and Zephyr, had the instruments in a raised semi-circular binnacle positioned on the dash top in front of the driver, the fan-shaped speedometer being above a horizontal strip where the four supplementary gauges – fuel, temperature, oil pressure and amps – and warning lights were sited. The dash top was padded as was the lower edge, the first tentative steps towards the safety issues we now know so well. As was the trend at the time, bench seats with centre armrests were fitted front and rear.

Mechanically the Phase III carried on with the well-proven 2.1-litre OHV wet-liner four that had served so well. After all, it was more than capable so why mess with it? It was still rated at 51kW (68bhp) at 4200rpm and 146Nm (108lb-ft) at 2000rpm. The only real change from before was the adoption of a crossflow radiator to lower the bonnet line; and the differential ratio was raised to 4.3:1 to give more responsive acceleration, and first gear of the three-speed gearbox was now synchronised.

While the front suspension retained the upper-and-lower wishbone and coil spring arrangement, it was now ball-jointed (replacing king pins) and mounted on a separate subframe that was bolted up to the bodyshell. Carried over with virtually no changes was the recirculating ball steering system, semi-elliptic rear leaf springs and the Lockheed braking system with its 228mm (9in) cast-iron drums all round.

Modern Motor published a full road test in its April 1956 issue and tester Bryan Hanrahan was highly impressed with it. His comments included, "Outwardly it is an extremely clean-looking, low-built six-seater saloon, the lines of which do not have to rely on ornamentation;" "Inside you drop into a driving position that has been determined by a driver's needs;" "Ahead is a full, neatly-cowled set of instruments – a refreshing change from the usual battery of warning lights" and when carrying out the performance checks he commented, "the remarkably consistent figures recorded left no doubt that the Vanguard can hold our most popular six-cylinder car". Cratered road surfaces did not faze the suspension and the brakes took all the punishment he handed out. At the end of the test he had recorded a maximum speed of 132.8km/h (83mph) with 0–80 and 96km/h (0–50mph and 60mph) times of 14.0 and 21.9 seconds respectively and fuel consumption of 9 litres per 100km (31mpg). *Wheels* magazine also tested a Phase III and came away with the figures of 124.8km/h (78mph) maximum speed, 0–80 and 96km/h (0–50 and 0–60mph) times of 15.8 and 23.0 seconds and ended their test by saying, "We consider the new Vanguard a very good type of car for Australian conditions and note that a large part of its content is Australian. Its ability in hard going should win it friends in the country." Its showroom price tag was £1410 which included a heater/demister and electric windscreen washers making it more expensive than the Ford Zephyr but that did not unduly hamper sales.

Interestingly, Standard Motor Products were able to get the Vanguard Phase III made the official car for the 1956 Melbourne Olympic Games.

To add some spice to the Vanguard range the engineers in Coventry carried out a little cross pollination using parts mostly available off the shelf. By using a slightly detuned Triumph TR3 engine – it was a 1991cc version of the famous four – that gave 67kW (90bhp) at 4500rpm and 164Nm (121lb-ft) of torque at 2500rpm plus a completely new grille that was evocative of Triumph grilles of yesteryear (including the famous globe emblem) they created the Vanguard Sportsman that was introduced in England in August 1956. However, only 20 were brought into Australia, many of them have luckily survived.

There had been van versions of the Vanguard from the early days but it was not until the Phase III that a true Estate was added to the range in 1957. It was a steady seller for the company during its life on the market here. Like most station wagons from that time, the Vanguard's consisted of a lengthened roofline, squared-off window frames for the rear doors and extra side windows. At the rear was a two-piece horizontally split tailgate, the top half lifted up and was held by a ratchet mechanism and the lower half dropped down and was held by a two-piece link. The fuel tank was a new 64-litre (14-gallon) unit that was wide and low with the spare wheel under it thus keeping the luggage floor flat and clear. Also available was a half-ton utility that proved popular in rural areas and with tradies.

By late 1957 the Port Melbourne engineers had come up with the Australia-only revised Phase III that had a new mesh grille, modified bumpers and a 'fin' stuck on the rear fenders to emulate the styling silliness that was coming here from America. It came with a wide variety of colour schemes and the Deluxe version sold for a whopping £1595 which slowed sales considerably; a price drop of £300 came the following year to try and kick-start sales again.

The Phase III had been on the market for two years and was in need of freshening up, particularly from a styling point of view although many critics also believed that the four-cylinder engine was well beyond its use-by date. In late 1957 one of Standard's engineers, Harry Webster (who would later go on to be the Engineering Director of Triumph) made contact with Italian styling genius Giovanni Michelotti and through him Alfredo Vignale. This triumvirate would create the Vignale Vanguards (saloon and estate) that were released in Australia in September 1958 and sold for £1298 (sedan) and £1389 (wagon).

The styling touches of Michelotti and Vignale were minor in relation to the overall design but had a significant effect on the car's appearance. The grille was changed from a mesh to one with four horizontal chromed bars with a small extension to the surround on each side that housed the separate clear park and amber indicator lights. It gave the front a far more modern look; the front and rear windscreens were enlarged slightly and the taillight units were altered, from round to rectangular and positioned vertically in a new housing bolted onto the rear fender. Two-tone paint work was standard as were chromed wheel trims on the new 15-in wheels, there was a new motif on the bonnet and a flag emblem on each rear guard. Inside was plush (for the time) vynide upholstery and available for the first time as an option was a Borg Warner three-speed automatic gearbox.

It was a comparatively inexpensive make-over for Standard but one that gave the car a boost for the next two years of its model life and AMI had to instigate three-shift production rosters to meet the demand.

Australian Motor Manual published performance figures in its February 1959 issue, figures that were basically unchanged from before because nothing mechanically had changed. Top speed was 134km/h (84mph) and its economy ranged between 11-and-9.5 litres per 100km (26-and-30mpg). In the same month, *Modern Motor* published a full test of the new Vanguard automatic. It was a Borg Warner unit with three speeds and controlled by a steering column mounted lever that was unusual insofar as it was on the right of the column, not on the left; a five-position quadrant on the column showed the driver what range was engaged.

The *MM* folks found the joining of the Vanguard four-cylinder engine with the automatic gearbox to be one of the better installations available. That, along with standard fittings like a powerful heater/demister, windscreen washers, four door courtesy lights, full instrumentation and so on helped justify a price of £1497. The car's performance was rated as excellent with its 129.6km/h (81mph) top speed and 0–80 and 96km/h

(0–50 and 60mph) times of 17.9 and 24.2 seconds plus fuel consumption of 11 litres per 100km (25.4mpg). How expectations have changed!

A long forgotten part of the operations at Standard Motor Producers was the assembly of the TR3 and 3A sports cars from 1957 until mid-1959. They were assembled from CKD kits and had very little local content apart from labour. Priced at £1630 including wire wheels and overdrive, the TR3 was more expensive than the MG A by around £400 but the two cars were not really showroom competitors. Powered by a slightly reduced in capacity engine – 1991cc versus 2088cc – through liners with an 83mm bore (down from 85mm) it developed 74kW (100bhp) at 5000rpm on an 8.5:1 compression using with twin SU carburettors; weighing in at a fairly hefty 1132kg (2490lb) the TR3 would accelerate from 0–80 and 96km/h (0–50 and -60mph) in 9.6 and 13.6 seconds respectively and run to 166.4km/h (104mph) in direct top gear or 161.6km/h (101mph) in overdrive top. It was a quick and relatively inexpensive sports car in the 1950s. These were the only TR cars assembled locally, the others which followed were all fully imported.

With the Big Three in England – Austin, Ford and Morris – cleaning up the market between them in the small family car segment, Sir John Black and his deputy, Alec Dick, decided that it was too good an opportunity to let go any longer. Accordingly, in September 1953 the company released their competitor, the Standard 8. It was a completely new car in virtually every respect and the second 'clean sheet' design to come from the Standard Motor Company following the resumption of car production after the war.

New for the Standard 8 was the relatively light weight monocoque

body construction that was made as a 4-door saloon although its main rivals, the Ford Prefect, Morris Minor and Austin A30, were available with either two- or four-doors. What was unusual, and was the outward sign of financial skimping on Standard's part, was the lack of a boot lid. All access – loading and unloading – for luggage was through the rear doors and the fold-down rear seat while the door window glass slid open rather than wound down and up, another cost cutting measure. Stored under the luggage area was the spare wheel that was accessed through a small panel at the rear. Initially there was not even a grille, just an unadorned air intake pressed into the front panel; and like the A30 it had a simple flat pane of toughened glass for the windscreen. A first in the British small car class was made with the Standard 8 having pendant clutch and brake pedals instead of the more usual poking-through-the-floor type as used by Ford, Morris and Austin.

Cost paring was also clearly evident inside as well. There were no window winders as already mentioned and so there was a huge cut-out in the internal door panel that could be used to store things. Rubber mats covered the floor and the seats had simple tubular steel frames, springs and plastic upholstery. The dash was simplicity and cheapness personified – a single round plastic instrument binnacle containing a speedometer and a fuel gauge plus warning lights for the generator, engine temperature, oil pressure and high beam. A single, single-speed, wiper was fitted although a second could be fitted as an option.

Like its rivals, the Standard 8 was a four-seater family car designed for British conditions. It had an 803cc in-line OHV four-cylinder engine, a new design that intriguingly had exactly the same cylinder dimensions as the Austin A30's A-series engine – 58 x 76mm – and again like the BMC engine, both the block and head castings were of cast-iron. On a 7.25:1 compression ratio and using a tiny single Solex carburettor it developed 19kW (26bhp) at 4500rpm, 54Nm (40lb-ft) of torque at 2800rpm.

This power was delivered to the live rear axle through a four-speed gearbox with synchromesh on second, third and fourth gears and a long wand of a floor shift lever; suspension was by a simple upper-and-lower wishbone coil spring independent system up front and semi-elliptic leaf springs at the rear; braking was by tiny 178mm (7in) cast-iron drums on all wheels and the steering was by a cam and roller system. The body's wheelbase was 2134mm (84in), overall length just 3606mm (142in) with kerb weight at 675kg (1484lb).

The Standard 8 was released in Australia in February, 1954 and carried a retail price of £755 that compared well with the Morris Minor and Austin A30. It also compared well with its intended rivals where performance was concerned, being capable of a maximum speed of 104km/h (65mph) and 6.3–5.2 litres per 100km (45–50mpg) economy under the right conditions; its 0–80km/h (0–50mph) acceleration time was a sedate 22.0 seconds while its 0–96km/h (0–60mph) acceleration was timed with an egg timer, not a stop watch, at 54.4 seconds. *Wheels* said of the 8 after their test, "It is a very comfortable family saloon with brisk performance, good handling and notable economy. However, the interior is stark." Despite the obvious cost-cutting the little car, which was assembled by Standard Motor Products Ltd., sold well in Australia.

Within a year Standard released a Deluxe version with some of the obvious cost-cutting measures removed; for example, it now had two windscreen wipers and sun visors, the doors were now properly trimmed and fitted with wind down windows, each door having a quarter pane and the seats were upholstered with a better quality of vinyl plastic.

At the same time came the Standard 10 that was a variant of the Deluxe. The major difference was under the bonnet where an enlarged capacity version of the OHV engine now resided. Its capacity, intriguingly enough again, was 948cc achieved by increasing the cylinder bores from 58mm to 63mm; power rose to 26kW (35bhp) and with larger 5.60 x 13 tyres and a higher 4.55 rear axle ratio top speed rose to slightly more than 104km/h (65mph) while the 0–96km/h (0–60mph) time was reduced to 38 seconds, still slow but now more comparable with its rivals. *Modern Motor* tested a 10 and thought it a most worthy contender in the small car market, being more than competitive with its two BMC rivals in particular. Available as an option on the 10 was the semi-automatic 'Standrive' transmission that incorporated certain Newton Bennett patents that automatically operated the clutch during gear changes; it retained the gearlever but did not have a clutch pedal; a solenoid switch was built into the gear knob for the driver to operate during a gearshift. How many were sold in Australia is unknown but it was probably not many and the option was quietly discontinued.

By the end of 1954 an estate wagon and panel van joined the model lineup. Up to the B-pillar it was the same but from there back it was new panel work; the roofline continued straight to the rear where two van-type doors gave access to the load area. The rear seat lifted and folded to form a completely flat load floor with the back of the seat having the same protective rubber matting as the luggage floor. Interestingly, there was also a uniquely Australian 5 cwt utility version.

By 1956 further upgrades of equipment saw the arrival of a chromed grille – really a broad horizontal bar with an arched bar over it – and a proper bootlid for access to the luggage compartment together with fold-down rear seats for even more luggage capacity.

The next flowering of this design came in March 1957 with the release of the Standard Super 10 that carried on some of the fittings of the 10 but added a mesh grille, full body length chrome side strip that formed the divider when two-tone paintwork was applied, two-tone interior of washable Vynide plastic, a binnacle around the instruments (that were basically unchanged in themselves) and better seats. With this model came the 'Gold Star' 948cc engine that received a lot of publicity at the time. Every part of the exterior of the engine was painted gold as it went down the assembly line! The cylinder head had been modified slightly – higher compression, larger valves and better combustion chamber shape – to achieve 27.5kW (37bhp) at 4500rpm. On test *Wheels* achieved a maximum speed of 107km/h (67mph) with 32, 51 and 93km/h (20, 32 and 58mph) available in the indirect ratios, a time of 20.0seconds for the 0–80km/h (0–50mph) dash and the car returned economy figures from 7.6 up to 5.6 litres per 100km (37mpg up to 50mpg). Amazingly, the price for the Super 10 was £945, down from £1013 for its predecessor. They said in summary, "The keynote of the 1958 Super Ten is more value for less money." They added, "It is a keenly competitive model, and has much to offer the man who wants an economical light car, one which is brisk in performance and thoroughly at home on even the roughest of roads."

There was considerable turmoil within the company and in November 1958 the company's name was changed from Standard Products Pty Ltd to Australian Motor Industries having earlier in the year (May) also formed Mercedes-Benz (Australia) Pty Ltd in collaboration with Daimler-Benz AG in Stuttgart, Germany.

By early 1959 buyer interest in the Standard 10 had waned considerably. Rumours out of England suggested a rather radical new model was due soon to replace it and in a surprise move it was badged as the Triumph Herald. All cars were now badged as Triumphs because management believed the name had more cachet than Standard which implied a product of lower quality even though when the name was first used it was because the product *set the standard* by which others would be judged, how times and perceptions change!

The Triumph Herald was a radical re-think of the company's small-car segment model. Brilliantly styled by Giovanni Michelotti, it returned to the use of a separate chassis with the body components being stamped and assembled onto the chassis like in the old days, a manufacturing set-up forced on Triumph by its own lack of body manufacturing capabilities and as such it was a neat and simple way of overcoming a problem. Unusually for a British small car was the specifying of a fully independent suspension system that used upper-and-lower wishbones at the front with coil springs and telescopic dampers (it carried over some parts from the 10) and at the rear was a transverse leaf spring, longitudinal link, telescopic dampers and swing axles. The 948cc engine was carried over as was the four-speed manual gearbox (now with a remote gearshift) and the drum braking system. Like the Morris Minor, the steering was rack and pinion. To facilitate ease of servicing of the engine the whole front body assembly – bonnet and guards – pivoted at the front and lifted forward as a unit, a little like the Jaguar E-Type.

It was released in England in March 1959 and AMI had it on the market in Australia eight months later. *Modern Motor* published a full test in its November 1959 issue and was impressed. They recorded a maximum speed of 120.4km/h (75.3mph), ran the 0–80km/h (0–50mph) sprint in 18.5 seconds and found that it returned between 8.9 and 6.8 litres per 100km (32 and 42mpg). They liked the all-independent suspension, found its handling on dirt was superb and the steering was very accurate and light with a surprising 25-foot turning circle. "It is a remarkably revolutionary car for one designed in the UK," they opined, and put its performance on a par with the ubiquitous VW Beetle that in its time set the yardstick for all other small cars. Ironically, both the VW and Triumph possessed swing axle rear suspension geometry and both were prone to roll-overs because of this feature.

AMI released the Herald two-door saloon first at £970 (the VW Beetle cost £971) and followed it with the pretty coupe some weeks later, its engine featuring twin SU carburettors to raise power from 29kW (39bhp) at 4500rpm to 38kW (51bhp) at 6000rpm; it retailed for £999. Making a coupe out of the sedan was simple because of the method of building the body. The sedan's roof was removed and a restyled roof with a smaller rear window and no side glass was substituted, could not have been simpler.

The release of the Triumph Herald heralded a new era in the history of AMI and that will be covered in *Australian Cars of the 60s*.

1961 VAUXHALL VICTOR

CHAPTER 9

GENERAL MOTORS VAUXHALL, CHEVROLET, PONTIAC

Once Vauxhall had been incorporated into the world of General Motors in 1925 their manufacturing and marketing strategy changed completely. Rather than being expensive, bespoke high performance vehicles, moves were made to bring the marque down-market into the realm of the volume makers where it competed directly with Ford, Austin and Morris. Part of this move was to increase the volume of exports, predominantly to Empire countries, with a wider range of models on offer from the small 10hp model rising to the 12hp, 14hp and big 16hp. Vauxhall was a pioneer within the GM world in the adoption of an all-steel monocoque body that came onto the market in England in 1936.

Small numbers of Vauxhalls were assembled at GM-Holden's Woodville plant in the decade prior to the World War II as the make carved out a reasonably sized niche market for itself. After the war buyers could choose between either a fully imported or an Australian assembled Vauxhall that used the L series body and was badged either as a Wyvern (4-cylinders) or Velox (6-cylinders). The locally assembled versions were based on the pre-war chassis and the six-window J body, the imported English body having a conventional four-window style. This arrangement was changed in late 1949 when Holden's stopped pressing their own Vauxhall panels and reverted to importing panels from the UK thereby releasing press capacity for the growing demand for the 48/215 Holden. Locally assembled Vauxhalls had leather upholstery and a more rounded luggage compartment compared with the imported cars that were generally supplied with cloth upholstery and a flat rear panel.

Both models, the 1.4-litre OHV four-cylinder Wyvern and 2.3-litre OHV six-cylinder Velox, had suicide front doors, horizontal bar grille, bench seats front and rear, column gearshift, the unusual Dubonnet-type knee-action torsion bar front suspension that actually caused the front of the car to rise slightly when braking, and an abbreviated boot. An *Autocar* test in 1951 showed the Velox capable of 118km/h (74mph) and it took 19.3 seconds to go from 0–80km/h (0–50mph) which was slow when compared, for example, with the Jowett Javelin that with a smaller 1.5-litre four-cylinder engine would run to 128km/h (80mph) and took only 14.8 seconds to reach 80km/h (50mph) from a standstill.

In March 1952 the completely new E series was released although supplies were limited because of the lingering industrial effects of the war. Intriguingly, the model line included the unusually named Vagabond, a convertible Vauxhall that was unique to Australia as was the Velox utility. Both were built on the earlier J series chassis to give the body some rigidity but sales of the Vagabond were slow and it was discontinued by 1954. The Velox utility was continued before being quietly dropped in late 1957.

The E series had a monocoque body with the popular pontoon slab sides (there was just the faintest hint of a fender at the rear) with a chromed spear reaching from just behind the headlight to across the front door; the traditional Vauxhall bonnet flutes were there as was a large chromed grille that consisted of a broad rectangle around the perimeter with a bold horizontal bar across it; doors were opened by pushing a button alongside a chromed handle; there were small half-round taillights at the corner of the rear fenders; and the bootlid opened down to bumper level. Inside there was a new dashboard with round dials – speedometer in one, combination gauges (fuel, temperature) plus warning lights in the other – leather upholstered bench seats, foot pedals sprouting through the floor and the then obligatory column gearshift. Rubber mats sufficed on the floor and a heater/demister was an option.

Under the bonnet, which incidentally could be rather cleverly opened from either side, was a totally revised OHV engine. As before both the four-cylinder Wyvern and six-cylinder Velox engines shared their bore and stroke for maximum interchangeability of components. Both engines had cylinder dimensions of 79.37 x 76.2mm (3.125 x 3.00ins) for 1508cc (92-cid) for the Wyvern and 2262cc (138-cid) for the Velox; power outputs were 30kW (40bhp) and 48kW (64bhp), both at 4000rpm. The complex-to-manufacture and difficult to maintain Dubonnet front suspension was replaced by a conventional upper-and-lower wishbone system with coil springs and concentric telescopic dampers; the leaf spring rear suspension, drum brakes and steering were carried over with minimal change.

The retail prices for the Vauxhalls ranged from £1050 for the Wyvern, £1118 for the Velox, £1027 for the Wyvern Vagabond and £1076 for the Velox version. Again, *The Autocar* tested a Velox and was impressed. They described the new styling as “well proportioned and easy to clean because of its smooth surfaces”. The car’s spirited performance was appreciated, the sedan reaching 131km/h (82mph) and running the 0–80 and 96km/h (0–50 and 0–60mph) sprints in 13.5 and 21.2 seconds respectively. The Velox’s ability to cruise quietly and economically at 96–104km/h (60–65mph), too, made for positive comments. Despite the austerity of the times GM-Holden had little difficulty in selling all they could assemble.

Two revisions on the E series’ body took place, the first appearing in April 1955 featuring a new grille that had two horizontal bars with fine concave vertical bars between them and round parking lights included at each end, the Vauxhall name was in the top grille bar, a large V (for Vauxhall) on the leading edge of the bonnet, revised bumpers and a different chromed accent on the bonnet. Inside there was a completely new dashboard that was symmetrical to suit right- and left-hand drive (Canada was a strong market for the cars). All the instruments – speedometer, fuel and temperature gauges plus lights for ignition and oil – were contained within a single large diameter circular dial in front of the driver while the matching round pressing in front of the passenger housed the radio speaker; in the centre of the dash was the glove box and above it was provision for the fitting of a radio and a heater. Added to the range at this time was a luxury Cresta version

VAUXHALL CARS
1949 Vauxhall VELOX & WYVERN
MR-917
MR-909
MT-019

RVV-057

6549 AH

GCL-650

UUH-737

which featured leather seats, heater/demister, cigarette lighter, glove box light, electric clock in the centre of the radio speaker, whitewall tyres, several dual-tone colour combinations and added chrome accents. Retail prices were £1186 for the Wyvern (more expensive than the FJ Holden), £1264 for the Velox and another £120 for the Cresta.

The second revision came two years later, in April 1957, when another grille graced the body – it had 5 horizontal bars sweeping to large chromed round die-cast parking light/indicator assemblies – as well as a full body length chromed strip that dipped on the rear doors plus new taller vertical taillights with separate amber direction and red taillight lenses, and a wrap around rear window. The name Vauxhall was spelt out in large letters debossed into a prominent chrome strip across the top of the grille and there was a new badge and V in the centre of the bonnet's leading edge. Cheney's, the Victorian distributor, moved the badge from the grille to the front of the bonnet. Minor engine modifications saw the Velox/Cresta engine produce 50kW (67.5bhp) and the Wyvern 35kW (47bhp). During the latter part of the production run a completely new cylinder head was fitted to the Velox/Cresta six-cylinder engine; it now had 12 ports where previously there had been seven, and power rose to 58kW (78bhp) at 4000rpm. Another welcome change was to two-speed electric wipers and the circular speedometer displayed the road speed not by a needle but by a translucent moving disc that rotated as speed increased, its leading edge indicating the speed; it was more visible at night rather than during the day..... The Wyvern continued to sell at £1186 but the Velox had risen slightly to £1298 with the Cresta again slightly more expensive.

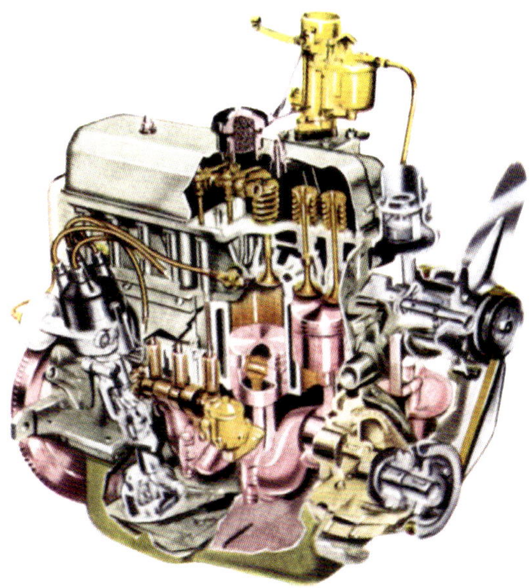

Modern Motor tested a Wyvern and commented that it was "a car combining generous size and capable performance with a moderate price". They coaxed 112km/h (70mph) out of it and it took 20.2 seconds for the 0–80km/h (0–50mph) dash – even by the standards of the day it was slow.

Rival magazine *Wheels* published a full test of the Velox (September 1957 issue) and declared "Following many years of development, the new Velox is a highly refined car with sharp acceleration, good handling, a quite amazing capacity for soaking up the rough, and commendable petrol economy. In short, the Velox is now fully adult." The testers liked the column gearshift with its short and positive movement and found the engine to be extremely flexible and smooth, pulling from 8km/h (5mph) in top gear. The only real negative they found were the drum brakes which faded when used in hard-and-fast motoring. Stability in wet and windy test conditions was considered exemplary.

The same year (1957) saw the arrival of a completely new medium-sized sedan to replace the Wyvern, the Victor. It was a case of America dictating to England where the styling was concerned as it was little more than a shrunken Chevrolet or Pontiac in many ways. It certainly did not *look* like an English car!

There was the vast wrap round panoramic front windscreen with vertical A-pillars, clap-hands sweep electric wipers, large chromed bumpers front and rear with what the Americans called 'Dagmar' protrusions each end (apparently named after a very well endowed model of the time), flutings pressed into the front fenders and accented with chromed strips to simulate what had been a Vauxhall tradition, a curved accent line pressed into the rear doors and the exhaust pipe poked out through the right rear bumper pod. At the rear were vertical taillight units with a separate round indicator lens at the top, the assembly being housed in a large chromed surround; at the front was a full width horizontal grille that had a chromed surround with the rectangular park lights each end under the hooded headlights; and there were two parallel raised ribs in the bonnet.

Inside there was a rectangular-shaped chrome rimmed instrument binnacle in front of the driver and odd-shaped pressings either side of the steering column to locate various switches, the heater/demister (when fitted) and the radio (also when fitted). The dash swept around at each end and into the doors as a styling feature. Passengers sat on Vynide upholstered bench seats front and rear with plastic-rubber mats on the floors. It was available in only one trim level and sold for £1123, slightly more than the last Wyverns.

The new Victor rode on a new platform that had a wheelbase of 2489mm (98in) (127mm/5in shorter) and an overall length of 4242mm (167in) (just 76mm/3in shorter) with a body width of 1594mm (62.75in) (102mm/4in narrower) and weighed exactly one Imperial ton. Power came from a re-energised four-cylinder OHV engine that had a bore and stroke of 79.37 x 76.2mm (the same as the last of the Wyvern's) for 1507cc. Running a higher 7.8:1 compression it developed 41kW (55bhp) at 4200rpm. *Modern Motor* managed 123km/h (77mph) and a 0–80km/h (0–50mph) time of 15.9 seconds in their January 1958 road test. *Wheels* tested a standard Victor sedan in its March 1959 issue and returned the figures 118.8km/h (74.3mph) for top speed, 14.3 seconds for the 0–80km/h (0–50mph) dash. Both appreciated the car's ride and handling and found few faults although the sparse equipment level came in for adverse comment.

Most of the mechanical components were carried over from the Wyvern so at least those parts were proven. In the rush to get the Victor on the market short cuts were taken in the body construction and finish that meant rust soon appeared to spoil the motoring experience. This spelled doom for Vauxhall in the huge American market and very nearly had the same effect in Australia.

For 1959 Vauxhall released the Series 2 in which the styling was toned down in response to conservative Britons complaining. There was a new bonnet pressing without the parallel ribs but with a single central rib and bonnet badge, new rear door outer skins, plain bumpers with a repositioned exhaust outlet, simple horizontal bar grille and a new dashboard that again was somewhat plain by comparison but worked better for the driver. GM-H was now offering two versions, the standard at £1046 and Super at £1090 that had polished stainless steel trim around the front and rear windows, chrome horn ring, door courtesy light and one or two other fittings.

Mechanically there were no changes.

In April 1958 the E series bowed out to be replaced by the PA series Velox and in June the Cresta sedan followed. Although the mechanical components were carried over largely unchanged (apart from the Solex carburettor being replaced by a Zenith), engine power rose slightly to 61.5kW (82.5bhp) at 4400rpm and the styling was very much again Detroit dictates to Luton. The new body style was garish like the smaller Victor but with some peculiarities of its own. Featuring prominently was the huge wrap round front screen with its knee crunching A-pillar and clap hands electric wipers; at the rear was a surprise in the form of a *three-piece* rear screen that curved

Symmetrical Instrument Panel

around into the C-pillar, rear 'fins' that started at the rear door handle and had the rear amber indicator lens in their ends above the oval-shaped red taillight lens that were in large vertical chromed oval-shaped bezels, the grille at the front was a narrow horizontal slot with five chromed bars flanked by separate indicator and parking light units. Along each side, starting from over the headlight, was a broad full-length fluted chrome strip that was a reminder of a past Vauxhall styling feature.

The new PA was a bigger and heavier car all round, the wheelbase being 50mm (2in) longer, length almost 152mm (6in) more, width was 50mm (2in) more and height had been reduced by a remarkable 152mm (6in), weight had increased by 68kg (150lb) and it rode on 13-in wheels instead of the 15-inch previously. Yet it was still a comfortable six-seater sedan with a 17-cubic-foot boot.

The dashboard was over-styled by English standards and, like the Victor's wrapped around into the doors for continuity of line. Two large round instrument pods were positioned in front of the driver, the left one containing the speedometer and the right one having the fuel and temperature gauges plus warning lights. Various switches – key start, wipers, choke, lights – were located either side of the steering column, the pistol grip hand brake was under the dash to the left and the driver had a large steering wheel with a half circle chrome horn ring and the Vauxhall griffin on the hub which resembled the instrument dials in style. Provision for a heater/demister and radio were in the centre of the dash.

As with previous Velox's and Cresta's, all passengers sat on bench seats front and rear with carpet on the floor.

Both *Modern Motor* and *Wheels* tested the Velox and came to similar conclusions – "Its styling is *very* US-inspired and is a matter of taste" – but having said that they praised its nice and airy interior, its quietness when cruising and found it to be an above-average performer. Top speed worked out at 140km/h (87.6mph) which was good for an English sedan, the 0–80km/h (0–50mph) time was 11.9 seconds and fuel economy was between 12.8 and 9.5 litres per 100km (22 and 30mpg).

Following adverse reactions from both the press and public, Vauxhall moved rather quickly to redesign the rear window and to make it a single piece of glass which in a stroke tidied up that aspect of the car's design. The grille opening was enlarged and fitted with a chromed mesh while more restrained taillights appeared at the back. This revised Velox appeared in mid-1959, the model selling well against its English rivals like the Ford Zephyr and Austin A95 that retailed at £1302 and £1398 respectively. Volumes were never high and with a retail price of £1393 it would never be a threat to the all-conquering Holden Special that sold for £1173.

All Australian-assembled post-war Vauxhalls had their body number prefixed with a single letter – A for Adelaide (Woodville or Birkenhead), M for Melbourne (Fisherman's Bend), S for Sydney (Pagewood), B for Brisbane (Acacia Ridge) or P for Perth (Mosman Park).

With the insatiable demand from buyers for Holdens all available production space at GM-H's plants was needed which meant that assembly operations for the Vauxhall range (and Bedford trucks) was moved to the Birkenhead factory in Adelaide.

CHEVROLET AND PONTIAC

By early 1946 GM-Holden was sourcing components from GM-Canada to assemble the 'new' Chevrolet and Pontiac sedans in Australia at its Woodville body factory where some panels were pressed to be mated with the imported rolling chassis. The sedans sold were from the Chevrolet Fleetmaster and Stylemaster series and Pontiac Streamliner and apart from minor trim items were carry-over 1942 models. In addition GM-H also assembled very small numbers of Oldsmobile and Buicks, the Olds having a 3022mm (119in) wheelbase and six-cylinder L-head engine of 238-cid and 74kW (100bhp), a conservative three-box body with a split-vee flat windscreen. The Buicks were, of course, famous for their OHV straight-eight engines, aero-back styling with big 'toothy' chromed grille.

This meant for Chevrolet they had three-box bodies – Ford and Chrysler had sloping fastback body styles – on a 2921mm (115-in) wheelbase, were 5029mm (198in) in overall length and were powered by the long-serving famous Chevrolet six of 216.5-cid displacement (3.5 x 3.75-in bore and stroke; 88.9 x 95.25mm for 3548cc) producing 67kW (90bhp) at 3300rpm. Under good conditions it would run to 128–136km/h (80–85mph) and give 15.6–14 litres per 100km (18–20mpg). Despite a market desperate for new cars the numbers sold was a fraction of the potential because of the difficulties GM-H had in obtaining supplies.

By late 1950 GM-H ceased importing CKD kits for both the Oldsmobile and Buick brands despite the seller's market conditions. Small numbers of private imports of those makes came to the country after that.

The first truly new post-war Chevrolets and Pontiacs to arrive in Australia came in late 1949 in time to be displayed at the Melbourne Motor Show but were not really available to buyers until sometime early in 1950. Delays occurred because of the huge demand for GM products in America. Not surprisingly, the styling of the 1949 Chevrolet bore a striking resemblance to the 48/215 Holden that had been developed at the same time in Detroit. It was a rather pleasant design characterised by the huge two-piece curved front windscreen, high cowl line sloping back to a quite low tail with small horizontal taillights; there was a prominent reminder of a mudguard over the rear wheels with a stone guard protector on its leading edge. The grille comprised a broad horizontal bar with a loop above and seven small vertical bars below with the parking lights included on the central bar.

Under the body was a separate X-frame chassis with coil-and-wishbone front suspension and a live axle suspended by semi-elliptic leaf springs at the rear. Low geared recirculating ball steering and four-wheel 279-mm (11in) cast-iron drum brakes rounded out the main mechanical specifications.

Power, all 67kW (90bhp) of it, came from Chevrolet's long-serving 'Stove Bolt' six now raised in capacity to 235.5-cid (3 9/16 x 3 15/16in; 90.48 x 100.1mm, 3848cc) that drove the rear wheels through a three-speed manual transmission with column shift lever. Pontiac followed a parallel course and shared its body with Chevrolet, brand differentiation coming from five parallel chrome strips – so-called 'silver streaks' – down the bonnet and boot lid, a unique grille, badges and taillights while under

1953 CHEVROLET
Entirely NEW
through and through!

Chevrolet
1956

Welcome to
CHEVROLET
The Sales Leader
GM-46

1957

the bonnet resided the division's similarly long-in-the-tooth side-valve straight-six engine of 239-cid (3905cc) giving 76kW (102bhp). Like Chevrolet, it featured a three-speed manual gearbox (non-synchromesh first gear) with a column gearshift.

Interior roominess was most accommodating for six adults on two wide bench seats, both having leather upholstery, door armrests and carpets on the floor but a heater was an option. The Chevrolet was priced at £1150 with a coupe utility available for £1002 while the Pontiac sold for £1275.

This body carried the name Styleline for the Chevrolet and Chieftain for Pontiac, and was carried through from 1949 to 1950, 1951 and 1952 with grille, badge and chrome accents altered each year, the basic sheet metal remaining unchanged. For the American market Chevrolet introduced the two-speed Powerglide automatic transmission in the 1950 model year. This option was not offered locally until the end of the decade but as part of that development program Chevrolet upgraded the specifications of the engine with improvements including larger valves, higher lift camshaft, stronger cylinder block with four main bearings for the crankshaft and a new pressure lubrication system that replaced the age-old splash system.

In 1953 a new style arrived, again the Pontiac being a derivative of the Chevrolet for the Australian market. As before the streaks, grille, badges and taillights were the main exterior differences and the dashboards were unique. The wheelbase remained at 2921mm (115in) while the windscreen was a now a single curved piece of toughened glass. This body's style was much more upright than previously which gave considerably more luggage room although not really that much more room inside; interestingly, it retained the suggestion of fenders over the rear wheels. Power continued to be provided by the 'Blue Flame' six as Chevrolet now called the engine that developed 82kW (110bhp) while Pontiac continued with its side-valve six.

A new dashboard faced the driver, the instrument binnacle in front of him having the circular speedometer on the left, space for a clock on the right and two parallel strips between them each containing two minor gauges.

With its Australian factories bursting at the seams trying to build as many FJ Holdens as possible to meet the seemingly insatiable demand, Holden made the decision to assemble only the Chevrolet from 1955 and to import the small numbers of Pontiacs that the market wanted. GM-Holden brought in CKD packs of Detroit's Model 210 which was another new design featuring the then fashionable wrap-around front windscreen and vertical A-pillar, six-window cabin and an L-shaped chrome side decoration that started at the slight dip in the rear door at waist level that showed up on the Vauxhall Victor in the same year and on the FB Holden for 1960. Small triangular-shaped taillights sat at the end of vestigial fins while the rectangular grille had an egg crate-like design.

The interior still had leather upholstered bench seats front and rear with carpet on the floor and armrests on each door but even though the Chevrolet cost £1681 a heater was still a dealer fitted option. A new dash graced the 1955 Chevrolet and it featured matching

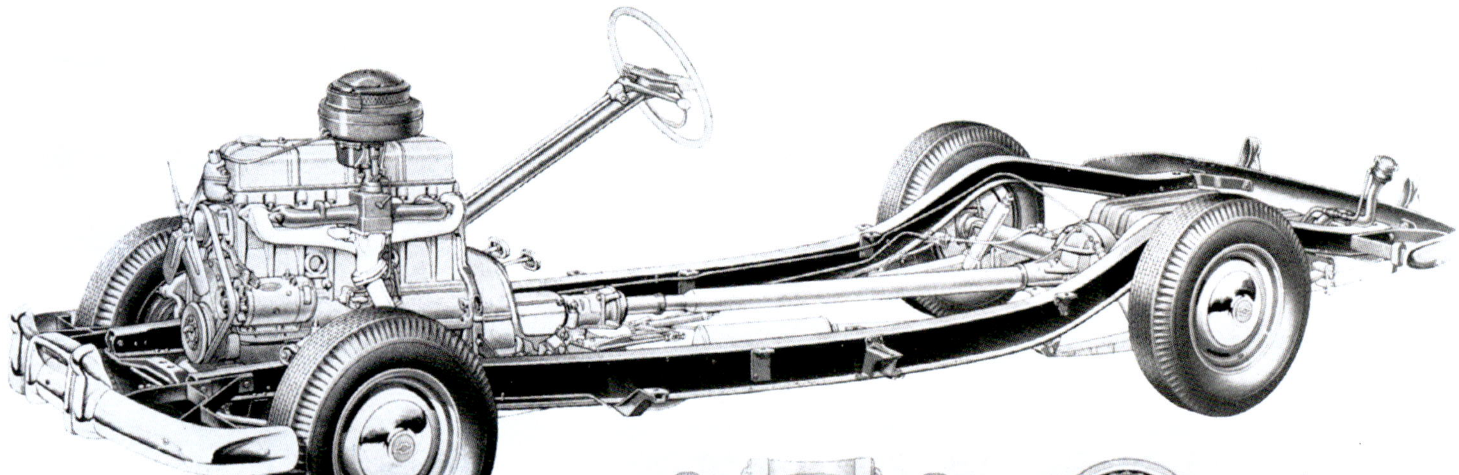

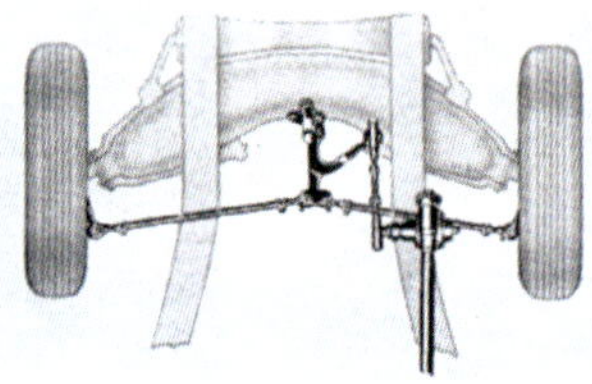

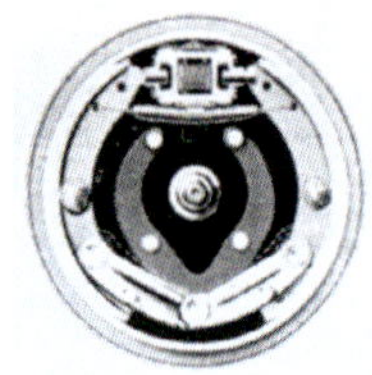

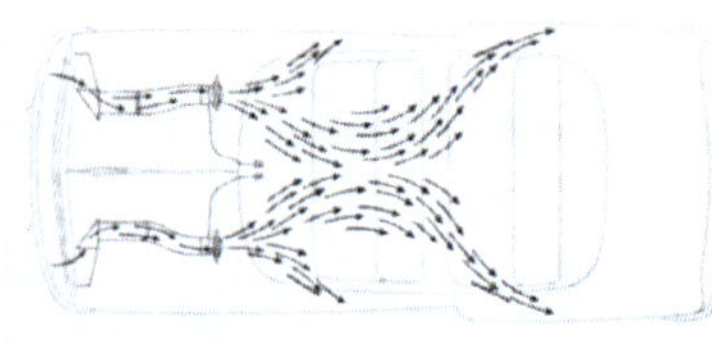

Vee-shaped binnacles, one for the instruments and the other (in front of the passenger) for the radio speaker; it also curved around into the front doors.

There were a number of small but significant improvements to the mechanical specifications of the Chevrolet, the most notable of which was the adoption of a ball jointed front suspension along with a new recirculating ball steering box that had a deplorable 5¼ turns from lock-to-lock, and the electrical system was now 12 volts. Revised breathing for the cast-iron 'Blue Flame' six-cylinder engine saw it now produce 89kW (120bhp) at 3800rpm. Running a 3.10:1 rear axle ratio, *Modern Motor* found the big and heavy 1527kg (3360lb) sedan would run to 153.6km/h (96mph) and do the 0–80 and 96km/h (0–50 and 0–60mph) dashes in 10.8 and 18.1 seconds respectively; fuel consumption for the test worked out at a surprising 15 litres per 100km (19.2mpg). The tester – Bryan Hanrahan – was impressed with the Chev's steering feel and the new-found suspension control on rough roads saying "the front end was quite outstanding". From a passenger's point of view he remarked that "the combination of soft suspension and bench seats demands at least central armrests in such a fast car. Their absence spoils the fun with passengers rolling about like peas in a drum."

For 1956 there were few differences apart from a new texture in the full-width grille with large rectangular park/indicator lights, new bumpers front and rear and slightly different tail lights. For the 1957 model year a more far reaching style upgrade was made based around the existing cabin sheet metal. There were now hooded headlights and a full-width mesh grille with a horizontal bar carrying the Chev bowtie badge and a massive wide-U shaped chromed bumper while at the rear were modest fins with half-moon taillights at the base and chromed strips gracing the edges of the fins. A *Modern Motor* test revealed the heavy sedan would just crest the 160km/h (100mph) mark, took 10 seconds to get to 80km/h (50mph) and consumed fuel at the rate of almost 18 litres per 100km (16mpg). At £2075 the tester felt that the fit and finish could have been better as should the level of standard equipment …

Pontiacs for 1955 through 1957 were imported although they shared most of the Chevrolet body. Forward of the A-pillar they had their own sheet metal with a prominent grille having closely spaced narrow vertical bars, imposing Dagmar-like round bullets and parking lights below; and slightly different rear fenders and taillights. Under the bonnet, now, was a V8 OHV engine which began at 287-cid (4689cc) in 1955 and was expanded year-by-year to 316-cid (5163cc) for 1956 and 347-cid (5670cc) for 1957 during which year GM-H mixed fully imported Pontiacs with locally assembled units. In the 1957-year model Holden fitted the US 55–56 Pontiac dashboard that had a slightly recessed semi-circular speedometer flanked by small round bezels containing the minor gauges and lights. From 1958 all local Pontiacs were Chevrolets with different trim, fittings, badges and some variation in sheet metal.

Another major restyle arrived for the 1958 model year over a longer 2984-mm (117.5-in) wheelbase for the new perimeter chassis that now had a four-link coil spring rear suspension with a live axle, the

front continuing as before. Both Chevrolet, now badged Biscayne, and Pontiac Strato Chief shared a common body with different front and rear sheet metal; both had a full-width grille within the same opening, the Chevrolet having dual parking lights under the dual headlights with the large chrome bumper filling in the lower part while the Pontiac had a single oval-shaped park light and different texture grille. At the rear the Chev had dual small round taillights in a single unit, the lights being embraced by the sweeping chromed-edged line of the 'rolled over' rear fenders; Pontiac had dual 'jet tube' rear lights and less extrovert fenders.

Inside both had bench seats and shared the same dashboard that had a wide, horizontal strip speedometer in a slightly raised binnacle with two minor gauges below in the flat panel that stretched across the wide interior; in the Pontiac was a clock which was the only difference between them. Under the bonnet was Chev's Blue Flame six of 235.5-cid (3848cc) capacity giving 108kW (145bhp) at 4400rpm while under the Pontiac's bonnet the engine had been enlarged to 261-cid (4264cc) and 112kW (150bhp) at 3800rpm. Prices had risen to £2165 for the Chevrolet and £2290 for the Pontiac which now came only with the Powerglide two-speed automatic transmission. Unusually for a GM model, the styling of the 58s was unique to that year alone with no connection to its predecessors or successors.

Modern Motor tested a Biscayne sedan in its February 1959 edition and found it typical of its genre – big in every dimension, heavy (1582kg/3480lb), incredibly roomy inside but blighted by a soft and floaty coil spring suspension system and drum brakes that were not up to par. Performance was more than satisfactory with the heavy sedan being coaxed to 163km/h (102mph) if the road was long enough, run

the 0–80km/h (0–50mph) dash in 9.2 seconds and use fuel at the rate of 17.5 litres per 100km (16mpg).

Country folk loved the big Chevs (as they did the Dodges and De Sotos) through the Fifties because of their absorbent ride and quietness, fuel economy be damned and their unruffled easy-going nature over poor roads and vast distances.

New and controversial styling arrived for the 1959 model year over a revised perimeter frame with a 3022-mm (119-in) wheelbase. The Chev's was by far the most outrageous with its vast horizontal fins picked out by chrome strips and culminating in a vee in the centre at the rear, wide cat's eye taillights each side and dinky round orange indicator lights hanging from under the fins, an after-thought and a requirement of Australian road law. For Pontiac GM stylists decreed rectangular-shaped taillights either end of a recess picked out with chrome strips and the small round indicator lights perched at the end of a shallow vee-shaped fin either side. The manufacturing of these complex designs was a tribute to the sheet metal bender's art. At the front was the first iteration of the Pontiac split grille theme that the division would adopt and use for many years.

Chevrolet continued with the 235.5-cid six – 1959 was its last year – developing 100kW (135bhp) now mated to the Powerglide 2-speed automatic transmission while Pontiac buyers had the 261-cid V8. To justify the extra cost of a Pontiac GM-H included a heater, power brakes, clock and windscreen washers in its specifications. In parallel with these models small numbers of four-door hardtop sedans were imported, the Chevrolet Impala and Pontiac Parisienne, powered by the 283-cid (4624cc) small block V8 engine.

Wheels carried a full test of the locally assembled Bel Air in its November 1959 issue. Not unexpectedly the writer expressed some dismay at the sheer physical size of the car which pushed its kerb weight up to 3808lb, or 1731kg. It was no shrinking violet! The writer was critical of the quality of finish inside (particularly the dashboard), seating and the comparative lack of standard equipment as well as the low geared steering (designed to be light in use), the puny drum brakes inside the 14-in wheels and the soft suspension.

The engine, now labelled the Hi-Thrift Six, developed 100kW (135bhp) at 4000rpm and 294Nm (217lb/ft) of torque at 2000rpm, enough to push the sedan to 156.8km/h (98mph) and run a 0–96km/h (0–60mph) time of 15 seconds; fuel consumption was 16.6 litres per 100km (17mpg) for the test. The engine-transmission combination came in for praise for its smoothness and quietness as did the silence and ability of the suspension to soak up road surface irregularities. In conclusion the writer said, "It is a welcome addition to the increasing range of sophisticated charabancs now in Australia. Comfortable, quiet, easy to drive under most conditions, at its price the Bel Air should find a lot of friends."

At £2793 the Bel Air was not inexpensive – the Pontiac Laurentian was even more expensive at £2945 – and one would have to say that it was poorly equipped for the money but it was a time when 'luxury' equated with physical size, at least where US-sourced automobiles were concerned. Nevertheless, both the Chevrolet and Pontiac were sales successes for GM-H in Australia.

More on their history in Australia can be found in the companion book *Cars of Australia in the 60s*.

1955
Pontiac
WITH THE 180-HP STRATO-STREAK
V8
PONTIAC

CHAPTER 10

VOLKSWAGEN

The biggest surprise of all in those days of industrial rebuilding after the devastation of war was the success of the most unlikely motorcar ever, the Volkswagen Type 1, or as it was irreverently named by Australian motoring journalists (much to Wolfsburg's apparent disgust), the Beetle or even more irreverently as the Pregnant Pasty. Some of the world's most eminent industry experts including Laurence Hartnett (later Sir), Henry Ford II and Lord William Rootes had rejected the car out of hand – too noisy, too slow, too ugly and so forth – and the bomb-damaged factory as war reparations, in other words they could have had the lot, lock, stock and smoking barrel for nothing! The British restarted 'production' in a limited way while the dust of war was still settling and was soon supplying the Allied armies and administration in Europe with transport. In 1948 they appointed a former Opel manager, Heinz Nordhoff, to step in and run the factory in the small town of Wolfsburg that was very close to the recently drawn East German border.

The key man to VW entering the Australian market was Baron Klaus von Oertzen who had established a small network of dealers in the late 1930s to sell the two-stroke DKW sedans here. He returned to Australia in the late 1940s as the Volkswagen AG representative and was keen to have the VW Beetle (and later the Kombi) sold here through the dealers from the DKW days. He also actively explored the idea of local assembly with the federal government.

Several VW Type 1 sedans (Beetles) were privately imported between 1949 and 1954; Regent Motors in Melbourne being appointed distributors for Australia in 1952. During this time von Oertzen was busy seeking a suitable partner company to begin assembling Volkswagens in Australia. He settled on the Melbourne company Martin and King Pty Ltd, a subsidiary of Clyde Industries of Sydney, who were based in the outer suburb of Westall (it was little more than a railway siding in those days) and who had the added advantage of a railway line going into their factory. They were coachbuilders and at the time had successfully tendered for a contract to build special rail coaches for the Victorian railways in preparation for the 1956 Olympic Games. From late 1951 until early 1953 Martin and King had assembled around one hundred (exact numbers are not known) Jowett Javelin sedans before the Bradford-based (Yorkshire, England) company succumbed to financial difficulties. There was also a flirtation with Renaults before the involvement with the Volkswagenwerke AG. Once the VW business began the factory was extended north to the Princes Highway and their address became Clayton.

In June 1954 the first VW Type 1 sedan rolled off the line with the first Type 2 kombi being completed in May 1955. It was the start of a roller coaster ride that nobody in Volkswagen AG or Australia could have imagined. This included Bill King, at one time Volkswagen Australia Chairman, who held grave concerns for the long term future of the business as he felt the Germans were too 'gung-ho'. Two years later Volkswagen AG purchased a controlling interest in Martin and King and renamed the company Volkswagen Australia Pty Ltd; it also purchased more land that took its frontage out to Dandenong Road, this being bought with the idea of establishing a second plant in 1958 as it gradually invested in its commitment to have 95 per cent local content in their vehicles. A new press shop, new paint facility and expanded assembly lines with a precision body jig manufactured and supplied from Wolfsburg, one of only three then in the world, saw the factory grow considerably during those years. Wolfsburg was serious in its intention to make its Australian facility one of its major production centres outside of Germany.

The Beetles that Martin and King were assembling were what Wolfsburg called their Export model, which meant that it incorporated many refinements designed to make it appeal to motorists internationally. These refinements included a softer suspension, bigger dampers, hydraulic brakes, synchromesh gearbox, swivelling quarter panes for ventilation and some chrome decoration on the body; there was also a new asymmetrical dashboard, the original being discontinued. It was a mirror image of its German cousin with the exception of paint, glass, interior trim and some electrical items that were locally sourced. Under the rear hood in 1954 was the 27kW (36bhp) 1192cc version of the famous 'boxer' aircooled engine that enabled the car to run to a maximum speed of 100km/h (62mph), a speed that was also its cruising speed, something that took Australians some time to become accustomed to even though it was commonplace in Europe. It had a 6-volt electrical system, trafficator-type indicators, taillights that included a small lens on top for the brake lights, 15-in wheels and a one-piece oval rear window.

Viewed from today, more than half a century later and with the benefit and wisdom of hindsight, the fact that Australians bought the Beetle in large numbers is amazing. We have always been very conservative in our attitudes to change – is it our British heritage? – and the little Volkswagen was a most unorthodox piece of transportation. Not only was its appearance totally different, so was its method of construction and the use of sophisticated materials like aluminium and magnesium in the engine and transmission castings. But it worked, and worked every time the key was turned and Volkswagen Australia, through its gradually expanding network of dealers, looked after the car and their clients rather better than everybody else. Perhaps there was the key to its success.

England began receiving supplies of the Beetle at around the same time as Australia and *The Autocar* carried out a full test in which they achieved a maximum speed of exactly 100km/h (62mph), a 0–80km/h (0–50mph) acceleration time of 22.9 seconds and a fuel consumption of 7.6 litres per 100km (37mpg). They commented on this performance by saying, "The car can be cruised continuously on full throttle at 62mph, for at this speed the engine is turning over at a mere 3000rpm." Longevity was both built-in and guaranteed. They concluded with the words, "The Volkswagen is a roadworthy, robust small car, bred on the *Autobahnen* and in the Alps. It gives a good performance without effort. It is nicely finished, easy to maintain and backed by elaborate service facilities at fixed prices." For a premier English magazine writing about a non-English car, its report amounted to the highest praise possible. In Australia *Wheels* achieved 102km/h (64mph), 16.0 seconds for the 0–80km/h (0–50mph) sprint and 7.4 litres per 100km (38-plus mpg).

In line with Volkswagen AG's policy of steady improvements from within, there were many apparently minor changes of specification through the ensuing years that included a redesigned fuel tank for a little more luggage space, slightly different exterior door handles, luggage compartment handle and steering wheel plus taillights that now incorporated turn signals, ever-so-slightly different license plate

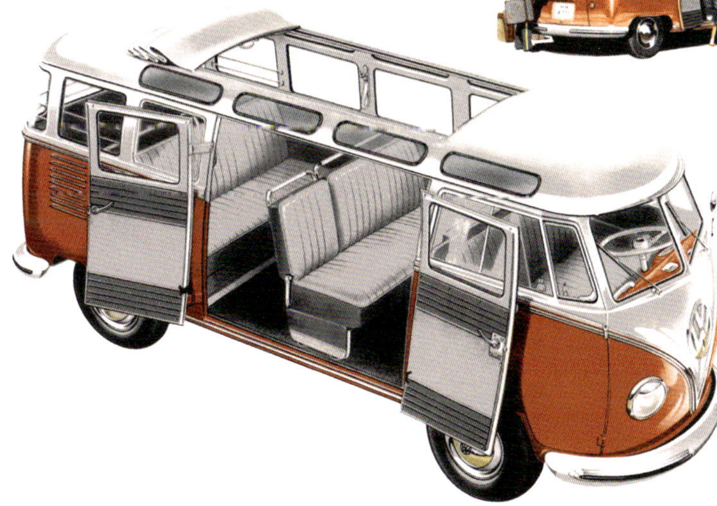

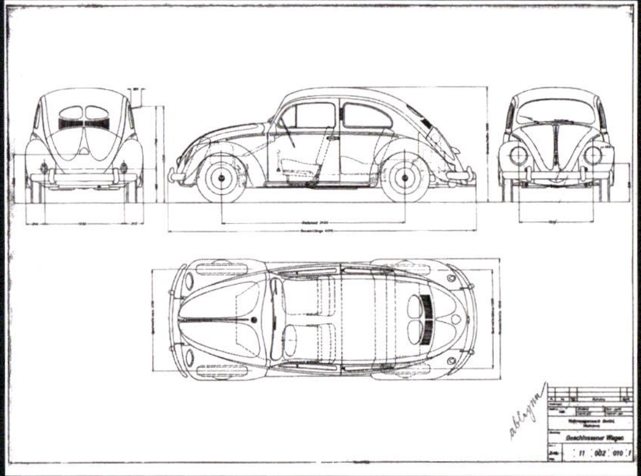

lights, larger interior mirror, organ-style accelerator pedal and in 1959 there was almost a revolution what with another new dashboard and a considerably larger rear window. During this time many of its rivals had undergone at least two major body changes!

From 1955 through 1958 VW Australia entered various long distance rallies with unprecedented success. The first was the 1955 Redex Trial in which only 57 cars finished out of 176 starters; the Regent Motors entry driven by Laurie Whitehead and Bob Foreman was the victor followed in second place by another VW driven by Eddie Perkins, father of Larry. For the 1956 Mobilgas Round Australia Trial, VW took out six of the first ten places with brothers Eddie and Lance Perkins taking the outright victory. The following year VW Beetles took the first six places and again in 1958 Beetles were victorious. It was an amazing run by a car that on first acquaintance would have seemed a most unlikely contender. If Australians were sceptical before, they were now buying the Beetle in ever-increasing numbers to the point where in 1960 the company built more than 29,000 units at Clayton.

Wheels magazine tested the Beetle in its April 1956 issue. Its comments were enlightening, saying, "Volkswagens represent a refreshing design trend. The car, although dating back over twenty years to the early 30's, is still advanced enough to make most others look backward." They liked the idea of 'sensible development'. On the handing they commented, "Overall handling at speed is still typically Volkswagen and tends to be chancy in the hands of inexperienced drivers. Nevertheless, the car handles very faithfully and will definitely do what is wanted under all circumstances." As for performance, they achieved a 115km/h (72mph) maximum and did the 0–80km/h (0–50mph) sprint in 11.4 seconds – half the time of *The Autocar's* Beetle! The magazine's writer concluded with, "This new Volkswagen is some of the best value on today's market. The finish is good, the motor is good and everything works. It is fairly noisy (not *too* much though), but that is about its only genuine fault." While its noise levels were criticised by most journals, there were issues with the lack of luggage space, having to lift the bonnet to fill the petrol tank, the battery hidden under the back seat and the feeble headlights.

Remarkably in those pre-inflation times the price remained almost static at £893 for most of the decade rising to £971, a price that it remained at into the 60s.

Running in parallel with the Type 1 was the Type 2, generally known as the Kombi but in Volkswagen terminology, the Transporter. A small number were imported in 1953 for the Australians to examine and determine whether it would be suitable for the local market. It passed all the tests and importation of both complete Type 2s as well as CKD kits began during 1954 and by early 1955 full production from CKD components was underway at Clayton.

The Type 2's impact on local industry, from the major fleet companies to the one-man self-employed contractors, was immediate and overwhelming to the point where the factory was unable to meet orders and waiting times stretched for many months into the future. The reason for this was quite obvious – there was no other manufacturer offering the kind of vehicle the Transporter, aka Kombi, was or in the diversity varying from a windowless van, windowed van, single cab utility, dual cab utility and microbus. Such diversity would follow later from various Japanese manufacturers but VW was the originator.

Like the VW Type 1, the Kombi was based on the same set of mechanical components although where the Type 1 had a platform chassis the Type 2 had a full length steel chassis with a box-section platform using the same 2400-mm (94-in) wheelbase where the load carrying area was; the engine, suspension, brakes and steering were all virtually interchangeable with the Beetle while the gearbox, casing was similar but the ratios were different.

The styling, such as it was, was controversial for its time in the same way that the Beetle was; after all no other manufacturer had thought to offer light commercial vehicles in this form so in many ways that was to be expected. The Kombi was very distinctive with its bluff front dominated by the vee-shaped pressing that rose from the mid-point at bumper level and swept up to the outer edges of the windscreen base and then along the body (including the utilities) at waist level encircling the vehicle. In the centre of the front vee was a large VW badge in a circle, generally painted white although other colours were available. The windscreen consisted of two pieces of flat toughened glass with a steel divider between them and a single flat-bladed electric wiper with a very limited sweep on each window, at the top of the windscreens where the roof overhung slightly, were air intake vents for the cabin ventilation system. Large, oval-shaped headlights graced the front panel while a single tiny round taillight was to be found on each side at the rear; also at the rear was the lift-up panel that allowed access to the engine for servicing.

Again, like the Beetle, styling changes were an anathema but nevertheless improvements were being incorporated. Between 1955 and the close of the decade changes were limited to a full-width dashboard, the fitting of an hydraulic damper in the steering system, a relocated fuel filler and flap, smaller engine access lid and the reduction of wheel size from 16 to 15in. From August 1956 all CKD kits for the Kombi came to Clayton from VW's giant Hannover-Stöcken plant that was dedicated to the VW Type 2.

Acceptance from government, fleet and private buyers meant that by 1959 the company was assembling and selling more than 3900 units each year. Because of the continuing huge demand for product Volkswagen Australia embarked on a massive £12 million expansion program in 1958 that took over more of the former Martin and King site.

Remarkably, Volkswagen Australia was by the end of the Fifties commanding around 10 per cent share of the new car market behind GM-Holden, Ford and a fading BMC, but well in front of the Rootes Group and Chrysler Australia.

VW's Australian history will be continued in the book *Cars of Australia in the 60s*.

CHAPTER 11

THE NICHE PLAYERS

There were many companies that courted commercial disaster in Australia in the 1950s by dabbling in the business of assembling cars in small numbers for the local market which was operating under a regime of government policy and tariff rates that favoured local assembly. Examples include the Bassin that was announced in 1950 and was apparently going to feature a wooden body, torsion bar suspension and a two-cylinder horizontally opposed 10hp engine; John Crouch Motors in Sydney assembled a handful of Berkeley sports cars; the Buchanan Cobra, brainchild of Nathan Buchanan, an early pioneer in the use of fibreglass as a body making material; the Edith micro-car from East Oakleigh in Melbourne of which maybe six examples were made and one was even road tested by *Modern Motor* (December 1956 issue) and reported a top speed of 70km/h (44mph) with just 7.5kW (10bhp) from its single cylinder two-stroke 198cc engine, its retail price was suggested as £455; the Tilli Capton – odd name! – micro-car from Moonee Ponds (same suburb as our Dame Edna Everage!) in Melbourne that had a stylish fibreglass body hiding an Anzani two-stroke engine of 348cc developing 11kW (15bhp) and tricycle chassis, it was shown in Melbourne in mid-1957 and was said to be ready for production at the rate of 50 cars a week; and the Wiles-Thomson tourer built in 1949 in Adelaide using DKW components that showed promise but the company lacked the capital required to productionise it. Another valiant attempt was the 1949 MCM car that was the brainchild of Jim McMahon, a speedway driver from Sydney. A single prototype was built and powered by a DKW two-cylinder two-stroke engine driving the rear wheels. The prototype was a sporty looking two-door four-seater with nicely flowing lines. McMahon had designed an air-cooled V8 for the MCM but sadly was killed while testing it in competition on the board track at Carpentaria Thunderbowl in Santa Barbara, California. His untimely death ended the MCM project.

The Hartnett Motor Company made two attempts at establishing an automobile manufacturing business, the first in a rented workshop in South Melbourne in 1950 and the second in Brisbane seven or eight years later; Australian Motor Industries whose activities have been covered in Chapter 8; Canada Cycle & Motor Company located in Port Melbourne and later Tottenham, both inner Melbourne suburbs; Continental and General who built a factory in West Heidelberg specifically to assemble cars; Volkswagen who took over an established local motor body company, Martin and King, and that story has been told in Chapter 10; Ira L & AC Berk in Belmore, a Sydney suburb, assembled small numbers of Renaults; Buckle Motors had a factory in Punchbowl, Sydney; and Continental Coachworks built the lovely Ascort in a factory in Tempe, Sydney. Kenneth Wright is believed to have assembled a small number of the Goliath 700 and 900E in a South Melbourne factory and although rumours suggested the much admired Borgward Isabella was also locally assembled there has been no confirmation of these activities. In addition, Willys Motors from Toledo, Ohio in America established an assembly operation for the CJ3 Jeep in Brisbane in 1958 and Land Rover did the same with its range of All-Wheel Drive vehicles in collaboration with Pressed Metal Corporation in Sydney.

They were very interesting times that also saw the component parts industry expand rapidly and exert some pressure on government.

HARTNETT (I)

The Hartnett saga is an interesting one that centred around one man, Laurence Hartnett (later Sir), who was largely responsible for saving General Motors-Holden from collapse in Australia in the 1930s and later set the wheels in motion for the Holden 48/215. However, he resigned his post at GM-H on 31 May 1947, some 18 months before the car was announced. He immediately set off on an overseas journey to see what he could find to import or manufacture in Australia on his own account. He looked at the smaller players like Jowett and Rootes in England, Willys in America as well as European biggies such as Fiat, Renault and Volkswagen who were all emerging from the rubble and ashes of war. Several meetings were arranged that did not bear fruit but he did meet Jean-Albert Grégoire, the visionary French engineer who had designed a small family car, the Grégoire, using largely aluminium alloy components. The French government tried unsuccessfully to persuade Henri Pigozzi at Simca to manufacture it post-war. It had been extensively tested during the war in great secrecy and following Simca's refusal to produce it, was taken on by Panhard & Levassor who altered it enough to circumvent any patent provisions and badged it as the Panhard Dyna.

A license to produce the Grégoire in England as the Kendall was granted but that failed because Lucas refused to tool up for a special positive engagement starter motor for it – the usual Bendix inertia drive system was apparently unsuitable – and through the collapse of Grantham Productions, the design was available to any interested entrepreneur. Hartnett was that man and he was able to buy a considerable amount of machinery and parts for a fraction of their worth. With this equipment he intended to set up the Hartnett Motor Company in Melbourne to build the car. Two prototypes were believed to have been imported (one has survived and is on display at the National Motor Museum in Birdwood, South Australia) and factory space in which the car would be assembled was rented from Kenneth Wright in South Melbourne, Wright also being a major shareholder in Hartnett's business venture. All of this was taking

place with support from the Chifley Labor Government in Canberra which did not want Holden to have a monopoly on Australian car manufacture. The Victorian Government, too, made offers of assistance.

The Hartnett would have been a small car by Australian standards; its wheelbase was 1981mm (78in), length 3226mm (127in), width and height were both 1397mm (55in) and it would have weighed a bantam-weight 568kg (1250lb). Its chassis was made up of six aluminium alloy castings (referred to as 'carcasse') that bolted together and formed an immensely strong and rigid self-supporting base unit; the running gear consisted of a fully independent suspension system – transverse leaf springs and wishbones up front, trailing arm each side at the rear with a coil spring in tension, most unusual, with tiny cast-iron drum brakes operated by a hydro-mechanical system. The prototype's engine was a simple aircooled flat twin with overhead valves, interestingly cooled by two four-blade fans driven directly off the nose of the crankshaft (one for each cylinder) that could be disengaged by the flick of a switch on the dashboard; bore and stroke were 72 x 73mm for a capacity of 594cc, its power output was 14kW (19bhp) at 4000rpm. There has been much speculation as to the source of the engines that would have powered the Hartnett. Whilst Grégoire may have designed the original French prototype engines they were never produced in any volume – Panhard redesigned the engine to suit their needs – and neither did Simca who simply refused to produce it. Some UK historians are of the opinion that Kendall had contracted with Frank Aspin, an English inventor-engineer who made a number of engines including a flat four with rotary valves; others have suggested Coventry Victor as the engine supplier based on the fact that they had displayed a flat four-engined prototype after the war and that CV were known to manufacture small volumes for outside companies. Perhaps a reader can shed more light on the subject?

With the use of the four-speed transaxle that directed all that power to the front wheels, the little Hartnett could scoot along at speeds up to 96km/h (60mph), slow down a little and it would consume fuel at the rate of 6.3 litres per 100km (45mpg). According to one road test published at the time the Hartnett's suspension was more than capable of absorbing the ruts and craters on local roads in the '50s and in fact showed up the inadequacies of the suspension systems of most of the other cars on the market. Inside was room for two adults and two children in an interior that could best be described as utilitarian.

Prototype testing proved that the twin-fan cooling arrangements as used in Europe were unnecessary and so a single (but larger) fan was substituted following test mileages that ran to over 88,000mi (142,000km) on one of the prototypes, this being in addition to the hundreds of thousands of kilometres other Grégoire prototypes had covered in Europe. What was apparent was the robustness of Grégoire's design, light in weight though it might have been.

It was intended that initially most components would be imported but gradually as much as possible would be sourced locally. Enough components were brought in from England for around 120 cars to have been completed but there the project stalled. Sadly events over which Hartnett had no control conspired against him. In 1949 Australians elected a new government, the Menzies Liberal government led by Robert Gordon Menzies. Hartnett was a Socialist by persuasion and this put him off-side with Menzies – it was Menzies' opinion that Hartnett had "gone over to the other side" by collaborating with the Chifley Government during the Holden negotiations and Menzies was determined to 'get even' with anyone who had taken that path. Brought into this political turmoil and acrimony was Commonwealth Engineering, a business that had been nationalised during World War II; management there would have been made aware of Menzies' feelings and undoubtedly would have been instructed to stonewall Hartnett who had commissioned them to press his body panels. After a long court case against his contracted supplier of body panels – Commonwealth Engineering – which he won, he closed the enterprise as the market had moved on and his project was now in tatters.

The Australian design was plainer than the French original to simplify and reduce tooling costs with Hartnett planning on three versions – a sedan, wagon and tourer – to be sold for around £495. In a progress report published by the company in September 1950 they openly talked about the all-Australian company formed with Australian capital with an all-Australian directorate and their optimism for the future while at

the same time thanking those who had paid a deposit and were patiently awaiting the delivery of their Hartnett. The same report mentioned that all the tools, gauges and jigs were ready for quantity production. Plans also existed for the assembly of the Hartnett cars to take place in the five mainland capital cities of Australia.

One issue that Hartnett may not have considered was his engineer's thinking about the car; from his personal point of view, even though the car made eminent sense and logic to him as a functional piece of machinery, Australians were a notoriously conservative bunch (still are!) for whom logic as applied to the purchase of motorcars did not exist. It is just possible that the Hartnett was too technically clever – aluminium chassis, fully independent suspension, front-wheel drive – for the average Australian who was lining up to buy the ultra-conservative Holden. Historian Max Gregory, however, disagrees saying, "The company had a full order book prior to the start-up of production and the public profile of Hartnett himself would have been a huge plus. Besides, the success of the VW tends to support the theory that Australians will buy cars that were non-conventional so long as the service back-up was good."

Wheels published a full road test of a Hartnett in its June 1954 issue and was quite impressed by it performance (for 600cc) and especially its road behaviour – "...it smoothed out potholes, sharp bumps and corrugations without jittering or wallowing" – that was a long way ahead of anything of its ilk at the time. While it was slow against the clock – 0–80km/h (0–50mph) in 24.1 seconds, 48–80km/h (30–50mph) passing acceleration in 24.0 seconds and a top speed of 93.6km/h (58.5mph) – it was extremely frugal in its use of fuel, returning up to 4.7 litres per 100km (60mpg) when touring.

Had this small car project succeeded Hartnett had intended to add a compact car (about the size of the VW Beetle) powered by a 1.2-litre OHV aircooled flat-four engine derived from doubling up on the flat-twin, and then he planned to add the technically brilliant Grégoire-Hotchkiss sedan with its 2-litre watercooled OHV flat-four engine, front-wheel drive and aluminium alloy construction to his burgeoning range. Pencilled-in in his Grand Plan was to have the major aluminium alloy components cast and machined locally using ingots bought from the then new aluminium smelter that had been established at Bell Bay, Tasmania.

Sadly this grand dream was thwarted by industrial short-sightedness, scaremongering and political stupidity and interference, sheer bastardry on a grand scale.

HARTNETT (II)

Undeterred by his earlier setback Hartnett set off for Europe again where, through industry contacts, he met Carl Borgward who ruled over his own motoring fiefdom in Bremen, north Germany, which included the marques Borgward, Goliath and Lloyd. The two men (both mature-aged engineers) apparently hit it off and soon came to an agreement to initially import and then assemble the little Lloyd sedan that was one of Germany's biggest selling cars, although later Hartnett was said to have regarded it as a poor relation to the Grégoire from a technical point of view. Apparently Hartnett's plans called for an increasing amount of the car to be sourced (and manufactured) locally with assembly taking place at the Buzacott Pty Ltd factory at Kangaroo Point in Brisbane using components initially brought in from Bremen.

Badged as the Lloyd-Hartnett (apparently Borgward's suggestion) here in Australia it had an advanced technical specification despite Hartnett's opinion. Like so many cheap European cars of the period it relied on a single substantial backbone tube to which all the major mechanical components and body were attached. Up front was a simple transverse leaf spring and wishbone suspension while at the rear was a semi-trailing arm arrangement that Lloyd called an 'A' bracket in their brochure material, the suspension being by a coil spring each side, with telescopic dampers all round; the steering was by a rack and pinion and tiny drum brakes did the stopping. The body was all steel with the

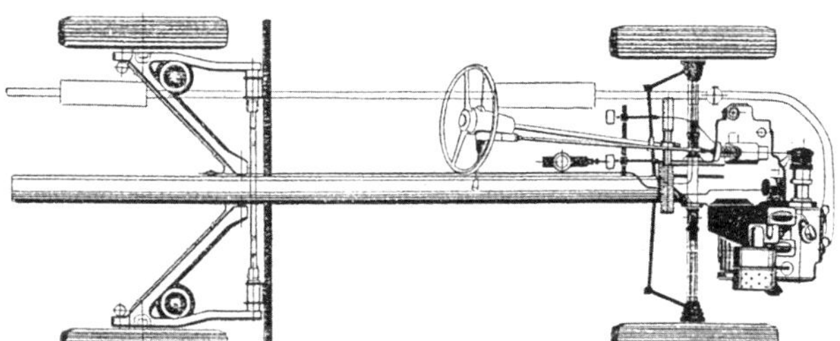

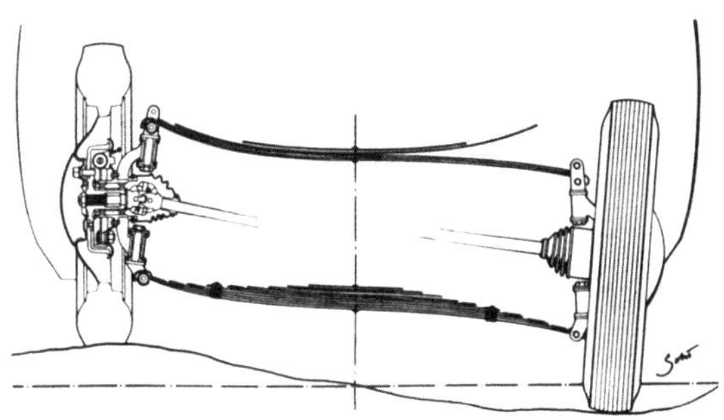

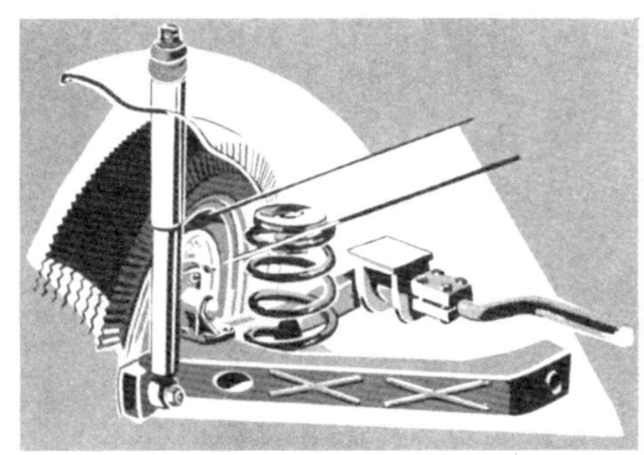

panels bolted onto the core structure for easy replacement. The Lloyd-Hartnett was not dissimilar in size to the Grégoire having a wheelbase of 2006mm (79in), length of 3073mm (121in), width of 1422mm (56in) and height of 1397mm (55in); kerb weight was 560kg (1232lb), and the fuel tank located on the bulkhead held just 25-litres (5.5-gallons) which was gravity fed the carburettor.

Under the bonnet was a jewel of an engine, a vertical twin cylinder aircooled unit with finned cast-iron cylinder barrels topped by an aluminium alloy cylinder head boasting hemispherical combustion chambers and a chain-driven overhead camshaft operating the valves through rockers; the crankshaft, big ends and camshaft were supported by roller bearings. It must have been the most expensive cheap engine ever made! Cylinder bore and stroke were 77 x 64mm for 596cc capacity, power output being 22kW (29bhp) at 5000rpm – the normal Alexander in Germany produced 14kW (19bhp) at 4500rpm – because Hartnett insisted on taking the TS version as the norm for our market.

Inside the seats (front buckets that tipped forward for rear access with no securing latch) and rear bench were upholstered in a hard, shiny plastic that was undoubtedly durable and cheap, rubber mats were on the floor and the dash was a simple metal pressing with just the single round dial facing the driver; it even had a very thinly padded top on the dash. Unlike many of its Continental rivals, the Lloyd-Hartnett had a reasonably-sized boot to take most of the belongings for four people on an extended trip. The noise levels from the engine might have meant that those trips were shorter than perhaps intended but the little saloon would readily buzz along the highway at 80–88km/h (50–55mph), slowing only for hills.

Modern Motor carried out a full road test of the Lloyd-Hartnett and published it in the March 1958 edition, the writer being the famous racing driver David McKay. He managed to push the little car to a top speed of exactly 96km/h (60mph) and took 25.0 seconds for the 0–80km/h (0–50mph) sprint in windy conditions while returning 7 litres per 100km (40mpg). In his conclusion he wrote, "Frankly, I enjoyed the Lloyd and imagine a great number of others will, too. The car has great merit, calls for hard yet sensible driving, and should become popular in Australia." Initially the sedan was priced at £820 with the station wagon (kombi) version an additional £25 but it was soon reduced to £790 making it a bargain.

Sports Car World tested a TS in its January 1960 issue – yes, really! – and found it would run to 103.8km/h (64.9mph) flat out and dash to 80km/h (50mph) from a standstill in 19.5 seconds; fuel consumption for the test worked out at 6.8 litres per 100km (41.3mpg), pretty damn good. The *SCW* guys were surprised to find a heater/demister was a standard fitting as well as windscreen washers. Although not enamoured with the gearshift's odd pattern they enjoyed the precise rack and pinion steering, the ride and the roadholding once they became accustomed to the front-wheel drive.

With the politically-motivated collapse of the Borgward Group in late 1961 the Lloyd-Hartnett venture faded into the history books with around 3000 cars having been assembled in the Brisbane factory according to Hartnett in his book *Big Wheels and Little Wheels*.

CANADA CYCLE AND MOTOR COMPANY LTD

Canada Cycle and Motor Company Ltd started out in Australia in 1901 as a subsidiary of a company of the same name formed in Canada in 1900 that was preparing for the motoring age by amalgamating the cycle-making operations of Massey-Harris, who was at that time the largest farm machinery manufacturer in the British Empire, with Goold Cycle Co ('Red Bird' cycles), Welland Vale and Gendron. Branches were established in each Australian state as well as in New Zealand. In Victoria, the business was run by Charles Neunhoffer, a German immigrant who was a well-known competition cycling champion of the era.

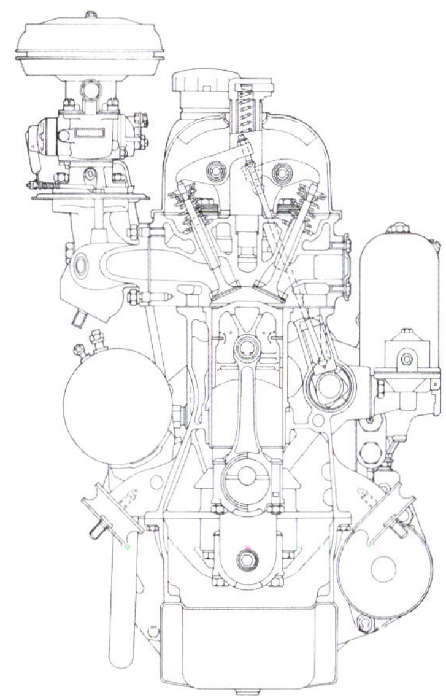

In 1914 the whole operation became a private company with the Buxton family buying the business, thus ending the connection with Canada other than in the name; Neunhoffer was retained as manager. The franchise for Dodge Brothers cars was obtained in 1915 with the first deliveries being made at the beginning of 1916 following arrangements for the bodies to be made locally at the rear of their Latrobe Street premises and then mounted on the imported running chassis; this was achieved with the nation involved in what has become known as the Great War in Europe. Motor car distribution was supplemented by the importation of small stationary engines for industrial use.

After World War II the company's general manager, Alexander Chapman, travelled to Peugeot's headquarters in Paris (together with a colleague from Harden and Johnson in Sydney) in 1948 where they witnessed the unveiling of the Peugeot 203 at the Paris Motor Show. Chapman negotiated the assembly and distribution rights for the southern states of Australia – Victoria, South Australia and Tasmania – while Harden and Johnson landed a similar agreement for

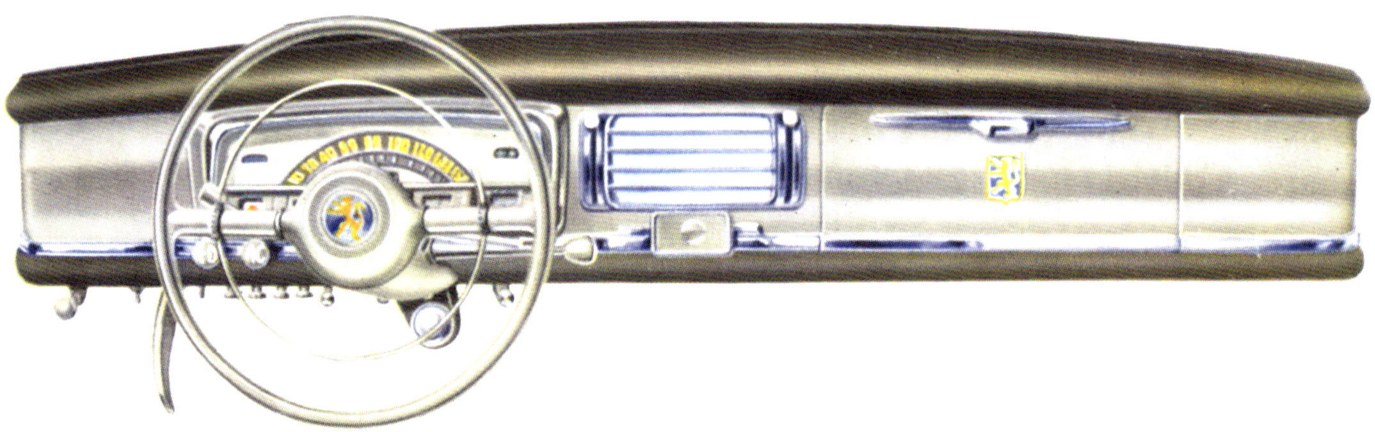

New South Wales and Queensland. The Peugeot 203 took its place alongside the Dodge cars on their Latrobe Street, Melbourne, showroom in October 1949, the premises having been the Cobb & Co stables around half a century earlier. According to Mac Chapman, son of the then general manager and who worked in Sales at the company for many years, sales were not spectacular because there was this perception that the 203 "was one of those peculiar French cars and was more expensive than the new FX Holden".

Initially the 203 came into Australia as a full import but starting early in 1953 it came into the country in a semi-finished form – they were without wheels and tyres, front and rear bumpers and their bodies were in primer only – with their assembly being completed in a primitive old factory in Ingles Street, Port Melbourne. This meant that Australian-assembled 203s had a different range of exterior colours when compared with their French cousins.

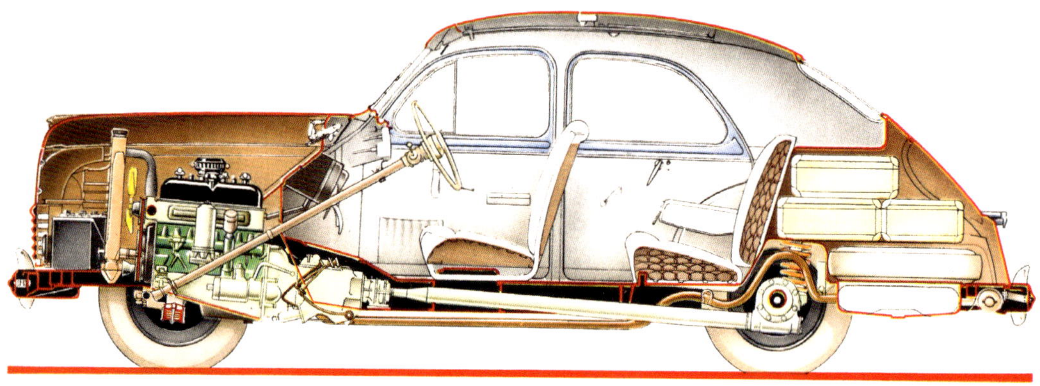

When Ken Tubman and Doug Marshall won the 1953 Redex Trial against all the odds in a privately-owned Peugeot 203, Canada Cycle was faced with a massive surge in demand sparked by the remarkable win and, to better cater for this demand, had to look for a larger capacity factory; this was found in Gwelo Street, Tottenham. Mac Chapman said, "The Tottenham factory was commonly known as 'The Birdcage' because of its high ceilings that provided an ideal place for birds to nest and to do what birds do best … you know what I mean!"

In the October 1953 issue of *Wheels* was a road test of the 203 that highlighted to readers just what a surprise package the car really was, in particular the suspension system's ability to absorb any conditions with little effect on passengers. In outright terms the 203 was not especially fast with a top speed in the overdrive fourth gear of 123km/h (77mph) and acceleration times of 18.6 and 25 seconds for the 0–80 and 96km/h (0–50 and 60mph) runs. However, its point-to-point times were on a par with many far more powerful cars because of the superb suspension, accurate rack and pinion steering and strong brakes.

Until the Redex victory it was not unusual for Canada Cycle to have 203s parked behind the factory awaiting completion on the assembly line such was the slow rate of sales. However, in the first full year after the Redex Trial the number of locally assembled 203s rose to 1196 units, with the number growing each year after that. In 1954 the mildly modified 203A was announced that had a larger rear window, separate quarter vent windows in the front doors and a slightly restyled single taillight design positioned in the centre of the boot lid above the license plate as was common at that time, and the upholstery pattern was changed. Power from the engine rose slightly to 33kW (45bhp). At the end of 1954 came the 203C (there was no 203B for some reason) that had more subtle improvements including a new all-synchromesh gearbox and larger dual taillight units. Peugeot continued the 203 in France until 1960 but in Australia it was phased out during 1959.

The Peugeot 203 was one of those unlikely cars where the whole was far more than the sum of its parts; after all, its specification was nothing out of the ordinary combining as it did a monocoque-built four-door body (the first for Peugeot) with the then-fashionable sloping back (with small rear screen) and flat one-piece windscreen, doors hinged on the centre B-pillar and an alligator-type bonnet opening. Mechanically it was all

203
Peugeot
1960

203
Peugeot
1958

BERLINE LUXE 203

203
Peugeot
1959

403
Peugeot
1958

403
Peugeot
1959

new and featured an independent front suspension by upper wishbones and a lower transverse leaf spring and a coil sprung rear axle that had a worm-drive differential, Peugeot being the last mass manufacturer to use this system. The all-new engine was a simple four-cylinder in-line unit with a bore and stroke of 75 x 73mm for a capacity of 1290cc; the camshaft was high in the side of the cast-iron block and there was an alloy cross-flow cylinder head with the spark plugs down a deep recess and needing a special spanner to remove them. What this valve arrangement gave was a hemispherical combustion chamber, a feature until then seen only on far more expensive and sophisticated machinery. Power output initially was a modest 31kW (42bhp) at 4500rpm but it was enough to allow a maximum speed of up to 128km/h (80mph) and an easy loping cruise (top, 4th gear, was an overdrive) at that speed with 8.4 litres per 100km (34mpg) economy. Available as a sedan, station wagon, panel van and utility, the sedan was priced at £1090, a comparative bargain at the time and that had risen only to £1098 in its last months on the market.

The American magazine *Road & Track* published a full test of the 203 in its May 1955 issue and it made interesting reading, especially the performance chart, when compared with the standard American sedan of the time that invariably had a large six-cylinder or, more likely, a new modern V8 engine. Having just 33kW (45bhp) to propel 995kg (2190lb) (slightly more with driver and co-driver) meant that a maximum speed of 115km/h (72mph) and a 0–80km/h (0–50mph) acceleration time of 21.2 seconds were pretty good going. In conclusion the magazine said, "The Peugeot 203 is in the truest sense a family car – roomy, comfortable, good trunk space, yet husky enough in body and engine to withstand long, hard usage with a minimum of maintenance."

Modern Motor tested a 203 in its October 1953 issue and came away most impressed with its performance, ride and roadholding. Against the clock it took 18.6 seconds for the 0–80km/h (0–50mph) sprint and ran to an excellent 123km/h (77mph) – almost as fast as the 48/215 Holden – and returned more than 8.8 litres per 100km (32mpg).

In November 1955 Peugeot introduced the 403 in Australia, a car styled after consultation with the famous Italian design house Pinin Farina, and was assembled by Canada Cycle from the beginning at the Gwelo Street factory. It was a major improvement in many ways over the 203 (that was continued for the moment) with more passenger room, larger boot and more power from an enlarged 1468cc engine – the bore was widened to 80mm – with the suspension and worm-drive differential being carried over from the 203. The 403's body was built on a lengthened 2667-mm (105-in) wheelbase and was nearly 152mm (6in) longer overall, 76mm (3in) wider and 101mm (4in) lower; it was also three hundred pounds heavier which negated the extra power (43kW/58bhp at 4900rpm) from the engine. Its retail price was £1398 at a time when the Holden Special cost £1204 but that was no real impediment to sales.

Like the 203, the 403 quickly established a reputation for ruggedness, reliability and longevity that

had become the hallmark of the marque. Over the next decade little changed apart from cosmetic touches to distinguish one series from the next. In 1957 the 403 adopted flashing indicator lights to replace the original trafficator arms in the C-pillar, the external sign being the large round lights directly below the headlights, and the old-fashioned pull-start button on the dash was replaced by a press-button. During 1958 a more highly specified 403 Deluxe was made available and soon became the better seller. Local content with the 403 consisted primarily of paint, interior trim and upholstery, tyres and some accessories and would have amounted to no more than 30 per cent when labour and materials were factored together in the opinion of Mac Chapman. Added to the range in 1957 were a Station Wagon, Vanette (a wagon with optional rear seats) and a cab-chassis.

Australian Motor Manual carried a comparison test between the 403 and the Singer Gazelle in its September 1957 issue, both cars retailing for similar money – £1366 for the Peugeot and £1249 for the Singer – and both were powered by 1.5-litre engines of some technical interest. They coaxed 124.8km/h (78mph) out of the 403 and a 0–96km/h (0–60mph) time of 22.7 seconds (almost the same time as the 203 took to reach 80km/h/50mph) but bald figures like those only told part of the story, especially with Peugeots. As they wrote, "The handling of the 403 in particular was outstanding" and added that "the suspension is an excellent compromise for Australian roads". The 403's ability to cover vast distances point-to-point at very high average speed was nothing short of remarkable. *Modern Motor* concluded their test (January 1956) by saying, "So there goes the 403 – an outstanding combination of the elegant, lively and robust."

During 1959 Canada Cycle lost the distribution and assembly contract for Peugeot to Continental and General Distributors, a subsidiary of Austin Distributors that in turn was a member of the vast Cheney group of companies. "It was a worrying time for my father," said Mac Chapman, "because the company had a factory and no work. He flew to America – South Bend, Indiana to be precise – and was able to negotiate a distribution and assembly deal with the Studebaker-Packard Corporation. It was a lifeline for the company." Not only was the Lark

PEUGEOT
BERLINE 403/7 CONFORT

403
PEUGEOT
1964

important to Canada Cycle but it was a huge fillip for its parent company achieving sales levels previously unknown at the company.

The deal with Studebaker was agreed in April 1959 but it took almost a year for the Gwelo Street factory to be converted to the assembly of the Lark sedan, Hawk coupe and Champ pickup with the Lark station wagon coming on stream a year later. In the meantime, the company began importing and distributing Larks through its national dealer network.

CONTINENTAL AND GENERAL DISTRIBUTORS LTD

Austin Distributors had been formed by S A 'Bert' Cheney in the 1920s after he had moved from Adelaide to Melbourne and after he had successfully gained the Dodge distribution rights for Australia. He was also responsible for Holden and Frost, an Adelaide coachbuilder, moving into the automobile business and making bodies for Dodge cars. Through Austin Distributors he distributed both Austin and Morris cars in Victoria and had a small assembly operation. At the time when Continental and General was formed out of Austin Distributors, BMC Australia was going through a rationalisation of its whole national dealer and distributor arrangements and one of the casualties of this process was Austin Distributors who was therefore looking for new assembly contracts to keep its business going.

Continental and General had a relatively new assembly facility at Dougherty Road, West Heidelberg, an inner northern suburb of Melbourne, and it was to there that all the assembly jigs and components were transferred so that the assembly of the 403 could continue. For the 1959 model year more detail changes took place – the Peugeot Lion emblem on the front of the bonnet was removed and replaced by the model number, 403, and a chrome strip was added running up the spine of the bonnet pressing; the horizontal bar in the grille was narrower with the Lion badge attached in the centre. On the side of the body there were two chrome decorative strips about 6in apart that were used for a second, contrasting, paint colour – for 1959 the lower strip featured a vee-shaped dip on the rear door. Inside there were new seats using moulded Pirelli foam instead of springs to shape them; engine power had crept up to 48kW (65bhp) and it had a new all-synchromesh four-speed manual gearbox still with a column shift.

The 403 segued into the new decade without further change and continued to be a strong seller in both sedan and station wagon forms.

M-NP 495

M-NP 495

F
ROSSBACH
PARKPLATZ

HN-ES 853

NSU

In 1958 the small German manufacturer NSU re-entered the automobile market with its diminutive Prinz two-door sedan that was a challenger to the Lloyd Alexander in Europe. NSU had been the world's largest motorcycle manufacturer in the decade after WWII but a declining market saw them invest in the Prinz, their first passenger car since they sold their car division to Fiat in 1929. Gradually the company sold off its motorcycle manufacturing equipment to Yugoslavian interests and concentrated once more on automobiles with some success.

With large numbers of German immigrants living and prospering in Australia the company decided to export the Prinz with company representatives meeting senior management from Continental and General Distributors where an agreement was signed to assemble the Prinz at the Dougherty Road factory alongside the Peugeot 403, supplies of kits coming through from Neckarsulm by mid-1959. Only the sedan was locally assembled, the pretty Bertone-styled Sport Prinz coupe being imported in very small numbers; prices were £765 for the sedan, reduced to £625 in 1961, and an expensive £1075 for the coupe.

As with the Peugeots, the local content amounted to components that were readily available in Australia, items like paint, tyres and trim. The little Prinz had been modelled deliberately by NSU engineers to mimic the Volkswagen Beetle; afterall, it was far and away the biggest-selling car in Germany so they believed something must be right about the rear engine-rear wheel drive formula. Power came from a delightful vertical parallel twin-cylinder aircooled engine that owed a lot to the NSU Max motorcycle unit, bore and stroke were 75 x 66mm for a capacity of 583cc, output was 27kW (36bhp) at 5500rpm, a remarkable output for such a small engine in 1958 although those familiar with NSU's motorcycle racing activities probably would not have been surprised. One unusual feature of the engine was the drive mechanism for the single overhead camshaft – it was by an eccentric shaft driven off one end of the crankshaft, unlike a chain drive it was silent and proved to be utterly reliable over big mileages and as had

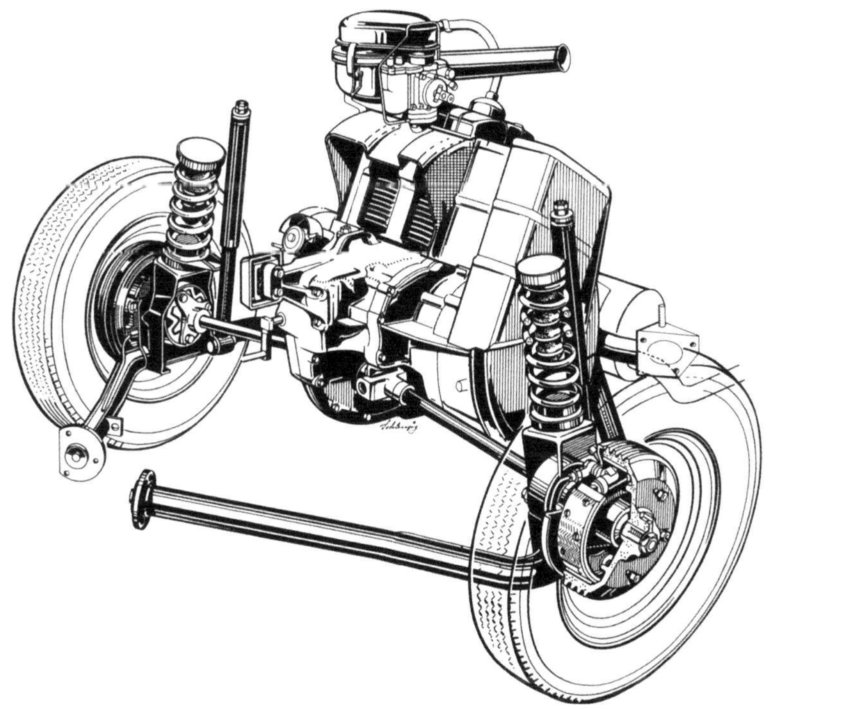

been proven in competition it could withstand very high engine revs.

Drive went to a four-speed all-synchromesh gearbox and out to the rear wheels through equal-length drive shafts; steering was by a very direct rack and pinion system, braking was by four small cast-iron drums and the suspension was fully independent by coils and wishbones up front, coils and swing axles at the rear using fabricated tubular steel lower wishbones whose pivot points were parallel to the car's centreline and very widely spaced. Despite the doomsayers, the system worked and worked well by providing a most absorbent ride and drama-free roadholding.

The Motor in England carried out a full road test of the little Prinz in its 25 February 1959 issue and came away impressed with most aspects of its design. The testers wrote with praise about the engine's amazing flexibility and its ability to rev smoothly to very high revs without apparent discomfort and that the gearbox ratios were well-suited to the engine's power and torque characteristics. On the test strip they achieved a maximum of 100km/h (62mph), a 0–80km/h (0–50mph) acceleration time of 25.8 seconds and an economy figure of 5.6 litres per 100km (50mpg). As a two-plus-two family car with a small luggage compartment up front they thought it worked well; they admired its nimble behaviour on the road but lamented the hard ride and high noise levels. Nevertheless, for its price they believed it to be good value for money. *Road & Track* in America tested it and published better performance figures – 115km/h (72mph) maximum and 16.5 seconds for the 0–80km/h (0–50mpg) run – and concluded their test by saying, "Taking everything into consideration, the NSU Prinz is clearly the best designed of all the mini-cars. Unfortunately, although it is the best of its class, we can't imagine very many people wanting a car as small as the Prinz." That was America in late 1959 when b-i-g was certainly regarded as better.

However, the NSU was not the sales success in Australia that was hoped for – according to Mac Chapman reliability surprisingly was not what you'd expect from a German car – and by early 1962 it was discontinued as the Prinz was being replaced in Germany by the boxy-looking Prinz IV of which a small number was imported. Interest in the marque waned quickly and little was heard of it until the release of the sensational NSU Ro80 at the Frankfurt Motor Show in September 1967, but that was the beginning of another story.

MERCEDES-BENZ

Mercedes-Benz's post-war sales in Australia began with the pre-war 170 sedan pending the arrival of their all-new post-war range. This was hampered by the Australian Government's introduction of licenses for all imports, a situation that affected all motor manufacturers one way or another. Discussions were held in late 1956 between Daimler-Benz and two companies – Martin and King, and Commonwealth Motors – in Melbourne regarding the assembly of Mercedes-Benz products in Australia but no agreement was reached. At around this time Australian Motor Industries (AMI) had examined the prospects for the assembly of the little DKW cars with their front-wheel drive and small two-stroke engines but again nothing came of these studies. The small German economy cars had been sold in Australia in the 1930s through the agency of Baron Klaus von Oertzen who was a board member of the Auto Union GmbH in Saxony. He would be an important contact when Volkswagen was looking at local assembly of their Beetle sedan.

In May 1955 Daimler-Benz appointed a factory representative, Willy Zeh, who was based in Camberwell, Melbourne, with a colleague Peter Quartz. By 1957 they were actively involved in a feasibility study for local assembly of the company's passenger cars. Through industry contacts two companies (Daimler-Benz and AMI) learned of each other's needs and discussions were held locally before two key AMI executives – Keith Horner and Allan Cheetham – travelled to Stuttgart in 1958 to sign an agreement. Mercedes-Benz (Australia) Pty Ltd was formed with joint ownership by AMI and Daimler-Benz AG. An area of the expanded Port Melbourne factory was set up with body assembly jigs supplied by Daimler-Benz and on 12 February 1959 the first Australian-assembled Mercedes-Benz sedan – a 220S 'Ponton' model – rolled off the new assembly line and into history followed by a 190 sedan. Local content consisted primarily of paint, glass and some trim items.

The 'pontoon' series of Mercedes-Benz cars were the right luxury cars for the times – classy-but-conservative styling that clearly identified them as Mercedes-Benz, that regal-looking grille topped by the three-

W83-5197

pointed star – combined with a sophisticated technical specification that included a single chain-driven overhead camshaft for the engine, a separate bolt-on sub-frame that supported the upper-and-lower wishbones, coil springs and telescopic dampers of the independent front suspension, steering gear and the engine-gearbox assembly, and a swing axle independent rear suspension with coil springs. A clean sweep of most of the world's Grands Prix and long distance endurance races during the early-to-mid Fifties certainly helped in promoting their heritage.

The 190 and 220 shared a great many components, particularly in the body. Both were built on a platform chassis (not dissimilar to the VW Beetle in concept) with a substantial fahrschemel (sub-frame) bolted to it at the front which supported the major mechanical components. For the 190 the wheelbase was 2650mm (104in) and 2820mm (111in) for the 220 with their overall lengths being 4500mm (177in) and 4715mm (185.6in) respectively, weights were 1147kg (2523lb) for the 190 and 1325kg (2915lb) for the 220. The differences between the two were all concentrated at the front (all forward of the A-pillar) where the 220 had a longer nose to accommodate the six-cylinder engine.

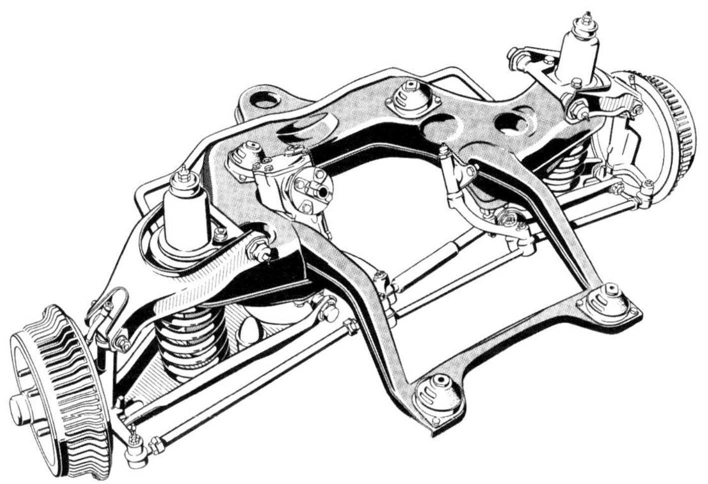

Although the two engines shared a similar design with a cast-iron cylinder block running three main bearings for the four-cylinder 190 engine and four main bearings for the six-cylinder 220 engine, non-crossflow cast-iron cylinder head and a single duplex chain-driven overhead camshaft their dimensions were not common. The 190 engine's bore and stroke were 85 x 83.6mm for a capacity of 1897cc while the 220 engine's dimensions were 80 x 72.8mm for 2195cc; power outputs were 60kW (80bhp) at 4800rpm and 74kW (100bhp) at 4800rpm respectively using a single Solex carburettor each. Late in the career of the 'Ponton' 220 a Bosch mechanical fuel injection system was introduced that raised power output to 86kW (115bhp) at 4800rpm and pushed the maximum speed to just over 160km/h (100mph).

Modern Motor was able to road test one of the early 190 sedans off the assembly line and after a searching examination of the car's finish was able to write, "The paint work is superb – eight coats of baked enamel – with excellent chrome work; everything fitted as you would expect." Most media people who examined and tested the early AMI-assembled Mercedes-Benz sedans came to pretty much the same conclusion, that AMI had made the effort to make sure the cars were as well assembled as their German counterparts. Inevitably there were people who declared that the locally-assembled Mercedes-Benz were nowhere near as good the real thing imported from Stuttgart. Having known a wealthy businessman who owned an AMI-assembled 220S all that can be said was that he drove it for over 250,000mi (400,000km) with nary a complaint and he was not one to hold back!

As for performance, *Modern Motor* published a top speed of 145.6km/h (91mph) for the 190, a standing quarter mile time of 21.1 seconds, 0–80 and 96km/h (0–50 and 0–60mph) acceleration times of 12.0 and 18.7 seconds and fuel consumption of 10.5 litres per 100km (27mpg) overall for the test. For mid-1959 and a heavy four-cylinder sedan those figures were more than competitive. The 220, by comparison, would run to the magic 160km/h (100mph) in favourable conditions, and cut seconds off the 190's acceleration times as well as cruise at 128+km/h (80+mph) in almost complete silence.

With retail prices of £2270 for a 190 and £2852 for a 220S, assembly and sales of the 190 and 220 saloons continued through the remainder of 1959 and into 1960 using locally made seats and upholstery and interior hood lining. The story will continue in *Australian Cars of the 60s*.

RENAULT

After World War II importation of new motor cars in Australia was limited by government decree as the economy of the country was gradually rebuilt on the back of Merino wool and wheat exports. One of the first companies to introduce a completely new model in those difficult post-war years was the nationalised Regie Renault whose head quarters were in Boulogne-Billancourt, Paris, France. The company created quite a storm at the 1947 Paris Motor Show with their 4CV (as it was known in Europe), France's most affordable family car at the time. It boasted a rear-mounted, longitudinally positioned water-cooled four-cylinder OHV engine driving the rear wheels through a *three*-speed manual gearbox, had fully independent suspension and four-doors for relatively easy access.

The Renault 760 as it was known in Australia, became available from February 1949 initially as an import with local assembly beginning in May 1949, and soon had a five-month waiting list. Ira L & A C Berk Pty Ltd, who were the importers and distributors based in Sydney, established a small assembly facility – it covered an area of 70,000 square feet – in Belmore, an inner western suburb, where the assembly of the 760 took place with some local components. It needs to be remembered that the plant capacity at the time was between 4 and 6 vehicles each day. Pound Motors in Carlton were distributors for Victoria, Tasmania and the Riverina, Ira Berk was also the distributor for Queensland, City Tractors had the agency for South Australia and the Victor Motor Company had the west. In August 1950 Berk's celebrated the assembly of the 1000th Renault 760.

This continued until April 1951 when the 760 was superseded on the assembly line (but stocks were available until 1953!) by the Renault 750 that was exactly the same car but with the engine's bore slightly

S·17375

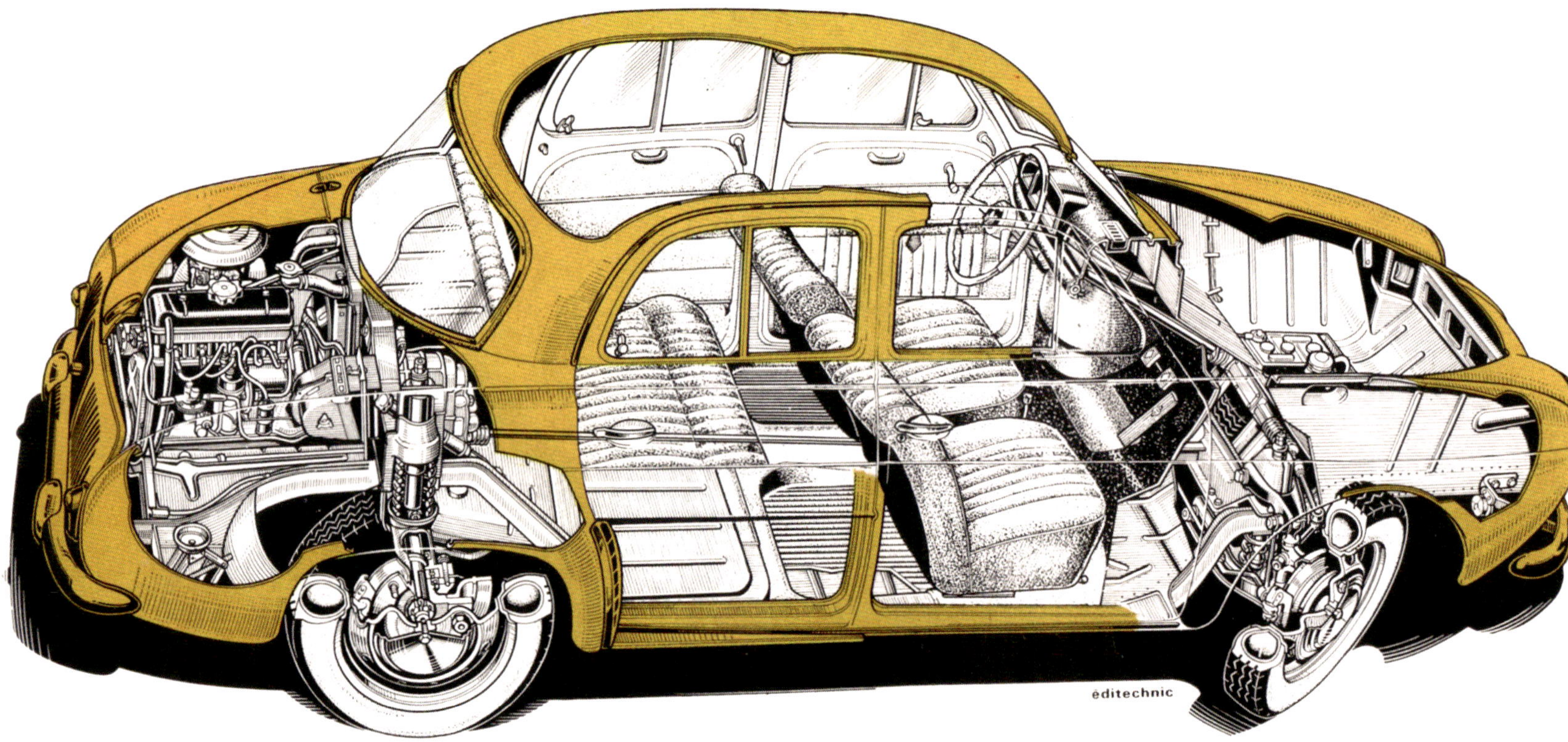

reduced to bring its capacity under 750cc, the limit in a popular class of racing in Europe. Apart from one or two minor cosmetic changes the two models were the same. The little engine (747cc, bore and stroke of 55 x 80mm) produced 16kW (21bhp) at 5000rpm, enough to push it to a maximum speed of just 91km/h (57mph) and the 'acceleration' took forever from rest to 80km/h (50mph), making it one of the slower cars on the market. However, with a 6.3 litres per 100km (45+mpg) economy not many buyers cared. Minor changes progressively took place over the next few years – new dashboard with the speedometer now flanked by water temperature and fuel gauges in 1952 along with telescopic dampers replacing the old lever arm type; the following year a Standard version was introduced as a price leader at £749.

Berks added the Prairie to its local range in 1952, this being a seven-seater multi-purpose wagon powered by a 2.38-litre side-valve four-cylinder engine driving the rear wheels. These vehicles were assembled from CKD kits. Have any survived I wonder?

March 1954 saw the release of the Mark 54 which had three wide aluminium strips as a 'grille' at the front with a round plastic Renault badge in the centre of the middle bar, the 6-volt battery was relocated to the engine compartment to make more room in the luggage compartment, the spare wheel was repositioned to the vertical position at the front (it had been horizontal), the engine cooling system was pressurised and gained a radiator blind plus new interior heating arrangements and demisting vents were located at the corners of the windscreen.

In 1956 a revised air intake system for the engine was introduced to prevent it sucking in dirty air on unpaved roads; at the same time a completely revised dashboard was fitted having the instruments in a binnacle directly in front of the driver, the 'safety' dash was made from plastic with a crushable rubber cushion along its lower edge, there was provision for a radio plus a larger Renault badge on the front. During

1958 full disc wheels with three-stud attachment were phased in replacing the previous detachable rim wheels and the fuel filler was moved from within the engine compartment to the right-hand C-pillar to minimise petrol station attendant's confusion (this was Australia-only!), the seating was improved as was the Sofica heating system. The price was now £835.

Also during 1958 came a shake-up of the distributor network in Australia. Ira Berk was replaced by Harden and Johnston in New South Wales, Canada Cycle replaced Pound Motors in Victoria and the assembly operations were gradually transferred to Martin and King at Somerton, Victoria, before they took on the Volkswagen contract.

Production in small numbers continued until July 1962 by which time demand for the lovable little car had evaporated.

The 750 was supplemented by the universally admired Dauphine – the first French car to achieve the magic million unit production milestone – that was really more of the same but wrapped in one of the prettiest small sedan bodies ever created. Its assembly at Belmore began in November 1956. Intriguingly, Renault France announced a proposal to the Australian Government for the *manufacture* of the Dauphine locally with local content beginning at 45 per cent and progressively rising to 100 per cent and a volume of 20,000 units by 1963. The idea quietly faded into the sunset …

At the rear was an enlarged 845cc (58 x 80mm) in-line water-cooled OHV four-cylinder engine driving through the same three-speed manual gearbox. *Wheels* magazine published a full test and was highly complimentary towards the small sedan, loving its ride, nippy handling, comfort, comparative silence and Gallic charm. It was quicker than the 750, having a top speed of 110km/h (69mph), a 0–80km/h (0–50mph) time of 18.3 seconds and 6.6 litres per 100km (42mpg) economy. Like the 750 it was a four-door sedan based on a floorpan with a wheelbase of 2260mm (89in) and length of 3937mm (155in) and weighed a light 678kg (1490lb). The Dauphine, for all its charm, was Renault's first big seller in Australia and America although the demon rust has meant that few remain to be enjoyed and appreciated today. And as noted historian Max Gregory wrote to the author, "It certainly was a pretty princess but was fragile in comparison with the VW."

Two versions were available, Dauphine Special and Dauphine Deluxe that differed in trim details with two-tone paint and a Ferlec clutch available only on the Deluxe; both versions had the spider-type detachable wheel rims. In 1958 the Special cost £988, the Deluxe £1115 with the Ferlec clutch adding £44; by December 1959 the Deluxe price had dropped to £964. Developments for the Dauphine in the early days were restricted to relocating the fuel filler to behind a flap in the right-hand C-pillar and the introduction of full disc wheels, just like on the 750.

To capture part of the executive market in France – remember, post-war France had a Socialist government and Renault was state-owned – the company announced the Fregate in 1951 to compete with the well-established Citroen Traction Avant. The model was withheld from the market for over a year while development continued but when it became

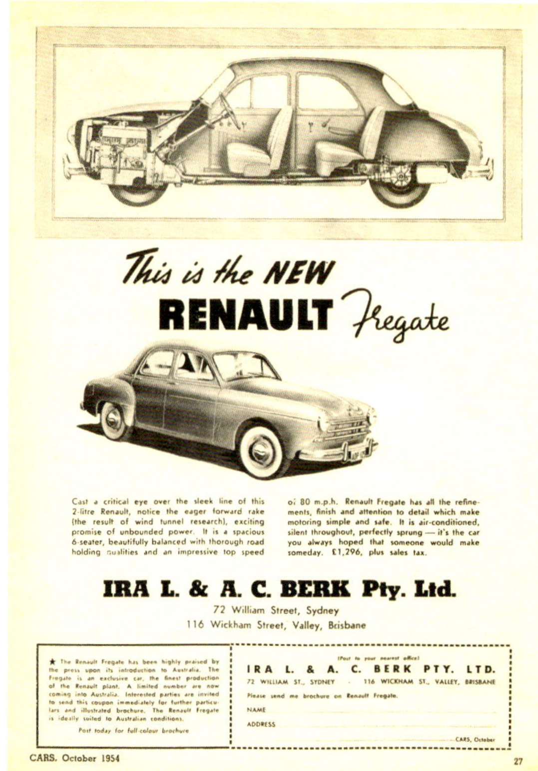

available it was only marginally successful in France despite a reasonably competitive price and specifications. It bombed in Australia. Its specifications read well enough: big, torquey in-line four-cylinder OHV engine with replaceable 'wet' cylinder liners (as on the 4CV and Dauphine), commodious four/five-seater body (it was 4699mm/185in long on a 2794mm/110in wheelbase) with smoothly rounded lines that allowed good aerodynamics, nice interior fittings for the era, and a supple fully independent suspension system. The engine's capacity was 1997cc (85 x 88mm) and produced 46kW (62bhp) at 3800rpm which was sufficient to push the heavy (1336kg/2940lb) and well appointed sedan to a top speed of 131km/h (82mph) and for a 15.1 second time for the 0–80km/h (0–50mph) run. Its forté was sustained high speed cruising – 104–112km/h (65–70mph), fast for the '50s – for four passengers who would have been travelling in comfort. From 1956 the engine's capacity was increased to 2141cc by widening the cylinder bore from 85mm to 88mm; power was increased slightly to 57kW (77bhp) but there was barely any discernible difference in performance, or sales.

Berks added the Fregate to their local assembly operations in 1953 with various versions – Affaires (standard, £1366), Amiral (deluxe) – coming off the line during the following six years along with the Domaine station wagon. Five years later came the fully imported Grand Pavois (super deluxe) that cost £1483. *Wheels* tested a Gran Pavois in its March 1958 issue and found it to be a car with some character saying "the Fregate has several major virtues and its fair quota of faults". On the positive side of the ledger were the car's ride and roadholding, the engine's flexibility, excellent windscreen wipers, interior room and comfort and the general style of the car. On the debit side were the 6-volt electrical system and headlights that were inadequate for the car's performance, a very heavy clutch pedal and odd gear ratios and gearshift positions – it was a shift pattern not unlike that on the current 403 Peugeot, and the gearshift lever was on the right-hand side of the steering column. Despite the quirks they concluded by saying "Like all cars it has its faults but it is well worth considering when purchase of a car in this price range is contemplated. In many respects it has no peer."

With long distance round Australia trials enjoying huge popularity in the mid-50s and with the 760/750 enjoying considerable success in rallies across Europe it might have been thought that the same situation would occur here. Little has been recorded from the period but two private entry Renault 760s were entered in the inaugural 1953 Redex Trial – Cars 49 and 192. The former had engine troubles early in the event and was classified as a non-finisher while the second car finished having lost 1979 points. The following year four 760/750s were entered – Cars 3, 50, 195 and 223 – but none finished as they were unable to cope with the tough conditions.

Again in 1955 four Renaults were entered – Cars 28, 75, 112 and 181 – and again none went the distance.

BUCKLE MOTORS

Bill Buckle was an adventurous Sydney businessman who became involved in the car business his father had established in the late 1920s. He was a mechanical engineer who had gone to England after graduating from university and associated with Colin Chapman, Stirling Moss, Mike Hawthorn and Peter Collins, among others, and through industry contacts was introduced to the new wonder material called fibreglass. Buckle was also a racing driver and motor sports enthusiast who conceived the idea of building his own-design Grand Touring coupe using locally available components. The Buckle coupé was the result of these plans that were approved by the Board of Buckle Motors in 1954 with most of the following year spent producing various styling proposals and scale models.

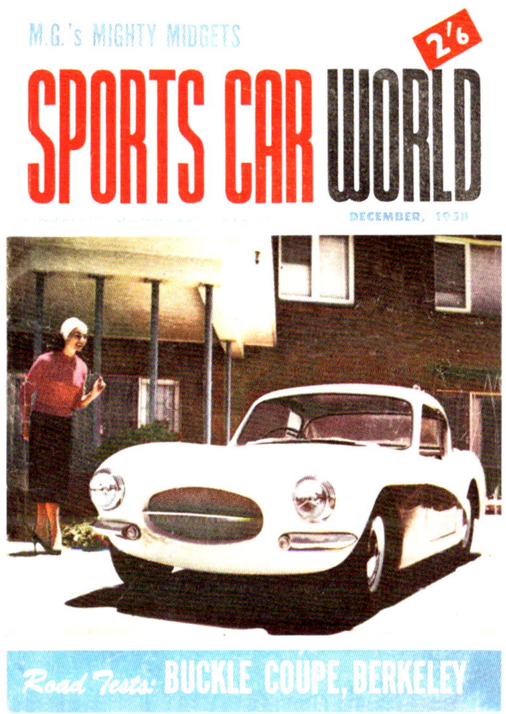

It was built on a separate steel box-section chassis with 5 x 7in fully-boxed side members with tubular cross members designed by Ron Tauranac – who went on to international fame with Jack Brabham – that featured an independent front suspension using a transverse leaf spring as the upper support with a Ford Zephyr transverse link and stabiliser bar that did double duty as part of the lower location and minimising body sway and the dampers were telescopic. At the rear was a conventional live axle with semi-elliptic leaf springs, Girling drum brakes all round with 147 square inches of lining area and a recirculating ball steering system. All these major components were from the Ford Zephyr parts bin. Power for the prototype came from a Ford Zephyr Mark I 2.3-litre OHV six-cylinder engine that, with twin SU side draft carburettors in place of the single Zenith downdraft, produced 63kW (85bhp, up from the standard sedan's 50kW/68bhp) at 4750rpm. Drive went to the rear wheels through a Zephyr three-speed manual gearbox fitted with a floor gearshift in place of the column shift in the sedan; a Laycock de Normanville overdrive was planned to be an option. The chassis had a wheelbase of 2387mm (94in), with the front and rear tracks being identical at 1245mm (49in) each.

The first prototype had a roadster body onto which a hardtop was bolted; it was completed and undergoing road tests by October 1955, its styling being a mixed bag having a large almost square opening with egg-crate grille at the front that was reminiscent of several Ferraris of the era (the Type 166 and 195 Inters particularly) giving it a bluff, high frontal appearance; there was no front bumper but at the rear was a chromed Zephyr bar. There was no external access to the luggage area, the vacuum-operated wipers were hidden under a panel in front of the windscreen, the dash was flat and very plain with just two round Smiths dials and the two-seater interior was accessed through doors that were rear-hinged. The bonnet included the tops of the fenders and lifted forwards (like the later Jaguar E-Type) for access exposing the 12V battery in the space behind the left front wheel with the spare wheel in the corresponding space on the right. Interestingly, Bristol in England began using a similar system from 1954 with their 404.

It was shown at the Sydney Motor Show of that year (1955) where potential buyers liked what they saw except for the rather brutal frontal styling. It also featured on the cover of *Wheels* October 1955 magazine. Buckle took nearly two years from then to bring the coupe to market during which time he really redesigned it completely. For production he developed a much lower, sleeker nose with an oval air intake, quarter bumperettes front and rear, a boot lid was included and it became a

BB·818

68

OTORS
PTY. LTD.
Trucks & Commercials
Phone FA 6688
BB·818

stylish coupe that had the rear window curve around into the pillar – it looked very much like the Hillman Minx rear window but it was in fact made from Perspex, the front windscreen being from a Mark I Zephyr. Mechanically the production Buckle coupe had the larger capacity 2.6-litre Mark II Zephyr engine with twin SU carburettors and an extractor exhaust manifold that produced 71kW (95bhp) at 4750rpm compared with 63kW (85bhp) of the standard unit. The front suspension was changed to incorporate Austin A70 upper arm with lever arm dampers as part of their pivot, these being substituted for the telescopic units because of a lack of room underneath the lower bonnet; the transverse leaf spring had been relocated to become the lower arm of the front suspension to make room for a thermo-couple engine cooling fan; the windscreen wipers were changed to a clap-hands sweep and were fully exposed, the 68-litre (15-gallon) fuel tank that was in the boot floor was changed to two inter-connected 34-litre (7.5-gallon) units that were integrated in the rear wings and the spare was relocated to a well in the boot floor.

The production body was moulded in one piece with the doors, bonnet, boot lid and floor being separate pieces, the floor and body being laid over the chassis and bonded together with fibreglass and polyester.

For its time it was well finished and well equipped, having push-button electric door locks (an early version of central locking) and a fold-down rear seat for added luggage carrying capabilities. The dashboard was a fibreglass moulding with a neat Bristol-like binnacle in front of the driver containing three round Smiths dials with Buckle-specific graphics, speedometer with trip and total mileage was on the left, a combination gauge with dials for fuel, amps, temperature and oil pressure in the centre and the tachometer graduated from 0–6000rpm on the right.

Buckle-made seats were standard although available as an option were the more expensive Recaros of the time and there was provision for a heater/demister and radio, cars not being so opulently appointed then as they are today.

Production of the fibreglass-bodied two-plus-two seater coupe commenced in May 1957 at Buckle's factory in Punchbowl and continued until December 1959 by which time just 20 examples had been made and sold. Sadly for Buckle Motors every one was sold at a loss.

Sports Car World was able to road test a Buckle coupe in its December 1958 and February 1960 editions, although to be fair the latter test was of a privately owned coupe that had been further modified. The standard coupe – it was pictured on the front cover of the magazine – ran to a maximum speed estimated at 179–184km/h (112–115mph) and did the 0–96km/h (0–to-60mph) sprint in 11.4 seconds with the in-gear speeds being 51km/h (32mph) for first gear and 104km/h (65mph) for second. In conclusion, writer Ian Fraser wrote: "The Buckle coupe is a very fine automobile in the best sporting tradition and, although the £1950 price tag may come as a shock to those interested in the car, it's well to remember that there is very little else available at this price which offers the same performance, comfort and finish. A very good car indeed."

While not the sales success that Buckle would have desired, many owners (including Buckle himself) successfully raced their Buckle coupes on tracks up-and-down the eastern seaboard. Drivers from Buckle, Brian Lawler, Peter Williamson, Clive Kane, Dick Newell and others competed at Bathurst, Warwick Farm, Catalina, Gnoo Blas, Amaroo Park, Oran Park, Sandown Park, Hume Weir, Winton, Phillip Island and Lakeside.

GOGGOMOBIL

Before ending production of the Buckle coupe the company had negotiated the Australian concession for the Goggomobil brand as a result of a meeting with Hans Glas, founder of the company. The deal was for Buckle to import the chassis beginning in 1958, although a small number of German-made Goggos with steel bodies – believed to have been 2 – arrived during late 1957. The Goggomobils were products of Hans Glas GmbH located in the town of Dingolfing in upper Bavaria, about an hour's drive east of Munich. In those days it was a small town in an area where the main occupation was agriculture but today it is a bustling city with a huge BMW factory on its doorstep following the takeover in late 1966.

Having gained enormous experience and expertise in the use of fibreglass Buckle tooled to mass produce the Goggo sedan's body as a one-piece moulding (the German cars had an all-steel body) mounted over the Glas made-and-supplied mechanical components. At the rear was an aircooled two-stroke twin-cylinder engine of 293cc (bore x stroke of 58 x 56mm) producing a mere 11kW (15bhp) at 5000rpm; its technical sophistication included ball-and-roller crankshaft bearings and needle bearings for the connecting rods with twin-breaker ignition and a combined starter-generator. The rear wheels were driven through an oil bath clutch and four-speed constant mesh gearbox whose gearshift pattern was in an H but laterally configured which was initially confusing for anyone getting in to drive for the first time. The suspension was fully independent by coil springs all round (swing axle at the rear) and the tiny sedan ran on 3.00 x 10 split rim wheels shod with 4.40 x 10 tyres. On a good day with a tail wind the little Goggo could run to 96km/h (60mph)!

Modern Motor published a full road test (December 1958) and the writer thought the Goggo could be regarded as a 'serious' car in that it easily coped with daily life as a city runabout with more than acceptable ride and handling, handy turning circle and with ample room for its purpose. Obviously its 300cc engine limited performance but it was able to keep up with traffic – its 0–80km/h (0–50mph) time was 23 seconds and its top speed was 95km/h (59.5mph) – and was frugal in its use of fuel at 4.8 litres per 100km (58mpg) overall. At £622 they thought it a bargain.

In May 1959 Bill Buckle surprised everybody in the industry by announcing the Goggo Dart Sports, a car that was designed to satisfy three criteria: low initial price (£685), low running costs (40+mpg) and maximum fun. It was designed by Buckle himself and the model for the first running prototype was hand-built by North Sydney racing personality Stan Brown who made a tubular aluminium space frame over which he fashioned alloy panels, the actual platform and running gear being from the Goggo sedan. For production, however, the body material was fibreglass just like the Goggo sedan and the Buckle coupe before that.

The styling was very attractive with a smooth rounded front rising to a Lotus-like rear that gave it a small frontal area and aerodynamic lines; tiny vertical taillight units were fitted and the headlights were recessed into the front fenders while there was a black decorative strip encircling the whole body hiding the join between the two halves from the mould. There were no doors and weather protection was minimal although a hood and side curtains were standard equipment. A single round instrument (the speedometer) was positioned in the centre of the moulded dashboard with switches for lights and wipers below it and there was a two-spoke plastic steering wheel; the seats were able to be slid back for really tall drivers and rose to help people enter and exit the car. The windscreen was sourced from a Renault Dauphine – it was that car's rear window!

The mainstream media gave the Goggo an amazing amount of editorial and the three main motoring magazines from the time – *Wheels, Modern Motor* and *Australian Motor Manual* – also carried numerous articles and tests of the Dart. For the local motoring scene in the late '50s it was a veritable breath of fresh air, something different, slightly irreverent perhaps. As Bill Buckle commented, "I wanted to do something unusual using the basic Goggo platform and it occurred to me that I could do a 'sports' car, so I did!"

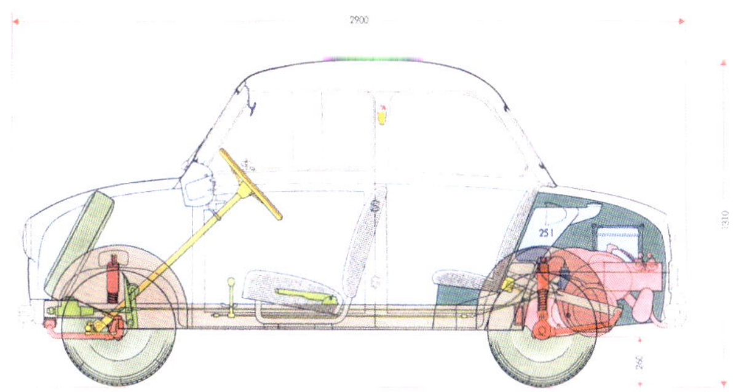

For a time the Dart was the darling of the alternative crowd and the company could not build them quickly enough to satisfy the demand. Today those that remain of the approximately 700 made are very much coveted.

Buckle extended the Goggomobil range when he released the Goggo Coupe in 1959. Where the little sedan had fairly utilitarian styling the Coupe had a sense of chic about it – it had been designed by Andreas Glas (son of the founder) and chief engineer Karl Dompert. And like its siblings, it had a fibreglass body over the Glas-supplied platform although with imported steel doors that were hinged at the rear. It achieved that most difficult feat for a small car in looking balanced with neat touches like the heart-shaped 'grille' flanked by oval-shaped air vents housing the front parking/indicator lights.

It was a car for two adult people with maybe a couple of kids on the small bench seat in back and a small amount of luggage when nobody was carried as a passenger. There was no lid at the front giving access to any luggage space – the battery and spare wheel had to be accessed from the front seats! The Goggo 400 coupe was primarily aimed at suburban commuters.

The small seats had a cloth facing with vinyl edgings; the driver faced a triangular instrument dial with a similar-shaped panel in front of the passenger as a glove box lid – the whole dash looked like a 1957 Chevrolet but on a smaller scale.

It was small, being only 2997-mm (118-in) long by 1372-mm (54-in) wide by 1219-mm (48-in) high, with a 392cc aircooled two-stroke twin (67 x 56mm) at the back like the sedan and Dart. Power was 15kW (20bhp) at 5000rpm so performance was nothing to speak about other than to say it would keep up with traffic if flogged and would cruise at 80km/h (50mph) on the highway. *Sports Car World* tested one and found it ran to 89.6km/h (56mph), took 26.2 seconds to 'dash' to 80km/h (50mph) and found the handling to be safe given the lack of power.

As well as the sedan, coupe and Dart, Buckle also made perhaps 15 Goggomobil Carryall vans over the sedan rolling chassis with the 400cc engine. All told Buckle Motors made around 3500 Goggomobils and reportedly made money on them. Their demise locally was brought about by the arrival of the Morris Mini which completely changed people's perception of an economy car.

CONTINENTAL COACHWORK PTY LTD

Continental Coachwork was formed in 1958 by an immigrant Czechoslovakian engineer, Mirek Craney, for the purpose of manufacturing the Ascort sports coupe that he had designed. For readers younger than 50 years of age the name probably would be unknown but older enthusiast motorists might remember it. It has been something of a well-kept secret over the years.

Born in July 1925 in Czechoslovakia and named Miroslav Krajnik he was fortunate that his parents were wealthy by the standards of the time. He studied engineering at the university in Prague and after graduating began working in the plastics industry. In 1950, after the Communists had taken complete political control in Czechoslovakia, Mirek (he changed his Christian name and Anglicised his surname) and his wife Anna escaped to Australia where he established the Hermex Corporation in rented premises on Wolseley Road, Point Piper specialising in the then new material of fibreglass.

Through these years Craney yearned to build his own car using fibreglass as the body material. Having admired the Volkswagen Karmann Ghia he decided that he would base his car on the KG but it would be better: Craney was something of a perfectionist. Work on designing and making the first prototype began in 1956 using a slightly modified VW Beetle floorpan. Two years later he was ready to manufacture it and for this purpose he established a new company, Continental Coachwork Pty Ltd, to build and market it, and rented an old tram depot in Tempe, a Sydney suburb.

The Ascort – the name was a blending of Ascot and Escort – was one man's interpretation of what his perfect Volkswagen coupe would be. It was in some ways a cocktail of influences and components – from its VW mechanical basis to its Karmann Ghia–inspired body design – although Craney did admit that as the style evolved he also tried to incorporate some styling ideas that he liked from the Beutler VW, which he had seen at one of the European shows. Rumours at the time suggested that Anna Craney designed the Ascort's interior.

Being an Okrasa importer it was only natural that the Ascort be powered by an Okrasa-tuned VW engine. Using hot up parts – high compression and gas-flowed cylinder heads, new crankshaft, two Solex carburettors and extractor exhaus – Craney raised the capacity of the engine to 1296cc in the TSV1300 version (although the TSV1200 kit retained the 1.2-litre capacity) and power from the engine was raised from 27kW up to 40kW (36 to 54bhp) at 4300rpm, an improvement of better than 40 per cent. Craney retained the Type 1 Volkswagen Beetle floorpan complete with the famous torsion bar suspension, vague steering system and four-wheel drum brakes.

As a perfectionist engineer Craney could not resist making the Ascort far better than its donor cars and far better than perhaps it needed to be. While this attitude made for a superb car, it made it expensive to build at anything like a profitable price. Craney designed a tubular steel framework that was welded to the VW floorpan which dramatically increased the strength of the Ascort's moulded fibreglass body which was, unusually, double-skinned. Moulded into the body front and rear were 'bumpers' that hid steel beams that were the real bumpers while at either side behind the rear seats were twin 35-litre fuel tanks that gave it an 800km cruising range. Not content with using Recaro seats, Craney went to the trouble of designing and manufacturing his own seats front and rear, those in back being shaped for two people separated by a padded armrest.

Craney received good media coverage when he announced the Ascort and soon articles appeared in most newspapers and magazines of the country. *Modern Motor's* January 1959 issue featured an Ascort on the front cover and carried a detailed 4-page article inside; in its May issue it carried a full road test that revealed just how good it was. Journalist Bill Daly, then a major contributor to *Modern Motor*, was extremely impressed with the quality of construction, the meticulous detailing in the interior, the roominess for a coupe for both passengers and luggage and, above all, the performance. He tested the TSV1300 that had the larger capacity Okrasa-modified engine that gave the Ascort a maximum speed of 153.6km/h (96mph), ran the 0–80km/h (0–50mph) sprint in 12.0 seconds and gave between 8.8–7.5 litres per 100km (32–38mpg). "This is one of the nicest cars I have tested," opined Daly. He did qualify his remarks by mentioning the rather high price but he justified that by asking prospective buyers to closely examine the quality of its construction.

Australian Motor Manual featured an Ascort on the front cover of its January 1960 edition and a full test inside. Headed "Ascort is World Class," the writer opined from the beginning that "after driving one of the first models off the production line I was certain I had found the car of my dreams." The Ascort TSV1300 had that effect on people. Priced at £2250 the car returned a top speed of 154km/h (97mph) with 37, 72 and 109km/h (23, 45 and 68mph) in the gears, 0–80km/h (0–50mph) in 11.8 seconds and 15.6 seconds to 96km/h (60mph).

When starting out Craney had made arrangements with Volkswagen Australia for the supply of components but after around 15 cars had been built VW reneged on the deal with no explanation. This meant that Craney had to find other ways of sourcing his base material which meant either buying cheap used VWs or trying to do a deal with someone in the vehicle recycling business. Either way, costs escalated dramatically. Despite holding many deposit-paid orders and with international importers keen to do business with him, Craney made the painful decision to call it quits after only 19 cars had been built.

After *Road & Track* had published a report on the car that an American VW dealer had imported to study – it drew considerable interest – the dealer then contacted Craney with a deal to share the costs of the moulds and other pieces of equipment with the view to manufacturing and selling the Ascort in America. To his everlasting regret, Craney turned him down. Inquiries came from New Zealand, South Africa as well as England but that all depended on local sales being strong enough to support exports. At £1998 (initially) that proved an insurmountable hurdle but even at that price Mirek Craney was losing money!

The Ascort was really a very interesting might-have-been and could so easily have played a more significant role in the emerging Australian motor industry. It certainly had all the ingredients and really deserved to succeed. It is believed that 10 or 12 still exist and occasionally come out at classic car events.

WILLYS MOTOR CORPORATION

Willys' name was made internationally famous by the ubiquitous All-Wheel Drive Jeep that it made in the hundreds of thousands for use by the various Allied armies involved in World War II and a little later in the Korean War. After all the fighting had stopped and peaceful endeavours were again pursued there were thousands of Jeeps scattered all over the world that were suddenly redundant.

Many surplus stock Jeep MBs and Ford GPWs found their way to Australia and were a small but important cog in the return to a normal way of life. With their go-anywhere capabilities they were particularly popular with the rural communities. By 1946, less than a year after the end of the war, Willys Motors was building civilian versions of the Jeep, coded the CJ-2 followed by the 2A, in reasonable numbers but mostly for the vast and seemingly insatiable US market. A range of colours plus a new 3-speed manual gearbox added to their appeal. Australia was then a very small market in terms of numbers and while the parent company might have wanted to establish a local operation it would not have been viable. It must be remembered that in those austere times the Jeep really had no competition although the English Land Rover that was inspired by it was slowly beginning to be exported to former Empire countries.

Like the Land Rover, the CJ-2, 2A and 3A had a 2032-mm (80-in) wheelbase and were just 3276mm (129in) in overall length and weighed a solid 1020kg (2243lb). Under the bonnet was the famous cast-iron 'Go Devil' side-valve four-cylinder engine that had a bore and stroke of 79.37 x 111.12mm (3.125 x 4.375in) for a capacity of 134.2-cid, or 2.2-litres; on a 6.48:1 compression ratio it produced 45kW (60bhp) at 4000rpm and 142Nm (105 lb-ft) of torque at 2000rpm. Besides the Jeep, this engine was also fitted to the station wagon and pickups that had been added to the range.

Released in 1946 was a ground-breaking vehicle from Willys although that was not realised at the time – it was the Brooks Stevens-designed all-steel bodied station wagon, quite probably the first of its type in the world. Available initially only with rear-wheel drive (although powered by the 'Go-Devil' four-cylinder engine) it offered the Jeep all-wheel drive system from 1949; body types available included two- and four-door wagons and a four-door panel van. All were built on a 2654-mm (104.5-in) wheelbase and were 4470-mm (176-in) long; it would remain in production until 1965. In 1947 Willys added the Jeep Truck, or pickup as they were usually called, to the product line.

Late in 1948 the CJ-3A became available followed in 1953 by the CJ-3B that brought a more powerful engine to market, the F-head Hurricane of 134-cid capacity that developed 54kW (72bhp), up from 45kW (60bhp). Even though it was a new design from the drawing board of the legendary Dellmar 'Barney' Roos, the Hurricane shared the same bore and stroke 79.37 x 111.12mm (3.125 x 4.375in) and same three-bearing crankshaft allowing the continued use of existing machine tooling. Like its predecessor the new engine also went into the half-ton pickup and the wagon. The Hurricane engine was slightly taller than its predecessor which meant that the CJ-3B and CJ5's frontal structure had to be redesigned to accommodate it. The new engine's cylinder head featured an overhead inlet valve and side exhaust valve, hence the designation F-head. Interestingly, Rover in England used a similar system on their engines.

The most enduring Jeep arrived in 1954 after the takeover by Kaiser (in 1953) who renamed the company Willys Motors Inc and set out on a program of internationalisation that eventually saw Jeep manufacturing facilities established in thirty countries including Australia. It was the CJ5 that was to remain in production, with improvements, until 1983. It was slightly larger than the CJ3 – the wheelbase was now 2050mm (80.7in), length 3503mm (137.9in) that made it more than 178mm (7in) longer and weighed 1026kg (2259lb) – and had been based on the M38A1 military Jeeps built initially for the Korean War and later saw service in Vietnam.

Until 1958 the importation and distribution of Jeeps in Australia had been carried out by two companies, Dominion Motors in Brisbane and Stokoe Motors in Melbourne although it is probable there were others such as M S Brooking in Perth. Dominion Motors were already assembling Austin cars for the Queensland market during the early '50s and had, in fact, also assembled from CKD kits a small number of Jeeps. Willys Motors Australia Pty Ltd was formed in 1958 with 50 per cent Australian shareholding and a factory established at Salisbury North, a suburb of Brisbane, and assembly operations began of CJ-3B and CJ-6 versions of the Jeep. The Australian army, which was using Jeep MBs as a part of their fleet, began testing the CJ-3B with the view to replacing the MB with them. In the event Willys was not successful and the army purchased Land Rovers instead. This created a problem for management who now had to find ways to promote their product to the non-military market. Nevertheless the RAAF did purchase a number of CJ3Bs and other CJs as did many Queensland Government departments.

Apart from the conversion to right-hand drive other local modifications included converting the electrical system to 12 volts which meant that electrical components – starter motor, generator, regulator, wiper motors and headlights – were locally-sourced and the spare wheel was repositioned at the back.

The '50s was the decade of the long distance round Australia trials and Willys offered a CJ-3B to the organisers as an official support vehicle for the 1958 Mobilgas Trial. Suitably painted with advertising (including 'Australian Made' painted on its roof) the locally-assembled Jeep completed the 14,000-km-long (8700mi) event without mishap and generated a great deal of publicity for the company. Sales at this point were small in volume and came mostly from the rural community but the company was planning for a bigger future. *Wheels* unusually published a full test of a CJ-5 supplied by Dominion Motors in Sydney in the December 1958 issue. It had the 56kW (75bhp) version of the F-head engine driving though a 3-speed gearbox with a two-speed reduction box – hi and low – with a 2.4 reduction ratio; the normal setting of the transfer box was in high range but there was a small lever alongside the main gearshift to engage low range. The crew carried out tests in mud, soft sand, across country and generally put the Jeep through a stern test which it coped with without any fuss or bother. As they said, "It's designed to go anywhere and it will do so!"

LAND ROVER

For a vehicle that the directors thought they might be able to sell 5000 units of as a stop-gap while they got Rover passenger car production up and running again after the war, the Land Rover proved to be a huge and continuing international sales success.

Being a small company – its production of cars in 1947 had amounted to around 10,000 units – located in the British Midlands city of Solihull, near Birmingham, with meagre resources available to it plus the restrictions placed on industry by the newly-elected Atlee Labour Government in the UK, it meant that the engineers had to be creative in the way in which they used what was available to them. There was no thought, for example, given to designing and producing an engine specifically for the Land Rover, nor a transmission.

The starting point for the Land Rover was the desire by then managing director Maurice Wilks to have a practical and versatile work vehicle for use on his north Wales farm. Discussions with his engineers and designers led to a vehicle that ended up being something like the ubiquitous American war-time Jeep; not surprising since the soldiers of the British armed forces had experienced it during combat and so to that end Rover purchased two from surplus war stock to use as a template for their vehicle.

Between 1946 and 1948 the Rover engineers worked to develop the Land Rover and have it in production for the 1949 model year. It was displayed at the Amsterdam Motor Show in April 1948 where it created quite a deal of interest not only from the farming community but also the military and private buyers.

The first Land Rovers were relatively simple machines built on an 2032-mm (80-in) wheelbase, had a ladder-type chassis that was not dissimilar to the American Jeep's, rudimentary body panels stamped from sheet aluminium because steel was unavailable and the engine, gearbox and rear axle assembly came straight from the Rover P3 saloon while the rest of its mechanical makeup was either off-the-shelf from component suppliers or modified to suit. The four-cylinder engine was identical to that in the P3 saloon which featured a cast-iron cylinder block and head with Rover's unusual overhead inlet valve and side exhaust valve arrangement – so-called F-head. Of 1595cc capacity (69.5 x 105mm), it developed 37kW (50bhp) at 4000rpm on a low 6.8:1 compression ratio. The main gearbox was also from the P3 which meant that synchromesh was applied only to third and top gears, and a new transfer gearbox was bolted on behind. As for the axles, they were both ex-P3 but modified because of the offset of the differential unit while the front had to accommodate the steering mechanism. Cast-iron drum brakes of 254-mm (10-in) diameter were specified and the steering was a worm and roller system ex-P3 while the suspension was by extremely stiff semi-elliptic leaf springs all round.

During the 1950s Land Rovers were imported into each state in Australia by a distributor – Regent Motors in Melbourne, Grenville Motors in Sydney, Annand and Thomson in Brisbane and Champions Ltd in Adelaide for example. Small numbers of the 2032-mm (80-in) wheelbase Land Rover utility were assembled by Lark, Neave and Carter (LNC) who had a factory in Australia Avenue, Camperdown in Sydney beginning some time in 1952. All the mechanical components came direct from Solihull while the aluminium panels were stamped, spot welded and riveted in-house.

At the same time the company, later to become LNC Industries, was assembling various makes of cars for the New South Wales market. How many were assembled is not known. During 1957 LNC moved

Regular Land-Rover with basic equipment.

Long Land-Rover with basic equipment.

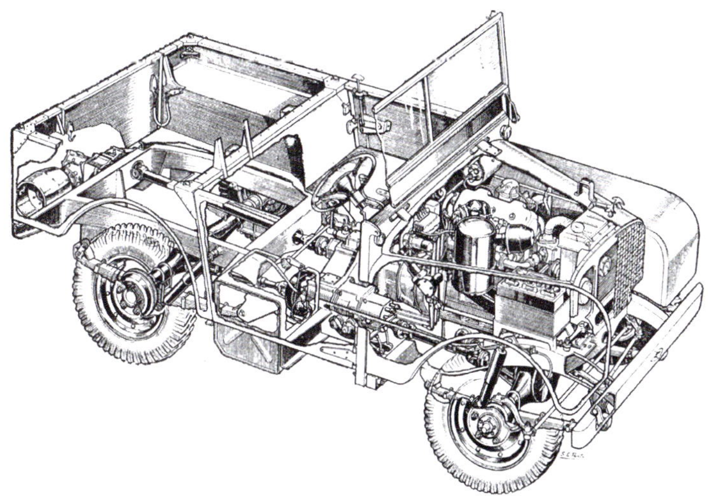

their assembly operations to a larger premise in Cosgrove Road, Enfield and not long afterwards the company's name changed to Pressed Metal Corporation and the car operation (as distinct from Land Rovers) was expanded to encompass the whole of Australia. By 1956–57 the Australian army was looking to replace its fleet of Jeeps and Austin Champs and with the release of the Series II models for the 1958 model year the army began seriously testing the Land Rover with the view to purchase.

Until then the largest buyer of Land Rovers had been the Snowy Mountains Authority who bought hundreds of them even though they came with a range of maladies that caused considerable frustration with the company. Their versatility was unquestioned but their lack of power was a telling factor in the mountainous terrain and there were some reliability issues, only some of which were corrected. Grenville Motors actually established a workshop in close proximity to the main works to help with a quick turn-around time for servicing, a most unusual move in those days.

Interestingly, the army already had a small number of Series I vehicles, the moniker Series I not being applied to the vehicles until after the arrival of the Series II. Only the Poms would do that! Land Rover was selected from those tests as the army's standard Ground Support (GS) vehicle and as a result of this the Rover Motor Company established Rover Australia Pty Ltd as a wholly owned subsidiary. However, it could not afford to set up a manufacturing facility of its own and so entered into a joint venture with Pressed Metal Corporation who had considerable experience in local assembly operations.

Slow-but-steady development began once production in volume got under way; in 1952 the 1.6-litre engine was replaced by a 2-litre unit of similar dimensions (77.8 x 105mm) and design with slightly more power and substantially more torque; the extra capacity came from slightly larger cylinder bores that were siamesed – cylinders 1 and 2 being together as were numbers 3 and 4. In 1954 in response to buyer demands the wheelbase was lengthened to 2184mm (86in) to allow for a larger cargo tray, and this was quickly followed by a 2718-mm (107-in) wheelbase version that had a load platform 1041mm (41in) longer than the original. This longer chassis was then utilised for a 10-seater station wagon.

For 1956 the Land Rover chassis was extended once more, to 2235mm (88in) and 2768mm (109in), dimensions that would become familiar to enthusiasts for many years to come. And the following year came the first diesel engine option, a Rover designed-and-built OHV 2052cc unit (85.72 x 88.9mm) that produced 39kW (52bhp) at 3500rpm.

There were more improvements made to the Land Rover for the Series II that was released in 1958 and it was this vehicle that the Australian army would contract to buy starting in 1959. The wheel tracks were widened by 3.8mm (1.5in), the front steering hubs were redesigned to allow more articulation (and a slightly smaller turning circle) while more power came from a new overhead valve four-cylinder engine of 2286cc capacity (90.5 x 88.9mm) that produced 52kW (70bhp) at 4250rpm and 168Nm (124 lb-ft) at 2400rpm. Because of the wider tracks the front fenders were reprofiled with more rounded top edges, the bonnet was reshaped slightly and the door skins, too, were slightly different; in addition, the door windows were changed from Perspex to glass although opening and closing was still by sliding and they still rattled, and the foot pedals were of the pendant type with plenty of floor clearance.

Rather surprisingly *Modern Motor* tested a Series II long wheelbase utility in its June 1959 issue, I say surprisingly because Landies were not the usual subject of local tests. At £1348 plus tax it was not inexpensive but that was of little concern to the army! On test it ran to just over 114km/h (71mph) in two-wheel drive and was happy to cruise at 96km/h (60mph) although as the tester noted, "tyre and transmission noise is rather wearing after a few miles". In low range 48km/h (30mph) proved to be useful maximum speed. From the test they concluded that the Series II was much more powerful, more stable, better riding, easier to manoeuvre and generally more comfortable all round.

Although originally intended to be nothing more than a stop-gap model, by the end of the decade Rover were building far more Land Rovers than they were passenger cars and their business had grown enormously on the back of it, the company was now selling its versatile Land Rovers all over the world. It was definitely no longer a stop-gap model!

CHAPTER 12

PARTS AND ACCESSORIES

It was inevitable that as the Australian automobile industry grew in the years after World War II so, too, would there be a corresponding growth in the parts and accessory supply industry. They both needed each other.

During the 1930s the local 'automobile' industry was somewhat fragmented and had evolved out of the earlier coachbuilding businesses. In Adelaide, for example, there was T J Richards & Sons that was building 40,000 car bodies each year, mostly Chrysler products but with a sprinkling of other marques on the side, Holden Motor Bodies across town that was a similar-sized operation building mostly General Motors products and Duncan and Frazer had been a major supplier to Ford; as well there was J A Lawton and Oke Motor Bodies operating in a small way. In Melbourne there was a scattering of companies – Tarrants, Ruskins, Martin and King, Waring Bros, James Flood and others while in Sydney there was Properts Motor Body Works, Clyde Engineering, Smith and Waddington and J E Steenbohm, Charles Hope in Brisbane and Campbell and Mannix in Perth. In virtually every case these companies were self sufficient insofar as they made everything in-house, very little was sub-contracted out. That would change in the new era.

Once General Motors-Holden had announced that they were committed to mass production of the 48/215 model and that would be aiming for a local percentage of content approaching 95 per cent that provided the impetus for other suppliers to invest in new machinery and methods to cope with the expected boost in business. The rate of expansion of these suppliers increased with the announcement by Lord Nuffield that he had acquired the old Victoria Park racecourse in Sydney and planned to manufacture his cars there. With the merger of Austin and Morris in 1954 here the Austin assembly operations were transferred from Ruskins in West Melbourne to Victoria Park where Nuffield invited suppliers like Joseph Lucas, Pilkington Glass and the Olympic Tyre and Rubber Company to establish factories within the old race course. Rootes, meanwhile, had purchased an old aircraft factory in Port Melbourne where they began assembling their cars and trucks while just up the road was Standard Motor Products (later to become AMI) and General Motors-Holden. Down the coast was Ford at Geelong together with International Harvester.

With the push from the federal government plus the states a number of companies built manufacturing facilities in Sydney, Melbourne and Adelaide. Possibly the largest supplier was Repco Ltd which was a holding company formed to take over the capital of several existing companies of which Replacement Parts Pty Ltd and Russell Manufacturing Co Pty Ltd were the most important. As the company grew its operation comprised manufacturing, research, export as well as retail sales through a chain of outlets around the country. It negotiated license manufacture with Borg Warner, Thompson Products Inc, Clevite Corporation and Bendix Aviation from the USA plus Birfield Ltd, Super Oil Seals and Gaskets Ltd and Associated Engineering in England. It was only natural that Repco look to both the USA and the UK for assistance because in those countries were vendors with a vast amount of expertise and experience in catering to the needs of an indigenous automobile industry.

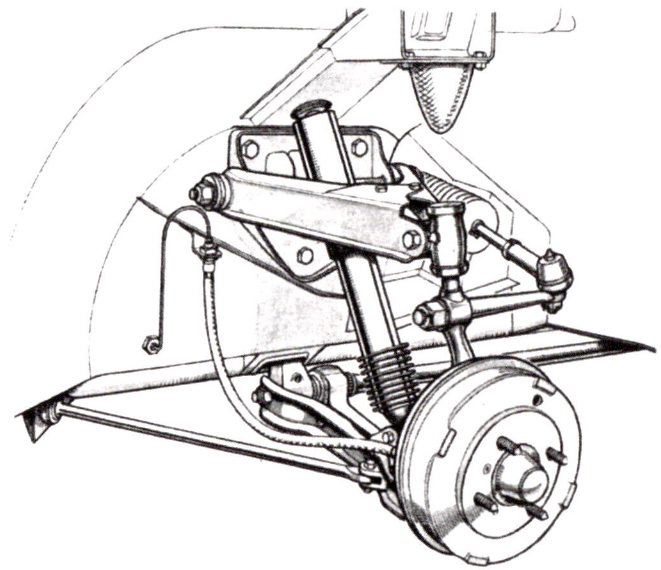

Paton Brake Replacements (PBR) specialised in braking systems and their components and Hardy Spicer (Australia) specialised in clutch mechanisms under license from Borg Warner.

In Sydney British Automotive Industries Pty Ltd, an associate company of Automotive Products Co Ltd, built a large new factory at Belmore to manufacture hydraulic braking systems, clutch assemblies, tie rods, suspension joints and filters. At least three other competitor companies were established at the same time – Duly and Hansford, Borg Warner (Australia) Pty Ltd and Automotive Components Ltd.

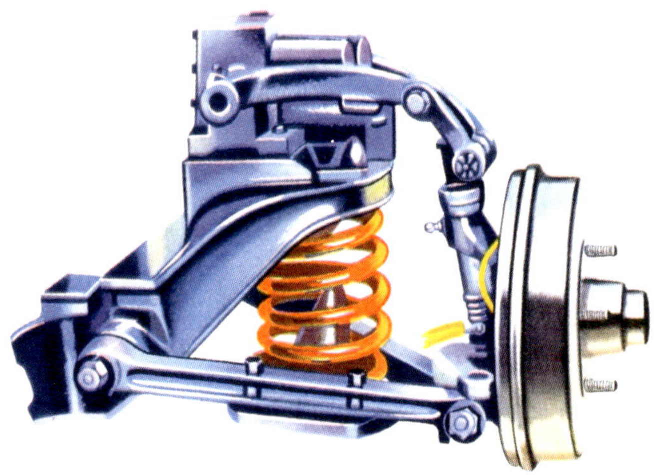

Two long-established companies also came to Australia at this time – Joseph Lucas (Australia) Pty Ltd and Robert Bosch (Australia) Pty Ltd – both constructed large facilities in Melbourne, Lucas in Cheltenham and Bosch at Clayton. Investment at the time (late 1950s) amounted to £4.5 million by Lucas and £3 million by Bosch but this was only a fraction of the total investment in facilities, tooling and infrastructure that was expended through the 1950s and into the 1960s as the industry continued to expand. BMC Australia expanded its Zetland site in 1957 and then Ford and Chrysler announced plans for the manufacture of cars in new factories in Melbourne and Adelaide along with VW Australia deciding to manufacture the ubiquitous Beetle locally.

S Smith & Sons (Aust) Pty Ltd established an Australian subsidiary to manufacture KLG spark plugs, a range of heaters and a wide range of instruments for the automotive, aeronautical, civil aviation and government projects.

Henderson Springs, National Motor Springs, Armstrong York, W H Wylie, Rubery Owen & Kensley Pty Ltd, Wilmott-Breeden, Coote and Jorgensen and AJ Sage also ventured to Australia to take a piece of the ever-expanding pie. All of these companies were involved in manufacturing 'hardware' for the automobile industry.

Of equal importance were the companies that were marketing rubber products and oil. By 1960 there were five companies making tyres, tubes and other rubber-based products. They were Dunlop Rubber Company that began operations here in 1899 amazingly enough and grew with the industry introducing the first tyre for a drop centre rim in 1926, the first cord tyre in 1927, the first balloon tyre in 1928 and the first tubeless tyre in 1953. By the 1960s it had 25 factories around the country and directly employed some 10,000 people and was a major supplier of tyres and batteries to the industry.

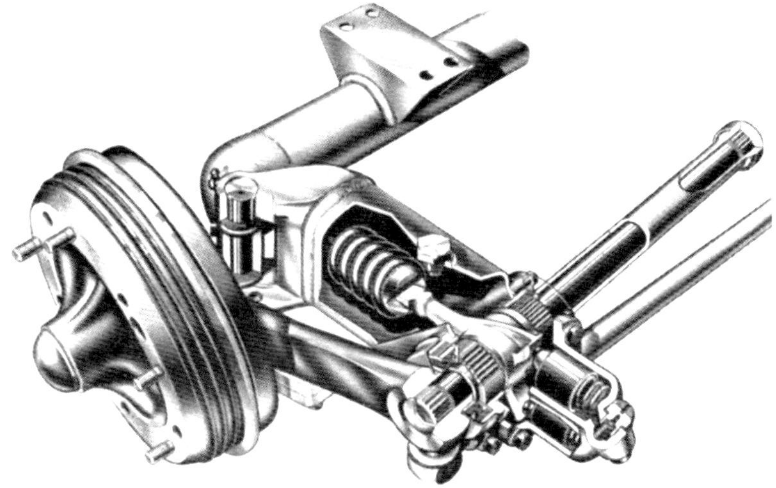

Olympic Tyre and Rubber opened its first factory in West Footscray in 1934 and rapidly expanded its product range as had Dunlop. Goodyear Tyre and Rubber, established in the USA in 1915, began operations from a new factory in Granville, Sydney, in 1927 and this was the first Goodyear factory operating outside the USA.

The smallest of the local rubber companies at this time, 1960, was James Hardie and Company Pty Ltd who had tyre manufacturing facilities in Sydney and Brisbane; they also manufactured brake linings (became Hardie-Ferodo) as well as batteries and asbestos products.

Starting locally in March 1960 was B F Goodrich that invested £3.5 million in a new factory in Somerton, Melbourne and initially distributed their tyres through the vast Ampol service station network. Ampol owned (then) 41.49 per cent of the company, the balance being owned by the parent company in the USA.

To cater for local tyre production the oil industry had to establish plants to make carbon black together with other petrol-chemical extraction units. Between 1951 and 1956 four oil refineries were built in Australia with a fifth coming on stream in 1962. The Standard-Vacuum Refining Company (later to rename itself Mobil Oil) built a refinery at Altona, then a far outer suburb of Melbourne (not any more!) at a cost of £22 million and soon after brought another plant on stream at Hallett Cove south of Adelaide at a cost of £16 million. Like Altona, it was a far outer suburb at the time but is now just another southern suburb.

Shell built a large refinery at Geelong at a cost of £30 million and a smaller one at Clive in New South Wales for £9 million. The largest refinery in Australia was built by BP at Kwinana on Cockburn Sound near Fremantle and this one also cost £30 million, a huge investment at the time. Caltex, through their affiliation with Australian Oil Refining Pty Ltd, had a £25 million refinery at Kurnell in NSW as well as interests in Bitumen and Oil Refineries (Australia) Ltd who had plants in Matraville and Hamilton in NSW.

Along with these refineries the oil companies had an extensive marketing system where they had service stations literally on every street corner in suburbia all across Australia! Some lovely old family homes were bulldozed in the name of 'progress' as the companies aimed at ever-greater market share.

There is no doubt that Australia came of age from an industrial point of view during the 1950s. It is true that we rode for a time on the sheep's back and on the exporting of our grain but gradually the momentum swung and brought some balance to our industrial landscape.

MODEL SPECIFICATIONS 1947–59

Year	Make	Price £	Engine	Capacity	BHP	Torque lb-ft	Trans	Wheel-base inches	Length inches	Weight lb	Max speed mph	0–50 mph	Economy mpg
1947–51	Austin A40 Devon	697 Aust 725 import	4-cyl OHV	1200cc	42/4400	59/2200	4-sp man	92	153	2128lb	70	26.9	34–40
1948–50	Austin A70 Hampshire	922	4-cyl OHV	2199cc	68/4000	116/1700	4-sp man	99	159	2760lb	83	15.9	21–25
1953–58	Austin A30	758	4-cyl OHV	803cc	28/4800	40/2200	4-sp man	79.5	126	1540lb	62	30	36–42
1951–54	Austin A40 Somerset	1027	4-cyl OHV	1200cc	42/4400	59/2200	4-sp man	92	158	2142lb	70	19.8	30–34
1950–55	Austin A70 Hereford	1259	4-cyl OHV	2199cc	68/3800	116/1700	4-sp man	99	167	2744lb	80	14.9	21–25
1955–59	Austin A50 A55 Cambridge	1104 A50 1240 A55	4-cyl OHV	1489cc	50/4400 55/4400	74/2100 76/2000	4-sp man	99	167	2296lb	76	17.6	30–34
1956–59	Austin A90 A95 Westminster	1317 A90 1449 A95	6-cyl OHV	2639cc	85/4500 92/4500	124/2000 130/2000	4-sp man	105.75	180	2464lb 2884lb	86 90	13.4 12.8	23–28 21–26
1959–63	Austin A40 Farina	915	4-cyl OHV	948cc	34/4750	50/2000	4-sp man	83.5	144	1680lb	67	19.5	33–40
1959–62	Austin A60 Cambridge	1160 sedan 1290 s/wag	4-cyl OHV	1622cc	55/4250	86.5/2100	4-sp man	99	178	2464lb 2548lb	78 82	13.7 15.3	27–35 25–34
1958–60	Austin Lancer	1025	4-cyl OHV	1489cc	50/4400	74/3000	4-sp man	86	152	2072lb	78	16.3	28–36
1959–61	Ascort	1995/2250	4-cyl OHV boxer	1192cc (VW) 1298cc (Okrasa)	54/4300	n/a	4-sp man	94.5	170	1624lb	94	11.9	28–34
1957–59	Buckle GT	1995	6-cyl OHV	2553cc	95/4750	n/a	3-sp man	94	156	1988lb	112	7.8	24–32
1954–55	Chevrolet Pre-54	1578	6-cyl OHV	3856cc	102/3600 120/3800	195/2000	3-sp man	115	196	3300lb	89	15.0	17–23

Year	Make	Price £	Engine	Capacity	BHP	Torque lb-ft	Trans	Wheel-base inches	Length inches	Weight lb	Max speed mph	0–50 mph	Economy mpg
1958	Chevrolet Biscayne	2164	6-cyl OHV	3856cc	145/4200	215/2400	3-sp man	117.5	196	3472lb	100	9.8	16–22
1959	Chevrolet Bel Air	2321	6-cyl OHV	3856	135/4000	217/2000	2-sp auto	119	210	3808lb	98	11	17–22
1957–60	Chrysler Royal AP1-AP2	1896 6-cyl 2059 V8	6-cyl SV; V8 OHV	3772cc (230) 4106cc (250) 5126cc (313)	115/3600 117/3600 220/4400	201/1400 205/1400 325/2800	3-sp man; 2-sp auto	115	200	3388lb 3584lb 3736lb	93 98 100	10.8 11.1 10.0	18–24 15–21 14–20
1953–57	De Soto Diplomat Plaza	2048	6-cyl SV	4106cc	112/3600	205/1400	3-sp man; 2-sp auto	114	192	3472lb (auto)	82	11.8	15–21
1958–59	De Soto Firesweep	3299	V8-cyl OHV	5733cc	275/4800	330/2200	3-sp auto	122	216	3800lb	108	7.2	16–20
1946–53	Dodge	1728	6-cyl SV	3562cc 3773cc	97/3600 101/3600	 179/1400	3-sp man	118.5	185	2990lb	85	14.5	14–22
1953–57	Dodge Kingsway	1787	6-cyl SV	3773cc 4106cc	101/3600 112/3600	179/1400 205/1400	3-sp man; 2-sp auto	114	192	3360lb (man)	87	14.0	14–22
1958–59	Dodge Custom Royal	3299	V8-cyl OHV	5733cc	275/4800	330/2200	3-sp auto	122	213	3800lb	107	7.2	16–20
1948–53	Ford Anglia, Prefect	534 561	4-cyl SV	933cc 1172cc	23/4000 30/4000	 48/2000	3-sp man	87 94	151	1680lb	61	22.8	30–36
1953–59	Ford Anglia Prefect	949 991	4-cyl SV	1172cc	36/4500	52/2500	3-sp man	94	152	1690lb 1788lb	71	19.9	30–36
1951–56	Ford Consul (Mk I)	1054	4-cyl OHV	1508cc	47/4400	74/2000	3-sp man	100	164	2435lb	75	19.7	28–34
1956–61	Ford Consul (Mk II)	1238	4-cyl OHV	1703cc	55/4200	87/2300	3-sp man	104	172	2504lb	77	15.9	28–34
1951–56	Ford Zephyr (Mk I)	1172	6-cyl OHV	2262cc	68/4000	112/2000	3-sp man	104	172	2591lb	80	14.1	22–28
1956–61	Ford Zephyr (Mk II)	1339 man 1458 auto	6-cyl OHV	2553cc	80/4200	128/2000	3-sp man	107	178.5	2691lb	88	11.1	22–28
1948–52	Ford Pilot	1066	V8-cyl SV	3622cc	90/3600	180/2000	3-sp man	108.5	175	3192lb	81	14.7	15–22
1949–52	Ford Custom	927	V8-cyl SV	3920cc	100/3600	191/1900	3-sp man	114	197	3290lb	85	12.5	16–22
1952–54	Ford Customline	1630	V8-cyl SV	3920cc	108/3600	194/2000	3-sp man	115	198	3360lb	90	11.3	16–22
1955–59	Ford Customline	1929 man 2089 auto	V8-cyl OHV	4460cc	164/4400	258/2200	3-sp man/2-sp auto	115.5	198.5	3472lb	103	10.1	17–22

Year	Make	Price £	Engine	Capacity	BHP	Torque lb-ft	Trans	Wheel-base inches	Length inches	Weight lb	Max speed mph	0–50 mph	Economy mpg
1959–61	Ford Fairlane 500 (Tank)	2463	V8-cyl OHV	5430cc	225/4400	325/2200	3-sp man/2-sp auto	118	208	3594lb	106	9.8	15–22
1957–61	Goggomobil sedan	622	2-cyl 2-str	293cc	15/4800	18/3800	4-sp man	71	114	1194lb	57	23.0	65–75
1959–61	Goggomobil Dart	715	2-cyl 2-str	293cc	15/4800	18/3800	4-sp man	71	114	865lb	60	21.5	65–75
1959–62	Goggo Coupe	775	2-cyl 2-str	392cc	20/5200	24/3900	4-sp man	71	119.5	1014lb	62	15.0	48–55
1949–51	Hartnett	655	2-cyl OHV Boxer	594cc	19/4000	26.5/2500	4-sp man	78.75	127	1200lb	58.5	24.1	45–55
1948–56	Hillman Minx Mk III	971	4-cyl SV	1265cc	37/4200	70/2200	4-sp man	93	157	2172lb	70	22.5	32–36
1956–58	Hillman Minx Series I	1099	4-cyl OHV	1390cc	51/4400	68/1800	4-sp man	96	162	2135lb	78	16.8	32–36
1957–60	Hillman Minx Series IIIa	1099	4-cyl OHV	1494cc	52.5/4400	78/2100	4-sp man	96	162	2260lb	80	15.3	28–35
1956–60	Hillman Husky	890 978	4-cyl OHV	1265cc 1390cc	37.5/4100 43/4000	70/2200 66/1600	4-sp man	86	149	1932lb	70	16.6	25–35
1948–56	Holden 48/215 & FJ	1074	6-cyl OHV	2172cc	60/3800	100/2000	3-sp man	103	173	2240lb	80	15.5	26–32
1956–59	Holden FE/FC	1204	6-cyl OHV	2172cc	70/4000	110/1200	3-sp man	105	176	2352lb	82	14	26–32
1948–57	Humber Hawk	1351	4-cyl SV	2267cc	58/3400	110/1800	4-sp man	105.5	180	2884lb	78	18.2	23–28
1957–62	Humber Hawk Series 1, II	1698 man 1873 auto	4-cyl OHV	2267cc	75/4000	120/2300	4-sp man/3-sp auto	110	184.7	3080lb	94	12.2	24–30
1952–58	Humber Super Snipe	1834 Aust 1942 import	6-cyl OHV	4140cc	116/3400 122/3600	206/1400 211/1400	4-sp man	115.75	197	3864lb 4144lb	92	10.9	18–24
1958–62	Humber Super Snipe Series I/III	1825 man 1974 auto	6-cyl OHV	2651cc 2965cc	105/5000 125/4800	138/2000 162/1800	4-sp man/3-sp auto	110	190	3352lb	102 103	11.2 11.5	20–26 17–24
1958–59	Jeep	1375	4-cyl SV/F	2192cc	60/4000 72/4000	105/2000 114/2000	3-sp man 4x4	81	139	2408lb	60	19.0	14–22
1947–53	Jowett Javelin	1168	4-cyl OHV Boxer	1485cc	50/4250	76/2600	4-sp man	102	168	2280lb	80	14.8	24–30
1959	Land Rover	1213 88in 1348 109-in	4-cyl OHV	2286cc	70/4250	124/2500	4-sp man 4x4	88/109	142 175	2900lb 3294lb	67	25.5	16–24

Year	Make	Price £	Engine	Capacity	BHP	Torque lb-ft	Trans	Wheel-base inches	Length inches	Weight lb	Max speed mph	0–50 mph	Economy mpg
1958–61	Lloyd Hartnett	790	2-cyl SOHC	596cc	28/4800	29/3000	4-sp man	78.5	133	1232lb	63	25.0	40–45
1959–61	Mercedes-Benz 190	2270	4-cyl SOHC	1897cc	84/4800	120/2400	4-sp man	104	176	2548lb	88	12.3	28–34
1959–61	Mercedes-Benz 220S	2870	6-cyl SOHC	2195cc	120/5200	137/3600	4-sp man	111	185	2898lb	98	12.4	22–30
1958–62	MG A	1376	4-cyl OHV	1489cc	72/5500	77/3500	4-sp man	94	156	2120lb	92	10.3	28–34
1948–54	Morris Minor	765 2-dr 810 4-dr	4-cyl SV	918cc	27/4400	39/2400	4-sp man	86	148	1792lb	61	38.5	35–40
1954–60	Morris Minor Minor 1000	888 2-dr 935 4-d	4-cyl OHV	803cc 948cc	30/4800 37/4750	40/2200 50/2000	4-sp man	86	148	1692lb 1705lb	66 71	18.0 15.0	36–40
1957–61	Morris Major Series I/II	1025 997	4-cyl OHV	1489cc	50/4200	74/3000	4-sp man	86 92	152 159	1975lb 2128lb	75 76	16.2 14.5	30–37 32–38
1948–55	Morris Oxford	1013	4-cyl SV	1476cc	41/4000	65/1800	4-sp man	97	167	2388lb	67	27.4	27–33
1955–59	Morris Oxford Series II	1046	4-cyl OHV	1489cc	50/4200	74/2600	4-sp man	102	171	2716lb	75	16.4	25–32
1955–58	Morris Isis	1335	6-cyl OHV	2639cc	86/4250	124/2000	4-sp man	107.5	178	3472lb	86	12.8	18–25
1958–59	Morris Marshall	1459	6-cyl OHV	2639cc	85/4000	130/2000	4-sp man	107.75	180	2968lb	91	14.0	21–26
1959–62	Morris Oxford Farina	1160	4-cyl OHV	1622cc	55/4250	86.5/2100	4-sp man	99	178	2464lb	78	13.7	27–35
1959–61	NSU Prinz	812	2-cyl OHC	583cc	36/5500	28/3000	4-sp man	78.75	124	1120lb	75	14.6	38–46
1948–56	Peugeot 203	1211	4-cyl OHV	1290cc	42/4500	59/2500	4-sp man	101.5	171	2190lb	72	18.6	28–36
1956–64	Peugeot 403	1353 Deluxe 1324 S/w	4-cyl OHV	1468cc	58/4900	74/2500	4-sp man	104.5	175	2576lb	78	15.9	26–35
1953–57	Plymouth Cranbrook	1776	6-cyl SV	3773cc	101/3600	179/1400	3-sp man	114	192	3136lb	90	11.4	16–24
1958–59	Plymouth Belvedere US	3024	V8 OHV	5215cc (318)	225/4400		3-sp auto	122	208	3790lb	109	7.8	16–22
1950–52	Pontiac Silver Streak	1875	6-cyl SV	3920cc	115/3800	197/2000	3-sp man	115	202	3416lb	90	12.8	15–20
1955–57	Pontiac	2290	V8 OHV	4692cc	180/4600	264/2400	3-sp man	122	203	3460lb	95	11.0	14–20
1958–59	Pontiac Laurentian	2643	V8 OHV	4537cc	195/4800	285/2400	2-sp auto	119	211	3584lb	103.5	8.5	16–20

Year	Make	Price £	Engine	Capacity	BHP	Torque lb-ft	Trans	Wheel-base inches	Length inches	Weight lb	Max speed mph	0–50 mph	Economy mpg
1949–62	Renault 760/750	869	4-cyl OHV	760/748cc	19/4000	32/1500	3-sp man	82.5	131	1337lb	55	50.0	40–45
1952–1958	Renault Fregate	1469	4-cyl OHV	1997cc 2141cc	77/4000	121/2200	4-sp man	110	185	2940lb	84	17.2	20–24
1956–1963	Renault Dauphine	986	4-cyl OHV	845cc	30/4250	48/2000	3-sp man	89	155	1500lb	69	18.3	38–42
1956–58	Simca Aronde	1128	4-cyl OHV	1221cc	45/4500	63/2800	4-sp man	96	160	2044lb	79	14.7	29–36
1959–64	Simca Aronde	1095 1127	4-cyl OHV	1290cc	48/4800	65/2800	4-sp man	96	162	2048lb	83	13.3	30–36
1959–61	Simca Vedette V8	1799 imp 1369 CAL	V8-cyl SV	2351cc	84/4800	112/2750	3-sp man	107.5	187	2576lb	93	11.9	20–24
1956–59	Singer Gazelle	1248	4-cyl SOHC	1496cc	52.5/4500	77/2000	4-sp man	96	164	2688lb	70	16.1	28–34
1959–62	Singer Gazelle	1179	4-cyl OHV	1494cc	60/4500	80/2000	4-sp man	96	164	2240lb	82	12.5	25–34
1953–59	Standard 8/10	802 945	4-cyl OHV	803cc 948cc	26/4500 37/4500	39/2800 52/2600	4-sp man	84	142	1484lb 1624lb	62 68	24.4	35–40
1948–56	Standard Vanguard	1164	4-cyl OHV	2088cc	68/4200	113/2000	3-sp man	94	165	2632lb	80	16.0	27–34
1956–61	Standard Vanguard III	1391 Std 1430 Deluxe	4-cyl OHV	2088cc	68/4200	113/2000	3-sp man	102	172	2688lb	82	15.8	28–34
1959–64	Triumph Herald	970	4-cyl OHV	948cc	39/4500	49/3000	4-sp man	84	142	1814lb	72	19.2	30–38
1951–57	Vauxhall Wyvern	1186	4-cyl OHV	1507cc	45/4000	76/2000	3-sp man	103	170	2772lb	67	22.7	26–33
1956–59	Vauxhall Victor	1079	4-cyl OHV	1507cc	52/4200	84/2400	3-sp man	98	166	2240lb	75	18.1	30–34
1951–57	Vauxhall Velox E	1267	6-cyl OHV	2262cc	68/4000	114/1400	3-sp man	103	172	2470lb	80	13.5	22–28
1957–61	Vauxhall Velox PA	1393	6-cyl OHV	2262cc	82.5/4400	124/1800	3-sp man	105	178	2520lb	91	11.8	23–28
1954–59	VW Beetle (Type 1)	971	4-cyl OHV Boxer	1192cc	36/3700 40/3600	61/2000	4-sp man	94.5	160	1624lb	72	16.2	32–38
1954–58	Wolseley 4/44 & 15/50	1355	4-cyl OHV	1489cc	50/4200	78/2400	4-sp man	102	173	2486lb	76	16.9	30–36
1957–60	Wolseley 1500	1120	4-cyl OHV	1489cc	50/4400	74/3000	4-sp man	86	153	2054lb	76	17	26–34
1959–62	Wolseley 15/60	1297	4-cyl OHV	1622cc	55/4250	86/2100	4-sp man	99	178	2408lb	80	15.0	20–34

SMALL CAR COMPARISONS 1954

	Price	Capacity	B x S	Power BHP	Max mph	0–50 mph secs	MPG	W/base inches	OAL inches	T/circle feet	Weight lb	Boot
Austin A30	£749	I4 803cc	58 x 76 mm	30/4800	64mph	22.0	42	79.5	136.5	35	1484lb	9 c/ft
Citroen 2CV	£796	HO2 375cc	62 x 62 mm	9/3500	41mph	n/a	55	93	146	35	1092lb	10.5 c/ft
Fiat 500		I2 570cc	52 x 67 mm	16/4400	60mph	43.0	50	79	128	28.5	1344lb	
Goliath	£1088	I3 700cc 2-stroke	80 x 70 mm	25/4000	61mph	32.0	39	90.5	159	39	1904lb	10 c/ft
Hartnett	£N/A	HO2 596cc	72 x 73 mm	19/4000	63mph	23.5	50	79	136	30	1120lb	
Morris Minor	£818	I4 803cc	58 x 76 mm	30/4800	64mph	26.0	37	86	150	31	1792lb	7 c/ft
Renault 750	£781	I4 748cc	54 x 80 mm	27/4000	64mph	22.3	47	83	142	29.5	1232lb	
Standard 8	£826	I4 803cc	58 x 76 mm	26/4500	63mph	22.5	38	84	142	32	1568lb	12 c/ft
Volkswagen	£893	HO4 1131cc	75 x 64 mm	25/3300	65mph	23.2	38	94.5	160	32	1652lb	

ASSEMBLY PRODUCTION MERCEDES-BENZ 1959–64

Code	Model	No Built
W121	190 Ponton	90
W121	190b Ponton	216
W121	190D	48
W121	190Db	90
W180	220S Ponton	354
W128	220SE Ponton	18

Code	Model	No Built
W110	190c fin	222
W110	190c fin automatic	78
W111	220Sb fin	2304
W111	220Sb fin automatic	912
W111	220SEb fin	810
W111	220SEb fin automatic	1248
TOTAL		**6390**

AUSTRALIAN REGISTRATION AUSTIN A30

Model	**1952**	**1953**	**1954**	**1955**	**1956**	**1957**	**1958**	**1959**	Totals
Saloon	6	3855	6456	6581	2949	1523	19	2	**21391**
Countryman			1	219	288	110	3		**621**
Van				205	228	34	3		**470**
Totals	6	3855	6457	7005	3465	1667	25	2	**22,482**

Note: These figures are for registrations and include cars locally assembled and imported. Figures provided by Craig Watson, *The BMC Experience*

HOLDEN PRODUCTION 1950S

48/215	120,402
FJ	169,969
FE	155,161
FC	191,724

MORRIS MARSHALL PRODUCTION 1957 TO 1960

Saloon	1341
Traveller	54
Panel van	30
TOTAL:	1425

CAR REGISTRATIONS IN AUSTRALIA FOR 1950

Austin	27,414
Ford UK	23,956
Ford US	4,204
Holden	18,293
Morris	15,838
Standard	15,390
Vauxhall	8,701
Hillman	5,797

RENAULT ASSEMBLY BY IRA BERK IN SYDNEY

1950 = 500; 1951 = 800; 1952 = 1000; 1953 = 1200; 1954 = 1500; 1955 = 2375; 1956 = 1235; 1957 = 1220; 1958 = 2560; and 1959 = 550.

Figures supplied by Regie Renault, Paris.

REGISTRATION FIGURES FOR THE PERIOD 1948–1959

	1948	1949	1950	1951	1952	1953	1954	1955	1956	1957	1958	1959
Austin	5463	16,924	24,528	17,258	10,498	9896	15,386	15,676	11,011	11,030	9450	9826
Chevrolet	4343	2068	2350	1878	2184	1930	2295	1887	1643	2079	1440	1736
Chrysler		504	470		6	8	11			2342	1947	2486
DeSoto		270	338	309	361	306	891	1604	1,158	356	180	93
Dodge	1317	1005	1279	1713	1576	1185	2237	2620	1909	651	226	190
Ford		11,883	23,883	17,054	21,164	24,147	28,677	34,626	24,011	22,205	23,469	25,701
Hartnett					1	21	22	1				
Hillman	3879	4192	5810	4177	4171	4269	6191	7372	6201	5030	5557	5665
Holden	112	7254	19,196	21,184	23,721	33,611	39,502	45,434	49,429	66,204	83,015	92,166
Humber	695	1593	3107	2657	1692	1537	2235	2053	1214	891	915	1528
Jowett	55	362	970	931	220	135	46	2				
Lloyd-Hartnett										31	563	284
Mercedes-Benz											383	729
MG	768	1167	989	358	276	131	795	946	336	148	667	592
Morris	8979	7485	14,507	15,944	15,285	9725	11,394	17,635	12,752	14,494	11,549	11,694
Peugeot	47	45	1472	1439	690	1186	1470	2035	1902	1340	1181	1334
Plymouth		685	1015		1852	1190	2118	2595	1882	627	278	178
Pontiac	861	301	357	229	260	299	253	299	306	201	224	247
Renault			2077	3449	920	800	1440	1954	1551	1669	1556	1104
Simca			27	133	55	35	65	200	953	1172	2032	3477
Singer	1049	1649	2428	1870	608	734	367	189	109	176	340	380
Standard	4663	9221	11,753	10,280	4975	4840	12,580	13,087	9076	5952	4732	4742
Triumph	165	141	156	2123	1921	736	56	127	67	56	38	1689
Vauxhall	6957	8888	9008	7676	5081	3512	8161	8954	6289	4741	6449	6560
Volkswagen				2			1816	6317	9983	11,065	14,231	18,131
Wolseley	1275	1033	3006	2009	1116	940	1969	1400	929	205	1624	1350

Data provided by Robert Simpson

BIBLIOGRAPHY

Motoring magazines from the period: *Wheels, Modern Motor, Motor Manual, The Autocar, The Motor, The BMC Experience*
Australian Car Trials, Bill Tuckey, Golden Press, 1989
Automobiles Australia, Australian Motor Sports Publication, 1960
Automobiles Australia, various, Wylie Publishing, 1960
Cars of the Fifties and Sixties, Michael Sedgwick, Colporteur Press, 1983
Great Ideas in Motion, Gavin Farmer, Ilinga Books, 2010
Jeep, Steve Statham, MBI Publishing Company, 2001
Knowing Australian Volkswagens, Dave Long & Phil Matthews, Bookworks, 1993
Land Rover Series One 1948–1958, Brooklands Books, 1991
Land Rover: Series One to Freelander, Graham Robson, The Crowood Press, 2003
Land Rover: The Early Years, Tony Hutchings, Tony Hutchings Publishing, 1986
Land Rover: The Formative Years 1947–1967, John Smith, Land Rover Series One Club, 2009
The Cars of BMC, Graham Robson, MRP, 1999
The Cars of the Rootes Group, Graham Robson, Mercian Press, 2007
The Heart of the Lion: 50 Years of the Australian Holden, J Wright, Allen & Unwin, 1998
The Holden Heritage, various publications, General Motors-Holden Public Affairs Department
True Blue, 75 Years of Ford in Australia, Bill Tuckey, Focus, 2000
Volkswagen in Australia: The Forgotten Story, Rod & Lloyd Davies, AF Publishing Pty Ltd, 2004
Wheels Across Australia, Pedr Davis, Marque Publishing, 1987

PHOTO CREDITS

Regie Renault Fronticpiece, 163, 165
GM-Holden Inside page, 11, 14, 17 (lower left), 18, 19, 21, 127, 129
Ben Davidson (Jeep Action magazine) 174
Ford Motor Company 26, 30, 31, 33, 45
Railmac Publications (Steve McNicol) 76, 77, 86 (upper)
Daimler Classic 159, 1260, 161
Carl Moll 137 (top right)
Jeff Morrow 168, 169
Splitting Image 136, 137 (top left), 138
Mark Agnew 172, 173
Gavin Farmer Library Collection 4, 8, 9, 10, 13, 15, 16, 17, 22, 23, 24, 25, 27, 28, 29, 30, 34, 35, 36, 38, 39, 40, 41, 42, 43, 45, 46, 47, 48, 49, 50, 51, 52, 54, 55, 56, 57, 58, 59, 60, 61, 62, 64, 66, 67, 68, 69, 70, 73, 74, 75, 78, 81, 84, 85, 86 (lower), 87, 88, 89, 90, 92, 93, 94, 95, 97, 98, 99, 101, 102, 103, 104, 105, 106, 110, 111, 112, 114, 115, 116, 118, 119, 120, 121, 122, 123, 124, 125, 126, 127, 128, 130, 131, 132, 134, 135, 139, 140, 141, 142, 143, 145, 146, 147, 148, 149, 150, 151, 152, 153, 154, 155, 156, 157, 162, 164, 166, 167, 170, 171, 176, 177, 179, 180, 181

ABOUT THE AUTHOR

Gavin Farmer has had a lifetime involvement with motorcars one way or another. He bought his first car magazine – *Modern Motor*, September 1959 – while in high school and this began a collection of magazines, books and model cars that occupy a special place in his life today.

He is one of Australia's leading motoring historians and has regularly contributed to such prestigious publications as *Automobile Quarterly, Collectible Automobiles, The Automobile, Bimmer, Sports Car International* and others around the world. In addition he has written many books relating to the post-war Australian motor industry which can be seen by going to the ILINGA BOOKS website at www.ilingabooks.com.au.

From the 70s through to the 90s he worked in the automobile industry in various roles from manufacturing, sales and public relations before turning his talents to writing. His original professional training was for teaching but he was looking for wider challenges in life. To this end he has been a State Manager for a multi-media educational publisher as well as a company that marketed computerised dispensary systems.

All the while he was adding to his knowledge of automobiles, the industry and the many new technologies. A colleague once described him as a "barefoot engineer!"

A man who is passionate about the automobile and its history, Gavin lives with his wife on a small property in the beautiful Adelaide hills where he enjoys occasional drives in his newly restored and quite rare Subaru FF-1.

INDEX

K

L

M

N

O

P

Q

R

S

T

V

W

Z